KEEPING FAMILIES TOGETHER
The Homebuilders Model

MODERN APPLICATIONS OF SOCIAL WORK

An Aldine de Gruyter Series of Texts and Monographs

Series Editor

James K. Whittaker

Ralph E. Anderson and Irl Carter, **Human Behavior in the Social Environment: A Social Systems Approach** (Fourth Edition)

Richard P. Barth and Marianne Berry, **Adoption and Disruption: Rates, Risks, and Responses**

Larry K. Brendtro and Arlin E. Ness, **Re-Educating Troubled Youth: Environments for Teaching and Treatment**

Kathleen Ell and Helen Northen, **Families and Health Care: Psychosocial Practice**

Mark W. Fraser, Peter J. Pecora and David Haapala, **Families in Crisis: The Impact of Intensive Family Preservation Services**

James Garbarino, **Children and Families in the Social Environment**

James Garbarino, Patrick E. Brookhouser, Karen J. Authier, and Associates, **Special Children—Special Risks: The Maltreatment of Children with Disabilities**

James Garbarino, Cynthia J. Schellenbach, Janet Sebes, and Associates, **Troubled Youth, Troubled Families: Understanding Families At-Risk for Adolescent Maltreatment**

Roberta R. Greene, **Social Work with the Aged and Their Families**

Roberta R. Greene and Paul H. Ephross, **Human Behavior Theory and Social Work Practice**

Roberta R. Greene and Betsy S. Vourlekis, **Social Work Case Management**

Jill Kinney, David Haapala, and Charlotte Booth, **Keeping Families Together: The Homebuilders Model**

Robert M. Moroney, **Shared Responsibility: Families and Social Policy**

Robert M. Moroney, **Social Policy and Social Work: Critical Essays on the Welfare State**

Norman A. Polansky, **Integrated Ego Psychology** (Second Edition)

Steven P. Schinke (ed.), **Behavioral Methods in Social Welfare**

Albert E. Trieschman, James K. Whittaker, and Larry K. Brendtro, **The Other 23 Hours**

Harry H. Vorrath and Larry K. Brendtro, **Positive Peer Culture** (Second Edition)

Heather B. Weiss and Francine Jacobs (eds.), **Evaluating Family Programs**

James K. Whittaker and James Garbarino, **Social Support Networks: Informal Helping in the Human Services**

James K. Whittaker, Jill Kinney, Elizabeth M. Tracy, and Charlotte Booth (eds.), **Reaching High-Risk Families: Intensive Family Preservation in Human Services**

James K. Whittaker and Elizabeth M. Tracy, **Social Treatment: An Introduction to Interpersonal Helping in Social Work Practice,** (Second Edition)

KEEPING FAMILIES TOGETHER
The Homebuilders Model

Jill Kinney, David Haapala, and Charlotte Booth

ALDINE DE GRUYTER
New York

About the Authors

Jill Kinney is Co-Director of Behavioral Sciences Institute (BSI) and co-founder of the Homebuilders model, which is housed at BSI. She received her Bachelors of Science/Honors in Psychology from the University of Washington, her M.A. and Ph.D. from Stanford University.

David Haapala is an Executive Director of Behavioral Sciences Institute, a nonprofit corporation created to provide, promote and study community-based family-centered services. Dr. Haapla is also co-founder of the nationally recognized Homebuilders program, which began in Tacoma, Washington in 1974. He received his M.A. from Washington State University and his Ph.D. in Psychology from Saybrook Institute.

Charlotte Booth is an Executive Director of the Behavioral Sciences Institute. She received her B.A. from Stanford University and her M.A. from the University of Washington.

Copyright © 1991 Walter de Gruyter, Inc., New York
All rights reserved. No part of this publication may be reproduced or transmitted in any form or by any means, electronic or mechanical, including photocopy, recording, or any information storage and retrieval system, without permission in writing from the publisher.

ALDINE DE GRUYTER
A division of Walter de Gruyter, Inc.
200 Saw Mill River Road
Hawthorne, New York 10532

The paper used in this publication meets the minimum requirements of American National Standard for Information Sciences—Permanence of Paper for Printed Library Materials, ANSI Z39.48-1984.

Library of Congress Cataloging-in-Publication Data
Kinney, Jill, 1944–
    Keeping families together : the homebuilders model / Jill Kinney,
    David Haapala, and Charlotte Booth.
        p.   cm.—(Modern applications of social work)
    Includes bibliographical references and index.
    ISBN 0-202-36067-9.—ISBN 0-202-36068-7 (pbk.)
    1. Family services—Washington (State)   2. Family social work—
    Washington (State)   I. Haapala, David, 1949–   . II. Booth,
    Charlotte, 1948-   ,   III. Title.   IV. Series.
    HV699.3.W2K56   1991
    362.82'8'09797—dc20   90-19973
                                                                            CIP

Manufactured in the United States of America

10 9 8 7 6 5 4 3 2 1

Contents

II. STAGES OF INTERVENTION

Preface

Our experience with keeping families together began amid much skepticism when we opened the Homebuilders Program in Tacoma, Washington, in 1974. Most of us thought families whose children were placed outside the home were probably hopeless. They probably didn't really care about their children and didn't deserve to have them.

Now, after providing intensive in-home family crises intervention and education services to 2,600 families and 4,700 children in imminent danger of out of home placement, we know most families are not hopeless. Depending on the presenting problems and the definition of out of home placement, between 73 and 91% are able to avoid out of home placement during at least the 12 months following intervention. Most show substantial improvements in functioning.

We hope this book will assist those who are considering beginning their own Family Preservation Services to evaluate whether or not the approach will be a good fit for them. We hope those who have already decided to begin a program or apply for a job in one will become aware of some of the complexities of program design and training so that they can make informed decisions. We would also like to stimulate others to challenge our methods and our conclusions, and to provoke us to continue refining our ideas and our practices.

This book is not a cookbook on how to begin a program. Every community is different, and requires careful, individualized planning and evaluation. The book will not teach people to be Family Preservation counselors. It cannot substitute for training, supervision, and hands-on practice.

Some of the challenges for us in writing this book have been organizing the material to be clear and easy to understand without sacrificing the complexity of reality. The way we have structured material is, as always, somewhat arbitrary. Everything is interconnected. Many topics that are separated in this book overlap in reality.

This book is about our efforts to learn to be helpful to families, and about families' potential to grow. We have struggled to put into words many areas where we are still guided by intuition and supposition. Families, human interactions, involve some areas we may never talk about very well, like the capacity of the human spirit to prevail over astounding odds. This capacity is what has kept us engaged for 16 years and moved us to put some of our observations on paper.

Acknowledgments

This book is the product of hundreds of people's efforts over 16 years.

Bud Wetzel, a former professor and long standing consulting psychologist, has mentored, inspired, and encouraged us for all of those years. He, more than anyone, helped us to write this book. We are grateful for his clarity, kindness, patience, editing and friendship.

Diane Johnson, our Administrative Assistant, took on this assignment as if it was her mission in life. She typed, organized, managed and encouraged. We rely on and appreciate her judgment, dependability, reliability, and cheerfulness.

The current and former Board of Directors of Homebuilders* have provided support for this book and the agency. Denzel Scott, John Briehl, Gerry Bresslour, Ricardo Cruz, Starla Drum, Kathleen Feely, David Giles, Jack Gretz, Betty Higley, Joan Meisel, Carmen Morris, Cliff Peterson, Diane Skaar, David Tobis, Bud Wetzel, D.J. Wilson, Mary Jo Uhlman, Don Rolstad, Hugh Armstrong, and Cheryl Richey have, and continue to be, wonderful contributors and friends.

The Edna McConnell Clark Foundation has supported much of our growth, and the growth of family preservation services throughout the United States. Peter Forsythe, Peter Bell, Susan Notkin, Courtney O'Malley and Joanne Edgar have been both inspiring and provocative and challenging. They, more than anyone else, encourage us to continue pushing back the frontiers in helping families.

Hugh Armstrong, Cor Bakker, Bill and Lyn Criddle, Richard Farson, Mark Fraser, Peter Newell, Peter Pecora, and Jim Whittaker have all made significant contributions to Homebuilders' concepts and technology.

Eugene Matsusaka and Catholic Community Services of Tacoma gave Homebuilders its first home, nurturing it, and us, and handling far more administrative details than we ever realized existed before moving into our own agency.

The clients, therapists, supervisors, trainers and office based staff are the people who have taught us the most. This book is for them.

---

*Homebuilders Ⓡ is the trademark of Behavioral Science Institute. Subsequent references to "Homebuilders" throughout the book should be regarded as implicitly carrying the registered Trademark.

I
THE OVERVIEW

1

Program Context and Philosophy

When a family's problems become so severe that the usual community resources are unable to help them effectively, caseworkers are usually advised to place children outside the home. Family Preservation Services (FPS), such as Homebuilders, are designed to give caseworkers and families another option: services that are more intensive, accessible, flexible, and goal-oriented than traditional supports. Instead of relieving family pressure by removing a child, we want to add resources to relieve pressure and to facilitate the development of a safe, nurturing environment for children within the context of the family.

Although this goal may appear straightforward, any decisions about children's welfare and living situations are complicated. Both family life and placement have advantages and disadvantages. Workers making decisions are pressed for time, making it difficult to consider all the factors. In this chapter we will present our views on when placement is necessary and desirable, but first, however, we wish to discuss our experience with families. During our work over the past 16 years, our clients have shown us that they had more capacity for growth than we had previously dreamed. This capacity now colors our views on the necessity for placement and the desirability of offering families one more chance to grow.

For as long as most of us can remember, child welfare workers have had high caseloads. Large amounts of time and expertise for children have typically been available only in residential settings. We have not known what would happen if we allocated similar resources to children while they were in their own homes. We have assumed placement was necessary partly because families couldn't change and partly because we felt many parents were unworthy of the privilege of parenthood.

When Homebuilders began in 1974, we did not know whether help for families would work either. We originally intended to develop "super foster homes": foster homes with lots of training and professional backup. Our funding agent, however, insisted that before placement, we try "sticking a staff member in to live with a family." This idea sounded outlandish, but it also seemed interesting. We knew we would learn about families, and since we wanted the super foster home funding, we decided to try the in-home services, assuming they would fail, our funding agent would be convinced, and we could then continue with our super foster home idea.

We were wrong: The approach was surprisingly effective. We learned quickly that we didn't actually have to move in with families to be able to facilitate significant change. After the first year, many of our initial assumptions were shattered. Most of these were beliefs about the types of families for whom we thought out of home placement should be considered.

Initially, we had assumed that families whose children were in danger of placement were different from us: well . . . , not really *nice*, not really as *good* as they should be. Sure, nice people had problems, but they usually got help from private psychiatrists and military schools. Their children would never go into State funded placements.

One of our families was a leader in its church and involved in numerous community activities. The father had a good job with an airline. They lived in a lovely, clean home on Puget Sound. They had four grown children with families of their own, all doing fine. The parents were charming, articulate, warm, and bright. At the same time, their 14 year old daughter, Monique, was taking all sorts of drugs they had never heard of and trying to kill herself. They didn't meet our stereotype. During our work with them, Monique clarified some of the issues that were upsetting her. She renegotiated some rules with her parents, and they all seemed to develop some new ways of understanding each other. We see Monique occasionally at the Public Library. She has a cute little girl of her own. They look fine and she says her parents are fine.

In another of our first families there was a single mother, Veronica, a 15-year-old daughter, Shanika, and two sons, Tyrone, 14, and Byron, 4. Veronica had been in a big fight with her ex-husband. He had grabbed her car keys and run out to her car. As he started it, she reached in through the window to turn the key off. He rolled the window up on her arm and dragged her for three blocks before he rolled the window down and she fell to the street. He later wrecked the car. She had a broken shoulder and numerous bruises and strains. She couldn't do her work and lost her job. She had $60. The 14-year-old boy was doing poorly in school. She had caught him trying to strangle the 4 year old. The juvenile court was considering placing all the children because the 4 year old was in danger and the mother seemed too overwhelmed to cope. During the second visit we found out that Shanika was pregnant. The situation did seem hopeless, but Veronica kept saying that her kids were all that were keeping her going. She wanted the family to remain together.

We started listing options and weighing alternatives. We sat at the kitchen table and began listing the problems and all the possible ways they might be resolved. We stayed for hours, and Veronica listed even more options after we left. We were surprised. She found a vocational school to fix her car. We helped her to arrange public assistance. We found an alternative school program for Tyrone who began learning anger management skills and put a lock on his bedroom door to keep out Bryon. Their physical confrontations stopped. Shanika decided to get an abortion. Finally, Veronica found a new job she could do with her injured arm. We were surprised at the progress the family had made, but though we were happy for the family when our involvement ended, we didn't really believe that the progress could be maintained. Veronica called us every month or so at the beginning, and they seemed to be doing well. Later, she called us to check in every couple of years. Twelve years later Veronica called to refer her sister who was having trouble with her kids. She said her oldest two kids had graduated from high school, were working, and had kids of their own. Byron was in high school and "doing fine." She thanked us again for our help, it had made a "big difference."

We also assumed that any child being considered for placement was not valued by his or her parents. Of those on the original team none was married or had children.

Our very first case was Donae, a 15-year-old girl who was constantly in trouble with her parents. She couldn't do anything right. She swore, she skipped school, she had "bad" friends, she smoked, she sulked, she ran away. Her mother, Lydia, especially, didn't seem to be able to come up with a kind word for her. Our expectations regarding lack of parental love appeared to be fulfilled. Then, one day, we role played different ways of communicating with Donae and one of our workers played the mother. She was very quiet after the session and on the way back to the office said that she had been wrong about the mother. Although she had stepped into the role expecting to feel hate, what she had felt in trying to communicate with Donae was a surprising warm flash of love and caring and commitment, covered by anguish and fear about what was happening. Later she discussed this with Lydia, who cried, and said "Yes, that's exactly how I feel. I just care about her so much, and I just want things to be okay." The experience made us more cautious about jumping to conclusions about parents' negative comments, and whether such comments meant that they had only negative feelings about their children. Donae stopped by our agency about 6 years after we had worked with her. She was proud of the new Tacoma Police Officer uniform she was wearing. She looked great, and said that her parents were doing well.

We also believed that most teenagers about to be placed didn't care about their parents.

In the Saney family, Becky cursed at her mother, called her names, and refused even to have eye contact with her. She seemed to hate her. Becky worked on chore charts for a week and earned 98 cents. She still didn't want to go anywhere with her mother, so our worker took her to the mall to spend her earnings. They walked up and down the mall for an hour, with Becky carefully considering her options for spending her money. Finally she spent it all on a special kind of small jelly bean that her mother liked. Then she took the bag of candy home and tossed it in her mother's lap and ran into her bedroom. Becky did care, but she just didn't show it very well.

At first, when we observed incidents like these we thought they were aberrations. These people couldn't have the capacities for change we thought we saw. Maybe we had just blundered into some really special people. As the months went on, though, and such incidents were repeated over and over with different parents, different children, and different presenting problems, we began to realize that we had been wrong. Most of the families we initially assumed to have minimal capacity for nurturing and minimal potential for change could eventually display more strength, sense, and compassion than we had thought. People could change.

We reevaluated our basic assumptions about change. As a result of our experience and observations we are now convinced that *everyone can learn.* People learn when they don't want to; people learn when they're upset; people learn even though they have failed to respond to many social services; people can learn even when social service providers say they cannot; people can learn even though they have dirty houses, little education, and a long list of problems. People are learning and changing all the time.

We abandoned the super foster home idea. Foster families were difficult to recruit and less interested in training than we had hoped. Besides, we weren't finding enough families who needed them to support a program.

After our initial work with families, we felt hopeful, but others remained skeptical. The process might work in Tacoma, but it wouldn't work in Seattle. Then, it might work in Seattle, but it would never work in Spokane. Well, it wouldn't work with children with mental health problems, or developmentally delayed children, or juvenile delinquents. A history of the program's development is shown in Appendix A.

We now hear stories from family preservation workers in different settings all over the country describing the same types of events we have experienced. When workers have the time to observe and interact with families in their homes, they see the same potential for change that we continue to see. The challenge now is to find ways to communicate this potential to workers who must stay at their desks and cope with loads of 40 or more families, so that they might learn to consider families' potentials for future change as well as their handicaps of the moment.

Details of program evaluation results are presented in Chapter 10. Depending on the client populations, definition of placement and length of follow-up, Family Preservation Services do prevent the need for placement in 67 to 95% of the families served. They do not help everyone, but the percentage they do help is high enough that we believe most families should be given this option for help before placement occurs.

Advantages of Children Remaining with Their Families

Usually, the safest, most nurturing environment available to a child is a family. Not necessarily a mother and father and two children, but some constellation of committed individuals who will provide continuity, stability, and guidance throughout his or her childhood. Families provide a nurturing setting for the development of self-esteem and self-discovery. They teach children how to solve problems, how to cooperate in small groups, and how to behave in culturally acceptable ways. Parents model and support commitment, love, and attachment. Long-term intellectual and emotional connectedness can affect children in a number of ways. Attachment can help the child to achieve his or her intellectual potential, cope with stress and frustration, and develop a conscience and future relationships (Fahlberg, 1979).

Families are the most socially accepted and valued means for raising children. Children who grow up in families have an advantage in respectability, credibility, and acceptability throughout their lives. They have grown up in the setting that society believes "should occur," and, as a result, they have a better chance of developing self-esteem and self-confidence. Perhaps because of this respectability, society is more willing to provide support for families than for other alternatives such as foster families. By the same token, natural families are more likely to have access to family preservation services or other types of counseling and education when they do have trouble.

Some Disadvantages of Children Remaining in Their Families

In our society, families are given a wide range of freedom and privacy in deciding how children should be raised. Parents are not screened or trained for the job, and many parents have few skills and make poor decisions. Family planning is not widely practiced so many pregnancies are unplanned. In family situations, children can be damaged emotionally and physically, or even killed (the leading cause of death in the United States in the first year of life is now *murder!*). These drastic events may happen without the larger community knowing that potential for harm existed.

Advantages and Disadvantages of Placement

Most foster parents, group home, and institutional workers are screened and trained. They have made a conscious decision to work with the children in their care and they are supervised and monitored by the State or private agencies or both. Many children in foster care show few negative effects (Festinger, 1983). For many individual children, foster families, group homes, and psychiatric hospitals literally have been and continue to be life savers, removing them from dangerous and unsupportive settings, and providing love, guidance, and help in resolving serious long-term problems.

In other ways, placement can have many weaknesses and potential disadvantages. Personnel are not always selected, trained, and monitored as carefully as we would like. Children can be emotionally and physically abused in placement just as they can be in families. Furthermore, children who are placed may feel rejected, inadequate, and alone. They may miss their families and envy siblings remaining at home. Children who are separated from their families miss out on significant portions of family history, making it difficult for them to have a sense of belonging and continuity. Often, when they do return to their families, nothing has changed, so that they still must cope with most of the problems they left.

Children who have had breaks in connectedness, such as those who have been institutionalized, show increased attention getting behavior, lack of selectiveness in friends, and slower intellectual growth (Rutter, 1972). and Pringle (1965) found that children separated from a primary care giver had lower IQs. Two hundred thirty-six children exposed to separation for at least 1 year from their parent(s) were reported to score higher on a trait depression scale (Parker, 1979). Some researchers view early parental loss as leaving children at risk for later depression (Rutter, 1972). Other empirical studies show foster children to be more anxious and aggressive than their adopted and biologically raised peers (Boostani and Tashakkori, 1982; Fanshel and Shinn, 1978; Larsson et al., 1986). Those who spend large periods of time in foster care may be more likely to suffer maladjustment or mental illness in adulthood (McCord, McCord, and Thurber, 1960; Baker and Holzworth, 1961).

Children in foster care may be placed frequently, so that attachment to a primary care giver never occurs (Solnit and Cauce, 1982). After multiple moves, children may learn not to attach, for fear of moving again. They may become defensive, fearful, and suspicious (Pike, Downs, Emlen, Downs, and Case, 1977). Little continuity and many broken relationships can be correlated with children's confused self-identities regarding who they are and to whom they belong (Fanshel and Maas, 1962). "A placed child, who becomes extremely afraid of yet another rejection by someone he loves may either try to stop loving by keeping everyone at an emotional distance, or may be involved constantly in rejecting people first" (Littner, 1960 as quoted by Fanshel and Shinn, 1978). This fear of rejection can be interpreted as lack of gratitude by foster parents, decreasing their efforts to reach out, and resulting in a vicious circle of rejection (Eisenberg, 1962). Some data indicate that the more times a child is placed, the more his or her emotional and behavioral problems intensify (Wiltse and Gambrill, 1973). Ultimately, the child may always carry within him a specific vulnerability to separation and to strangeness.

Even if they are in placement, children need parents. When they are in contact during placement, detrimental long-term effects on self-esteem and IQ are attenuated (Weinstein, 1960). Foster children who were visited by their parents showed a better sense of well being than those who were not visited (Weinstein, 1960, as cited by Fanshel and Shinn, 1978).

Placement may also be difficult for the remaining family members. Parents whose children are placed may experience feelings of failure and reduced self-esteem. Remaining children must still cope with their parents' lack of skills and the risk of abuse and neglect. They may wonder when they themselves will be taken from their homes.

Placement is expensive. Most communities today cannot afford placement alternatives for all the children whose current living situations are unsatisfactory. Placement costs can use resources desperately needed for other parts of the service continuum of care. Placement activities can require such a large percentage of the total resources allocated for children that child welfare systems essentially become bankrupt toward the end of their budget periods. As a result, children who need help are on the streets and services are unavailable for families whose problems might be relatively easy to solve. These family's problems are likely to escalate.

Necessary Placement

Some placements will always be necessary because some families will never be able to raise their own children safely and productively. When all the advantages and disadvantages of all potential settings have been weighed, when all the factors about potential for harm and change and political consequences have been considered, and when the equation yields more positives on the side of placement than on the side of family, it should occur. Family members wishes should play a major part in this decision.

Refusal of Services

Some family members do not wish to try any more to resolve their problems. In some cases with status offenders, the child absolutely refuses to consider trying to work things out with his or her parents. They feel so mistreated that they will not consider reconciliation. In other cases, the parents refuse to consider trying to work things out with their child. They feel so hurt and hopeless that they are unwilling to try any more. Assessment of these situations is complicated. In our experience, when either the parents or the children have an opportunity to vent their hurt, anger, confusion, and despair at length, without pressure to take any particular course of action, they often decide to give it one more try. Of course, for those who have, indeed, given up, placement should be available.

Lack of Housing

In some situations, no adequate housing is available for the family and the only way a child can have safe shelter is to be separated from his or her family. Although we want all families to have shelter and although it is illegal in some communities to place a child rather than find housing for the entire family, sometimes such a difficult decision must be made. A child in a rat-infested room with bare electric cords is better off away from his parents if that's the only place they have to live.

Dangerous Neighborhoods

Members of a child's family or people living nearby may be so violent that the physical safety of the child or of family preservation workers cannot adequately be guaranteed in certain locations. Though the family may have the potential to care adequately for the child, no one is able to protect him/her from others in the environment and the child must be removed. Likewise, if a family preservation worker cannot be reasonably safe when visiting the family, he/she cannot help the family or child and placement may be the better alternative.

Previous Family Preservation Failure

Sometimes a family preservation worker has previously worked with a family and the family and/or the referring worker believe that the services did not help enough to warrant another rereferral. In one of our cases, for example, a manic-depressive mother had stabilized with intensive help and monitoring of her medications, but adequate follow-up services were not available to support her progress. In such situations, it may be better for children to be placed rather than to remain in a continually unstable, threatening environment.

Avoiding Unnecessary Placement

Many placements would not be necessary if families had access to intensive services. We need to minimize unnecessary placement because of its potential disadvantages to children and because of its cost to communities. Unnecessary placement often occurs for three reasons: (1) caseloads are so high that workers do not have the time to identify and weigh carefully all the issues bearing on a case; (2) tradition strongly supports the notion that placement is the option of choice for troubled families; and (3) knowledge about the capacities of families to change has not been widely disseminated so that many caseworkers are unaware of possible alternatives to placement.

Sufficient Time to Weigh Alternatives

All of us in social service need to fight for caseloads small enough to allow thoughtful consideration of all the advantages and disadvantages of family life and of placement for each child we are considering removing from his/her home. We need to carefully scrutinize each aspect of the decision-making process.

Child Safety. As workers, we need to be demanding of proof about child safety with alternate caregivers as well as with birth parents. For both situations we need to ask whether our concerns are based on observation or on hearsay and interpretation. If hearsay, how credible is the source? Are we hearing descriptions of facts or speculation and interpretation? Workers must weigh the possible alternatives for support as well as the present circumstances of the family. Could the current danger be alleviated if a skilled worker could be with the family whenever there was trouble? Has the family ever received intensive help in learning to cope with problems? Are we assuming that the family members are unable or unwilling to learn new coping strategies? If so, why? How bad is the risk in supporting the family in comparison to the risks involved in placing a child? In neglect cases, is the child's health or development likely to be affected? If the child were placed, how long would the placement last? If the child were to be returned home fairly soon, would the situation be more safe then than it is now? Why? What is the likelihood that the placement will develop into a stable, long-term option for the child? To what degree is our opinion about placement based on real evidence of harm, and to what degree on values differences between us and the parents about parenting and life-styles?

As part of deciding whether or not to place a child, we need to assess the potential for maintaining the child's physical and emotional safety. A child may have a family with several deficits, but deficits in placement resources may be just as serious. One of our clients had been in 60 overnight foster homes in the 2 months prior to our seeing her. Group home staff believed that she was too difficult for their programs, long-term foster homes were filled, and all that was available was a succession of overnight placements. In some situations, teenagers have slept on the floors of public agency offices because there were no other places for them. We must come to terms with the fact that our current social service system cannot find desirable alternatives for many children. The options are inadequate. The fragility of many placements and the vulnerability of the children who will live in them require us to evaluate carefully each placement option—its potential for improving the child's welfare and its potential for providing the child with long-term social connectedness and support.

Worker Frame of Mind.   Present day child welfare, mental health, and juvenile justice work can be draining, depressing, and frustrating. These factors, along with the time pressures of the job, affect the decisions that workers make. We must be aware of these effects when we make decisions about children's lives. Are we, at the moment, personally frazzled and overwhelmed by our jobs? Could we be deciding to place this child because it is the easiest thing for us to do at the moment, or because our caseload is so large that it is overwhelming even to consider working with the family?

Political Factors and Tradition.   Individual workers and agencies continually need to assess their policies regarding placement. Families are changing, and so are the techniques available for helping them. Are we placing certain children because "we always have" or because placement is really the best alternative for them?

We also need to be aware that our decisions can be influenced by political factors instead of the specific needs of a particular child. Have there been recent media exposés about child abuse in natural families or in foster care? Are administrators fearful of losing Department support or of being blamed by supervisors lest they make a wrong decision?

Summary

Within a confusing, complicated, and, at times, disintegrating social service context, Family Preservation Services (FPS) offer a promising first step to helping families and individuals help themselves. These services also offer a cost-effective alternative to placement outside the home at a time when wise investment of social service dollars is a critical consideration. Although we still have a long journey ahead to realize the potential of FPS as an alternative to unnecessary placement, the first step has been taken and our experience tells us that the trip ahead will be worthwhile.

2

Basic Components of the
Family Preservation Approach

In this chapter we will discuss identifying characteristics of Family
Preservation Services as well as ways we, at Homebuilders, interpret
those characteristics.

Service Population: Families in Crisis

Family Preservation Services are often called *crisis intervention programs*. Crisis theory (Lindemann, 1944; Caplan, 1964) postulates that
when people go through periods of high stress, their regular coping mechanisms break down, leaving them more open to change in
either a positive or negative direction. Families seen in family preservation programs are usually experiencing one of two crises: (1) Child
Protective Services (CPS) has said that the family is not providing
adequate child care and is planning to remove one or more children, or
(2) problems between parents and children have grown so severe that a
parent is refusing to allow the child to continue to live at home, or the
child is running away. During times like these, family members are
usually open about their pain and their problems. Their old habits are
not working. If we can be available, and encouraging, the pressure they
feel can motivate them to change far more than they would when they
are more stable. Family members' increased vulnerability under such
conditions can serve as a catalyst for seeking help to resolve their
immediate problems. If we can be available and gently encouraging, the
pressure they are feeling may motivate them to give us a great deal of
information in a short time and to bond to us—partly out of gratitude
that we are there to share their pain, and partly because relationships
tend to form more quickly with intense exchanges of personal information.

Goals of Crisis Intervention

The goals of crisis intervention are resolution of the immediate crisis and restoration of the family to at least the level of functioning that existed before the crisis. We try to go beyond this point, to increase families' skill levels and resources so that they function better after the crisis than they did before.

Crisis theory postulates that in most cases, people will bring themselves out of the crisis without professional help. For many severely troubled families, a crisis has, in the past, been resolved by removing a child. We would like to support them during this time by the addition of new resources, so that the family may remain intact and its members grow (or survive) through the experience.

Appropriate Families

Family preservation programs differ in the ways they define families in crisis. Some require only that a State public agency worker feels out of home placement could occur sometime in the future. Others require that formal paperwork for placement has been completed or court proceedings have occurred before a client family is assessed as in imminent enough danger of placement. We, at Homebuilders, define "families in crisis" by the following criteria.

The Referring Worker Has the Power to Place. We want to get our referrals from workers who can make the decision to place a child because we want to be able to document that placement would actually have occurred without Homebuilders intervention. Usually, this means that referring workers are from public agencies. Sometimes, however, this power has been delegated to private agencies who then become appropriate referral agents.

Placement is imminent. Both referring workers and family members must believe that without immediate intensive intervention, out of home placement would be imminent. Workers must also have tried or ruled out other less intensive services for preventing placement. This process is never as simple as we would like. Sometimes referring workers really want to place children and placements are not available. Presenting problems and issues might change rapidly within 5 days. Referring workers gather information on the family: the complete legal names of family members, home address, home and work phone numbers, a brief case history, documentation of the imminence of placement, a summary of previous placements and dates, and reasons why more traditional services would not suffice at this time. Referring workers do not have to submit any paperwork to Homebuilders. Information they have gathered is shared during the referral phone call to our intake worker.

The definition of "imminent" is difficult. The actual power to place is delegated differently within varied social services systems. In some, judges have the power. In others, most power has been delegated to other agencies. In some locations, it takes days to go through the process of obtaining a placement. It would be possible to accept only referrals for whom a placement has been found, but that would mean a waste of the referring worker's time, and it would mean that the family had to wait for help instead of getting it when they needed it most.

We try to be flexible in different counties and cities, and with different populations, in negotiating the meaning of "imminence." Referring agencies have substantial stake in seeing that we get cases that really would be placed, because they want to save our resources for the families who are the most difficult. Some say a case must be placed within 3 days, some say within 5 days. With mental health cases in one county, the referrals had to be cleared for admission to the State Mental Hospital by the Office of Involuntary Treatment before we could accept them. Probably the thorniest issue is that in many locations, so few placements are available that even though a child might have problems severe enough to warrant it, placement is not available.

Whatever the chosen definition of imminence, it is an ongoing problem. Referring workers are often frustrated by high caseloads and want all their cases to get the most help possible. In many locations worker turnover is high and we must continuously educate new workers regarding our intake criteria.

The family lives in the catchment area. All our programs have a well-defined catchment area and it is unusual for us to see families outside those boundaries. The size of the area depends on the density of the population and the projected number of referrals. It also depends on travel time from one edge to another. We probably would not select a catchment area where it took more than a couple of hours to drive from side to side. So far we have avoided areas with no urban centers, except when workers can drive to our next area within two hours. We are concerned that an entirely rural setting will not have enough referrals to warrant a team of at least three counselors, and we believe workers need support from others doing similar work.

The family is available. The family needs to be willing and able to let the family preservation counselor visit within 72 hours. Counselors are available for intakes within 24 hours and almost all of our first sessions do occur within that time frame. Families can choose to wait up to 72 hours, and a few do. If family members are unavailable within that time, referring workers should wait to refer them when they can be seen immediately.

At least one family member needs to be willing to work with us for most of the 4-week period. Obviously, we would prefer that all family members want to work with us, but frequently they don't, at least at the beginning. We count on the fact that if one person changes, others will change, and that if we can make the change process positive, others will want to work with us. In 23% of our referrals, a child is living out of the home at the time the referral is made. In these situations, the referring worker and the family must have a plan to return the child home within 7 days of referral, so that we have time to work with the whole family while they are actually living together.

If family members are unwilling to meet with our counselors after they have told referring workers they would be available, we must be able to document a concerted effort to engage the parent(s) and gain their willingness to work with us. The expectation is that our counselors will persist in trying to engage the family. This could include multiple telephone calls to client home and work numbers, dropping by the home to leave messges, and involving the referring worker in attempts to contact the client.

Inappropriate Families

We do not accept families for whom placement is only speculative. If a referring worker thinks a family may need placement in a month or 6 months, but is not considering actually placing children now, the case is inappropriate. The family is also inappropriate if placement is an immediate threat, but there are less intensive (and less expensive) services available in the community that would suffice to prevent placement.

Family members may refuse our services. In some cases there is a court order stating that if they refuse, their children will be placed, but the family still has the right to decide not to have services, which will lead to placement. One way families can refuse services is to refuse to allow a child to live at home. Children, also, can refuse to go home.

Sometimes workers have made the decision to place a child, but cannot find a placement immediately. They would like to use Homebuilders to monitor and support the family until placement is available. Obviously, this is not a black and white situation. Referring workers change their minds. Families change their minds. Situations change. If, however, a worker is thinking of using Homebuilders to hold things together for placement only, the case is not appropriate. The worker must be willing to consider that the family could stay together before the case is appropriate for us.

Special Circumstances

Danger. Rarely, one of our counselors and a supervisor may determine that the family situation is so dangerous that the immediate safety of family members or the counselor cannot be reasonably ensured. This determination almost never occurs before we have seen the family, and happens in fewer than 1% of our cases, overall. One example would be a father's girlfriend shooting him in the shoulder while a Homebuilder had the teenage daughter out for dinner at McDonald's.

Illness of Family Members. Although many of our families have members with serious physical problems, sometimes they are too severe to allow for the safety and well-being of the children (or our staff). If key family members are too ill to participate at the beginning of the intervention, the child should be placed, unless support from other family members is available. If a key family member becomes ill after the intervention has started, and there are no concerns about the safety of the children involved, the family may be referred when the illness is over. Workers should not be asked to work with families experiencing serious contagious diseases. In New York, for example, a worker discovered on an intake visit that all family members had active tuberculosis. We did not accept the case.

Developmental Disabilities of Family Members. Many of our cases involve developmental disabilities of child, parent, or both. We use the same philosophy as with others; you can't tell whether a situation is hopeless until you try your absolute best to help people learn new ways to cope. One mother began intervention learning how to tell time, so she could get her children to school on time. Another family with a developmentally delayed boy needed help with toilet training.

The Sawyer family had a developmentally delayed 8-year-old boy, Joseph. He was not toilet trained. His parents weren't too worried, but were told something was very wrong with them or the boy because of this by other professionals and friends. They were overwhelmed and wondering about placement. They had two "normal" sons who also took time. Both parents worked.

We rented a buzzer pants device where any liquid hitting the pants would result in a low intensity buzz. When the buzzer sounded the Sawyers or daycare person took Joseph to the bathroom as rapidly as possible, removed the pants, and sat him on the potty. We also used reinforcement when Joseph used the potty appropriately. Although he was not completely toilet trained by the end of the 4 weeks, the parents felt so much more hopeful that he would be toilet trained at some point, that they were not concerned about placement anymore. Also, some respite care people had refused to take Joseph for weekends because he wasn't toilet trained so the Sawyers could never get a break. They had recently moved to Tacoma from Montana and didn't really have any social support here and no other options for respite. Much of the concern did revolve around the toilet training. I did lots of active listening to validate parents concerns and learn about all the issues.

Together, we structured a routine for toilet training. The parents were less stressed, the boy was well on the road to toilet training at the end of 4 weeks. (Mary Fischer)

Another family was ready to place their child because of his violence.

In the Porter family, Jason was developmentally delayed with an IQ of 70. He was 11 or 12 years old at a 5 or 6 year age level. The problems resulted from a difficult pregnancy. I saw the family December 6, 1985 to January 11, 1986.

Jason was first referred after he threatened his brother with a butcher knife. His brother had given him a direction, Jason became upset, and had gotten the knife to threaten his brother with it. The family said that as he grew older, he was becoming more violent in his outbursts, which concerned them since Jason was also becoming stronger.

During the intervention, we focused on education of the family members including giving them information about Jason's developmental abilities and how to actually make requests of him. We especially focused on behavioral principles/techniques and on using and practicing teaching interactions with Jason; the whole family participated. The teaching interactions that we practiced focused specifically on responding to Jason when he began to escalate—how to tell him "no" and to give him the option to come back when he had calmed down.

Also, since Jason was doing well in his special education curriculum at school, Jason's parents and I spoke with his teacher and the school social worker to learn how they worked with him at school and to coordinate between home and school. They used time-out with him and he was on a behavioral chart for his school work.

The family began implementing the skills we had discussed and reported that they felt more confident in their dealings with Jason and much more comfortable with having him in the home. There were no further incidents with the knife. (Sandy Edelstein)

Psychiatric Problems.   Many of our clients also have psychiatric problems. Some have been in psychiatric hospitals before being referred to Homebuilders. Some are on medication. Some have been diagnosed as psychotic. In some counties in Washington State, we accept cases where the goal is to prevent placement of a parent in a psychiatric facility if the parent's placement would mean the children would have to be placed in foster care. One of our first mental health cases was Albert, referred to Homebuilders as an option to long-term psychiatric placement.

> Albert was 14. He had an IQ of 140. Albert's psychiatrist described him as having "severe characterologic problems, involving a combination of schizoid disorder of adolescence with an early schizoid personality disorder as chacterized by poor attachment to individuals, preoccupation with his own thinking and peculiar thinking at times." Albert often sang instead of talking. He sang during classroom discussions. When he wasn't singing, he was constantly asking questions, especially about electronics, the functioning of tape recorders, televisions, stereo systems, and lighting systems at the school. He would interrogate his classmates about issues such as "Why is football more important than classical music?" He often had a glassy-eyed expression, what his brother called, a "genius stare." Albert smashed things at home and at school. He paced. He picked at his face until it bled. All family members fought frequently over a wide variety of issues.
>
> Albert specified his problems and began several change programs. We discussed social learning theory with him and school staff, and he began receiving rewards for appropriate school behavior. He worked with his counselor on basic social skills; how to carry on a conversation without singing or interrogating. He was fascinated with the videotape machine and enjoyed being taped and evaluating his performance. He learned to tone down his "genius stare" and discuss topics other than electronics.
>
> We worked with all family members individually at first, to help them learn cognitive skills to better control their emotions and to begin practicing new communications skills so that when they did meet as a group, they would experience some success.
>
> We worked with a school advocate to find a supportive placement for him. Ultimately, a program was tailored for him at a high school, involving more challenging classes, more structure, positive feedback for appropriate behavior, and time out when he yelled and sang. He attended a vocational school in the afternoons, taking electronics classes. We arranged for weekly sessions for him with a former Homebuilder who was now in private practice, and accompanied him for the first session.
>
> Four months after termination, Albert was doing fine at school and in his electronics classes. There were no complaints from anyone. Family fights were way down. If he felt like pacing, he walked around the block. He was still seeing his counselor once a week. (Mary Fischer)

Drug Abuse. Drug abuse involves a very complicated set of issues. Our jobs would certainly be simpler if none of our families used illegal drugs, but, in fact, a significant number do. The definition of drug abuse ranges from someone smoking marijuana every 6 months to someone being addicted to both crack and heroin. We can't work with someone who is always passed out or high on drugs. We feel uncomfortable leaving children in families where there are signs that parents are heavy drug users. If someone is addicted, our intervention will not cure the problem, although we may be able to get them into a long-term program that might.

On the other hand, many parents can learn to care for their children in spite of their own drug abuse. Sad to say, we all read stories about attorneys and stockbrokers who function while on drugs. We all have friends who grew up fine even though they had one or two alcoholic parents. We can teach other family members coping skills to deal with drug users.

The decision as to whether to place a child depends on the alternatives available. In New York, we had an 11-year-old girl whose mother admitted to heavy use of crack. We recommended that the public agency place the girl. She was placed, ran away, and began living with a neighbor who ran a crack den and used young girls as prostitutes. Every time she was placed, she ran back to her mother or the crack den. Restricted placements were full. None of the options for this girl was good. Maybe it would have been reasonable to have tried harder to get her mother into a treatment program and to teach the two of them to develop a functional daily routine. There are difficult moral dilemmas. We don't have the answers to them.

Other cases respond to help in a straightforward manner.

Dara (20) was the natural mother of Christina (9 months). Christina was in danger of placement in foster care due to the cocaine addiction of her mother. Her father, Matt, was serving time in jail on a drug charge. Christina's older brother, Jason, was placed in foster care prior to Homebuilder involvement. Dara's addiction prevented her from properly caring for herself and the children. Dara rented the upstairs apartment in her parent's home. Her 19-year-old boyfriend, Brian, spent a great deal of time with her and Christina.

I helped Dara find out about drug treatment centers and a schedule for Narcotic Anonymous (N.A.). She missed her first drug evaluation because of having an abortion. She and Brian went to one N.A. meeting and then missed many days. The CPS caseworker met with me and Dara and stressed the importance of her drug recovery. Dara agreed to complete the evaluation as well as attend N.A. meetings. Initially I accompanied her to the N.A. meetings for moral support. Sometimes Brian would go and the rest of the time her mother would accompany her. Dara successfully completed her drug evaluation and attended regular counseling sessions with a drug counselor. She volunteered for urinalysis, "just to keep her honest." Dara got involved with other young adults in N.A. They went to eat together and went out to dances and movies. She began associating with a new peer group. The CPS caseworker authorized maximum day-care to be paid for so she could attend her meetings and counseling.

Dara's mother volunteered to baby-sit Christina if Dara was with her friends from N.A.

Dara's husband got out of jail and wanted a divorce. He filed for custody of both of their children. I helped Dara arrange for legal aid. She said she was more determined than ever to "stay straight so she would look good in court" over the custody of the children.

Dara asked her boyfriend to move out so she could live by herself. She and Brian continue to stay in contact from time to time. Dara retained custody of Christina. She and Matt agreed on joint custody of their son, Jason, and Dara saw him every other weekend. She continued drug counseling and attending N.A. Her urinalysis always tested negative. (Monica Wafstet-Solin)

All Family Preservation Services have a commitment to reduce the barriers to service provision. We want to make it as easy as possible for families to learn and grow. We differ in the times counselors are available and the percentage of time that is spent in clients' homes. Few, if any of us, charge clients fees for services. We, at Homebuilders, interpret the challenges of lowering barriers in the following ways.

Therapist Availability

Workers are available to see intakes within 24 hours of referral. We have no waiting list and operate on a space available basis. The times referrals can be accepted are negotiated with referring agencies. In some areas, workers carry beepers to accept after hours referrals, or referring workers have Homebuilders counselors' home phone numbers to use for referrals. Some referring agencies do not work at night or on the weekends. Some prefer not to let night workers refer, because the paperwork invovled in transferring the case back to a daytime worker in the public agency after Homebuilders involvement has begun is too complicated. Usually after a project has become established, any openings are snapped up first thing in the morning, and after hours referrals lead only to frustration because there are never any openings.

Once cases are accepted, workers are on call 24 hours a day, 7 days a week to families. They routinely work some evenings and weekends. They are also available on holidays if family emergencies arise. Workers give families their home phone numbers, and the number of their supervisor, as well as a team beeper number. During periods of crisis, counselors also let families know other numbers where they might be reached. Knowing that their counselor is likely to be reached any time gives families a sense of security and makes them more likely to take risks in changing their behavior.

We prefer workers to give their home phone number as the first resort for families because we want families to call when they need to, and we believe they will feel more comfortable doing so if someone they know is on the other end of the line. Crisis calls also provide an opportunity for the worker to teach, and to gain critical information that could get diluted in the retelling by a teammate. For many workers, their home is their main office; after they are trained, they come to Homebuilders sites only for meetings and turning in paperwork. For them it is logical to give the number where they will be most of the time. Although the amount and time of visits to families vary a great deal depending on family schedules and presenting problems, workers average between 8 and 10 hours per week face to face with families.

A typical case might require 3 hours the first day, 3 hours the second day, telephone contact the third day, 2 hours the fourth day, 3 hours every other day for about a week, and 2 hours three or four times a week for the remaining time. Often there will be one or two additional emergency sessions within this period. It is possible, where necessary, for workers to take shifts with severely disrupted families, or even to stay over night, but these extreme measures are not usually necessary.

Appointments are scheduled at the convenience of the clients rather than at the convenience of the workers. Counselor availability means we are there when they need us. They appreciate it. All family members are more likely to participate if it is convenient for them. We can closely monitor potentially dangerous situations because we can be there when things are the most volatile.

Clients are encouraged to call whenever they feel they need help. At the beginning of the intervention, workers try to give examples of times it would be appropriate to call—if a family fight is occurring, if any threat of harm appears, if they are having trouble implementing new problem-solving skills, or if they are feeling anxious or confused. A counselor might joke, "It is probably not good for you to call me at 3:00 in the morning if you just thought of one more thing to tell me. Write that down and call me at 9:00 in the morning." Most clients would not be calling unless there was something wrong, and if there is something wrong, it's the counselor's job to help resolve the issue. Loneliness, frustration, lack of skills in using new techniques or controlling emotions are all seen as valid problems, deserving of the worker's time and effort. By far the majority of clients are thoughtful in calling workers. Those who call frequently may need to know that there really is someone around whom they can trust before they get the courage to share all their information or try some new coping behaviors. Most clients are impressive in their desires and abilities to work past depending on counselors to self-sufficiency.

Although counselors are clearly expected to be at clients' homes if there is trouble, sometimes family explosions happen very suddenly and the counselor must help stabilize the situation immediately over the phone. Although general diffusion techniques will frequently suffice, all counselors are trained in appropriate use of poison control centers, police, ambulances, and commitment offices.

Intervention in Clients' Environment

Except on rare occasions when clients request otherwise, all Homebuilders services are delivered in client homes, schools, work settings, and neighborhoods. Working in the natural environment makes it possible to reach a much wider range of clients and to reach more seriously disturbed clients. In times of troubles, many families are too disorganized to get themselves scheduled for and transported to office visits. In addition, many have had past unsuccessful social services and feel ambivalent about trying again, so that any barriers to service delivery may discourage them completely. The "no-show" or dropout rate is drastically reduced from what it would have been if we required clients to come to our offices.

In the natural environment, it is more likely that each family member will eventually participate even though they may choose not to at first. They get a chance to observe for themselves that no one is being blamed or pushed around. Even if they don't participate directly, workers often are surprised to learn how much family members pick up just by hanging around in the background.

We can see what is really going on in families' homes. We can observe their life-styles and routines. We can assess some of the environmental conditions and constraints such as the number of rooms, furniture, and toys. We can see and experience the natural kinds of disruptions and interferences that routinely occur—e.g., television, telephone, neighbors dropping in. The family knows we see and understand what's happening. Being there gives us more credibility and they are more likely to accept our advice.

Ultimately, families need to be able to use new skills at home. If they learn them in the office, skill generalization is often a problem. Many new behaviors never transfer to the environment where they are really needed. Generalization or transfer of learning is greatly facilitated if all services are provided in the natural environment of the client. We can model and shape new behaviors in the environment where they need to occur. Then we can watch family members try them, revise them if needed, and provide support until success is achieved.

Most family members like in-home services. Not only is it more convenient and functional, but many comment that it helps with some of their embarrassment at having to ask for help. They feel less subservient and vulnerable and say that it's more like having a friend or family member come over to help. This conceptualization is more comfortable for most than the traditional caseworker, social worker, or doctor/patient roles. Clients are more likely to experiment with new options when they feel comfortable. A few clients feel pressured to keep their houses especially clean if "visitors" are coming over. If they would prefer to meet in our offices, or some other location, that is acceptable to us. This probably happens in fewer than 1% of our families.

Although as Homebuilders we ordinarily counsel in our families' homes, all of us have had the experience of doing our work in some very unusual places.

> My most unusual counseling office has been a dairy barn where my client and I do our counseling work while two alternation rows of six Holsteins stand by in blissful attendance. My client works hard as a milker and she doesn't have much time to spend at home. So I visit her as she whistles the cows into stalls, sprays them off, puts on and takes off the milking machines.
>
> My client is very good at what she does. She knows and loves her cows and they produce more milk per gallon than the dairy has previously recorded. She loves her job and it is such an important part of her that I can't think of a better place to do some counseling. Of course, we do have an audience, but the cows are well known for keeping their mouths shut. (Jim Poggi)

No Cost to Families

There is no charge to families for Homebuilders services. Although sliding fee schedules have been considered in the past, the actual cost of the intervention ($2,600 per case in Washington state, $3,262 in the Bronx) is far more than most families can afford. Even if they could afford it, most families at the beginning of the intervention have minimal motivation to see another social services worker, let alone pay money for it. In most locations, public agencies would pay much more if these families placed their children. Both Washington and New York have decided it is worth providing services with no charge to families.

Flexibility

Scheduling of Sessions

Since sessions are scheduled when the clients wish, for as long as they wish, we can be available when it's convenient for them. We can stay long enough to hear their whole story, and we can come back again before the story is changed. We can take advantage of new crises and opportunities for change.

For many families, several hours are necessary to hear their stories.

The first time I met with Mary and Kevin they wanted me to know all about their case and wanted to know for themselves that I was not prejudiced against them. At the time of referral Mary and her baby, Gail, were living with Kevin's mother, Vera. Vera was the one who had made the report to CPS, claiming that Mary drank frequently and heavily and that when she did she was sometimes physically abusive to Gail. The first time I went to meet Mary she wasn't there; while I waited for her to return Vera gave me a detailed account of her view of the situation and of Mary's parenting skills, which she said were very poor.

It turned out that Mary's view of things was very different from Vera's. Although she agreed that she had a drinking problem, that she was capable of hurting Gail when under the influence, and that she needed to go to treatment, she felt much of Vera's account of her was untrue. Mary felt that Vera was trying to keep her child in her home so she could collect AFDC for her. Mary felt she and her baby were being held prisoner by Vera who had convinced the CPS worker that she was a caring, supportive person. Maybe she had even convinced me of this. Mary wanted me to know that just the opposite was true; Vera was emotionally abusive to both Mary and Gail. According to Mary, Vera would not let her hold her child and when the baby tried to come to her for comfort, Vera would restrain her. Vera would also tie Gail's arms down to her sides at night and prop a bottle in her mouth.

The CPS caseworker had ordered Mary not to remove Gail from Vera's home, but Mary had left and gone to Kevin's.

On my first visit Mary was very anxious to tell me all the details of what it was like at Vera's for her and Gail. She also wanted Gail to be removed from Vera's even if that meant she would have to go to a foster home. Because Vera had accused Kevin's stepfather (Kevin was living with him) of sexual abuse of children, the CPS worker was unwilling for Mary to bring Gail there. However, he met with Mary, Kevin, and me and agreed to move Gail to a foster home until Mary could relocate. I spent over 3 hours with Mary and Kevin on this visit. Much of the time I simply used reflective listening to encourage them to give me all the details they felt I needed to know and expressed empathy and concern for their difficult situation. At the end of this time we spent a few minutes making preliminary plans for working on their most immediate problem—getting housing quickly so they could get Gail back. They said they felt much better having a plan and someone to help them. (Dawn James)

Work and school schedules often prevent families who need services from receiving them. Fathers and teens especially may miss counseling sessions that are held during traditonal agency hours. If family members do not have to "give up" favorite activities or rearrange their work and school schedules to see their counselor, they are likely to feel more positive about the counseling and be more willing to actively participate. Encouraging family members to actively participate in setting up the time for appointments is a potentially useful teaching tool since it rewards them for taking control over part of their learning process.

This flexibility does not mean counselors have no say in when appointments occur. Particularly after the crisis period has passed, times can be negotiated, and some can be set up in advance so that workers can plan their personal lives. If a special event like a wedding anniversary is coming up, families can be told, and supervisors or teammates can provide coverage.

Services and Options

We provide a wide range of services. We try to fit the intervention to the family's life-style, skill level, and values. Rather than fitting the family to the service, workers aim to custom make or tailor the services to individual needs and preferences. We try to accommodate values, style, resources, and energy levels of our clients, and to approach change from many angles including behavioral, cognitive, and environmental. Concrete services we provide are described in detail in Chapter 8.

An example of the concrete services and advocacy is as follows:

Patty, age 28, and Bill, age 35, lived with their two children, Betty, age 3, and Joshua, age 7 weeks, at a low-rent hotel in the downtown area. The family had no cooking facilities so ate all their meals at a nearby hospitality kitchen. Some laundry facilities existed but had been overused and undermaintained and the heating system and plumbing in the building rarely worked properly. The children had nowhere to play as the single room was taken up by two single beds and a crib.

We focused on the family's housing needs and finding money for rent. Patty was taken to the housing authority but there was a long waiting list. We found classified ads regarding available rentals, made phone calls regarding cost and location, etc., and drove to look at possible residences. I helped Patty fill out rental applications as she had trouble reading and writing.

When a comfortable and otherwise suitable apartment was found we negotiated the rental agreement and payment of rent and located funds for the damage deposit [half paid by BSI ($100) and half by me ($100)]; a written contract was drawn up between the family and me regarding repayment of this loan of $100. The family did pay me $25 a month to repay this loan.

We moved the family's belongings out of the hotel and into their new residence with my pick-up truck. Three days later several Homebuilder counselors helped the family move other possessions out of storage and into their new house using one borrowed pick-up and my truck. After the move was completed and in following days, we helped unpack boxes and arrange furniture. (Peggy Mandin)

We do not require that all family members be present. We will work with whoever is present or whoever is interested in change at that particular time. We see some family members individually as well as in various combinations. We might use family sessions to assess interactions between people, to teach communications and negotiations, to set up contracts, or to review progress. We might use individual sessions when blaming is occurring at a high rate, when feelings are escalated, when working on individual goals, or when we have no choice because only one person is willing to work with us.

A list of clinical services we provide in shown in Table 1.

Intensity: Low Caseload

All family preservation programs serve only a few families at a time in order to provide time to take advantages of crises and monitor dangerous situations. At Homebuilders, our workers serve only two families at a time, the lowest level of FPS caseloads. Others vary from two to six families per worker.

With this low caseload we have the time to help families learn new skills as well as resolve their presenting crises. It's the only way to achieve the accessibility and flexibility that families need during high emotional times. The smaller the caseload, the more feasible it is to meet emergencies. The larger the case load, the more meeting emergencies disrupts planned visits. If safety is a big issue for referring agencies, then the ability to respond with as much flexibility as possible is important. If a worker must spend most of the next 2 days on a new case, the difference between rescheduling one other family and five

Table 1. Homebuilder Clinical Services Checklist

Please record the services you provided any family member, or the family as a whole, by indicating with a check mark whether the service was provided. Service categories not utilized for this family should be left blank.

1. Child Management/Parent Effectiveness Training:

   __ Use of reinforcement   __ Active listening skills
   __ Tracking behaviors   __ I statements
   __ Environmental controls   __ No lose problem solving
   __ Natural/logical consequences   __ Problem ownership
   __ Time out   __ Other_____

2. Emotion Management:

   __ Anger management   __ Use of crisis card
   __ Depression management   __ Rational Emotive Therapy concepts
   __ Anxiety/confusion   __ Rational Emotive Therapy techniques
      management   __ Pleasant events
   __ Self-criticism reduction   __ Relaxation
   __ Building self-esteem   __ Tracking emotions
   __ Handling frustration   __ Other_____
   __ Impulse management

3. Interpersonal Skills:

   __ Conversational/social skills   __ Appropriate sexual behavior
   __ Problem solving   __ Accepting "no"
   __ Negotiation skills   __ Improving compliance
   __ Giving/accepting feedback   __ Other_____

4. Assertiveness:

   __ Territoriality concepts   __ General concepts/skills
   __ Fair fighting   __ Other_____

5. Miscellaneous Clinical:

   __ Use of journal   __ Setting treatment goals/objectives
   __ Listening   __ Providing reinforcers
   __ Encouraging hope   __ Counseling referral
   __ Monitoring client   __ Treatment plans
   __ Building hope   __ Deescalating
   __ Relationship building   __ Values clarification
   __ Family council   __ Support/understanding
   __ Clarifying family roles   __ Structure/routine
   __ Process of change   __ Clarifying family rules
   __ Child/adolescent   __ Tracking/charting behavior
      development   __ Role playing
   __ Social skills   __ Providing literature
   __ Clarifying problem behaviors   __ Paper pencil tests
   __ Defusing crises   __ Multiple Impact Therapy
   __ Reframing

Table 1.   Continued

6. Advocacy:
    __ Referral to counseling   __ Educational system
    __ Referral to social services   __ Social service providers
    __ Consultation   __ Court hearings
    __ Utility companies   __ Other_____

7. Other:
    __ Money management   __ Informal support systems
    __ Time management   __ Recognizing potential suicide
    __ Leisure activities   __ Protective skills
    __ Job hunting/interviewing   __ Other_____
    __ Academic skills

others is dramatic. Staying longer with one family when they need more time is harder if there is another family scheduled soon and maybe another after that. A small caseload allows us to stay long enough during the first session to hear the whole story, even though the story is 5 hours long. It allows us to come back the next day to get to work on problems, without waiting until next week when the problems may all be different. Frequent contact with a family for hours at a time increases the opportunity to assess and promote a safe home environment for children and parents. It can reassure Child Protective Services workers that we are different from traditional services, and can provide the degree of protection and surveillance necessary to help them feel comfortable referring very difficult families.

Continuous, intensive involvement with families facilitates gathering more complete, qualitatively different information. Since the counselors are with their families for long periods of time, they "live their life with them: and see things as they really are." This continuous, intensive involvement with families also helps the counselor transcend the traditional worker-client relationship. The relationship becomes more equal, and deeper, closer to that of a supportive friend. With frequent contact and massed time, more work and better quality work can be accomplished than with conventional methods, because little time has to be spent on reviewing the problems each visit. Problems and solutions can be discussed exhaustively. Quick successes can be followed with additional success experiences, and initial failures can be corrected quickly to find more successful interventions.

The small caseload makes it possible to manage delivery of concrete services. In New York, it may take all day for a client to see a doctor, or to begin to straighten out red tape regarding public assistance. This capacity is critical in establishing trust and cooperation with seriously discouraged clients. It becomes less and less feasible as caseloads increase.

Low caseloads facilitate administrative scheduling. Often, cases can be terminated at the same time to allow for vacations. Coverage for compensatory time, crises, or sick leave is much easier than it would be if there were more cases.

A small caseload also helps workers stay on top of issues. Most families served by our program have needs in a number of areas, and the worker's experience with each family is often intense. Without adequate time, it would be difficult to keep track of everything that is going on with each family. The low caseload allows workers to keep all of the complicated problems and relationships and plans clearly in mind.

Low caseloads make it possible to give out home phone numbers. Having two families as potential callers is only one-third the hassle of having six families call, and only one-sixth the hassle of having 12 families who might call. Workers feel the low caseload is critical to both client safety and prevention of burnout.

I would feel frightened for the safety of the family and worried about my ability to keep more than two families safe when they experience serious and dangerous crises simultaneously. Usually only one of my families is experiencing a severe crisis at a particular time and I am able to implement a number of interventions to ensure their safety. Foremost among these options is staying with the family for as many hours as necessary in order to feel reasonably certain that they are safe. Even after leaving, it is often necessary to remain in close phone contact with the family and to make sure I am available to respond to any further escalation of the situation. I also schedule an appointment for the next day whenever possible in order to assess any changes in the situation, take further action if necessary, and take advantage of the crisis state to teach new skills. Putting a large amount of time into the intervention during a crisis often proves quite productive in terms of family safety and making progress in teaching skills. However, it could be very draining both physically and emotionally and sometimes required rescheduling appointments with my other family. I often find it necessary to take a day off after the situation had calmed sufficiently, although this was rare. Sometimes both families do escalate simultaneously and the same level of intervention is not possible without much support and assistance from my supervisor and team members. If more than two families escalated simultaneously, this task would become progressively more difficult, if not impossible. It would not be possible to stay a large number of hours and then return the next day. The rescheduling of 5 to 9 other families would prove to be a monumental task and if it happened several times, could prove harmful to the other families. I would also be concerned about the stress and strain placed on supervisors and team members with large caseloads. With ten families of my own, I believe I would be less likely to be willing or able to help out another counselor when one of his/her families was in crisis. An important element in a successful Homebuilders intervention is the support one receives from supervisors and other counselors. A large caseload would be detrimental to this support.

Part of the strain of being a Homebuilder is the knowledge that I can be asked to respond at any time. The more families I would cover, the more likely that I would have to make the shift from relaxed to ready for action. In my 4-1/2 years as a counselor, there have been numerous times that I had TV programs, books, conversations, and activities interrupted by the need to respond to a crisis. Although I get better at it over time, there was always an awareness that when the phone rang it might be time to go to work. Knowing that there were 6, 8, or 10 families who might require that kind of response at any one time would increase the probability of any single call being from a client and increase the anxiety each time the phone rang.

I would like to believe that if I carried more than two families at a time I would respond with the same intensity that I did when I carried two families. But if I did respond that way to 6, 8, or 10 families, I could not keep it up for very long. Even if I was a person who could tolerate the physical and emotional demands of such a response, I doubt seriously whether my wife and children could or would. At the point I felt I could no longer maintain that level of intense response or my family began to suffer inordinately because of it, I would have essentially two choices: find another job (often interpreted to mean someone is "burned out") or reduce the intensity of my response to the crises my families experience. I find neither option very satisfying. (Jack Chambers)

Even though they only see two cases at a time, our counselors may see the same or more cases per year (20) as workers in many other settings. Group homes, for example, may require 6 staff for 10 children who remain in the home all year. Their ratio would be 3 workers for 5 children as opposed to Homebuilders' 1 worker for 20 families. The difference is that we see families sequentially rather than concurrently. Thus, the cost per family is similar to many more traditional services. Most service providers are not accustomed to thinking about caseloads in this way. Often, program planners increase caseloads from two to six or twelve. Then they realize they need more time, so they increase the duration of the intervention from 4 to 12 weeks, or to 6 months. Whenever workers have a goal of seeing two families for 1 month, six families for 3 months, or 12 families for 6 months, they all will see the same number of families in a year.

Brevity: Length of Service Provision

By traditional standards for counseling, all family preservation programs are brief. The length of time usually correlates with the number of families seen at one time. If we hold costs constant and increase duration, it is necessary for counselors to serve more families at one time. Programs range from 4 weeks to 6 months. Often, because of the correlation between duration and caseload, families are seen for a similar number of total hours regardless of duration.

Homebuilders is the briefest approach. We see cases for only 4 to 6 weeks. This period may seem short to many. Often people are skeptical that significant change can occur in a month. Clients often say they would like more time. It is possible that with some families more could be accomplished if the intervention were longer. Counselors sometimes say they would like more time. A longer intervention could give workers more time to link clients with community resources having long waiting lists.

A 4 to 6 week time frame would probably not be sufficient for significant change in many more traditional approaches. The Family Preservation approach, however, has a number of differences that make it possible for change to occur more rapidly. Clients are in crisis. They are seen for intensive periods of time in the settings where the problems are occurring. They see workers when they need to see them, for as long as they need. Because of the low caseload, it is possible for clients to get the equivalent number of hours to a year's outpatient therapy in only 4 weeks. One participant in a training workshop referred to the short-term approach as a "microwave" intervention, where the outcome is comparable to other longer services. We do think that all the different aspects of this program design lead to a more powerful type of energy than is usually available. A short time frame has other advantages, as well. One of the most important is the expectation that change can occur rapidly. Workers discuss the 4 week time frame with the client during the first visit and continue to refer to it frequently throughout the intervention period. The message is that change can occur right away, and indeed it must, in order to fit into the time period. For many clients, this expectation is a relief: their problems may not have to drag on for many more years.

The short time frame also helps keep the worker and the family focused on specific goals and progress that is being made toward them. When they know there is a finite time period, they are more likely to use the time productively.

After 4 to 6 weeks, most clients are no longer in crisis. They have reached a plateau and are ready to take a break from the hard work of changing their lives. If they wished to continue, they would not wish to continue at such an intense level. Workers would have large amounts of extra time if they kept to their two caseload limit. If they gradually added more cases, they would lose the flexibility and accessibility that we think is necessary to help clients when the potentials for danger is high.

Both clients and workers tell us that it is easier to give their full commitment for a short period of time. The more severe the crisis, the less either the client or the worker should be holding back on energy, commitment, or attention, in order to pace themselves.

We believe the short time frame helps prevent worker burnout. Some families are extremely draining. Many are challenging. Workers say they can cope with anything for 4 weeks. If they thought they were going to continue for 6 months, it might be different.

The short period also diminshes the potential for dependence. When workers have the time and resources to do so much to help families, families might easily come to rely on them in ways that would not be functional in the long run. Workers and family members can keep in touch with the fact that family members need to care for themselves if the time they will be together is short. If one emphasizes time limitedness as well as duration, the longer the duration, the less meaningful time limitedness is as a motivator for a worker and family. To tell a family member we must be finished in 4 weeks may cause us to get hopping right now. Logic suggests that a deadline of 26 weeks will not motivate as well in situations where procrastination and avoidance of some problems can easily occur. The worker may be more likely to postpone things as well, since so much time is available.

Moreover, we have found that our success rate in averting out-of-home placement does not appear to be influenced by the length of the intervention (Table 2). Indeed, some comparisons have indicated no relationship between length of treatment and success in preventing placement.

Table 2. Mean Length of Treatment and Percentage of Cases Averting Placement for Five Home-Based Programs (Lloyd, 1982)

Program name location	Length of service (months)	Percent averting placement
Families of West Branch West Branch, Iowa	5	81
Home and Community Treatment Madison, Wisconsin	13	90
Homebuilders Federal Way, Washington	1½	92
Intensive Family Support Hillside Children's Center Rochester, New York	7	89
Oregon Intensive Family Support Sites in Oregon State	3	92

Over the years, we have tried varying the length of the intervention. We have experimented with 8-week, 6-week, and 4-week interventions, maintaining identical goals and intensity. The gradual decrease from 8 weeks to 4- to 6 was the result of pressure to serve more clients. We did not see a difference in our success rate.

Informal data indicate that most families who are unable to benefit from a 4- to 6-week intervention do not benefit any more from a longer period. If what we have to offer is not working for them, doing more of it still doesn't seem to work. From the referring worker/public agency point of view the increased cost of a longer intervention is difficult to justify if 4 to 6 weeks accomplishes the goal of placement prevention for 73-91% of the families referred. Even though we recommend a 4- to 6-week intervention period, this time limit is a guideline, not an absolute. Although most families can be terminated in 4 weeks, there will be some that need, and get, more time, and some families where placement can be averted in less than 4 weeks. This topic is discussed in more detail in Chapter 10. "Booster shots" are available and families can be re-referred for another complete intervention if necessary.

Accessibility

Although many families would like Homebuilders to continue longer, others see the short time frame as positive.

The child in danger of placement was an 11-year-old girl (Judy) who had been placed with her adoptive family (the Whites) 2 years previously, after a series of foster placements. There were three other children in the family, aged 15, 12, and 10. I am a researcher. Because this family was part of a special project, I visited the family soon after termination and asked them to discuss the intervention, their level of satisfaction with the services, and how things had changed in their family. Both parents reported being very satisfied and felt that things had changed significantly for the better although they were not "perfect." Mrs. White said: "When we first started Homebuilders I wasn't sure whether we were going to be able to keep Judy. I felt like it could have gone either way. Now I'm feeling more encouraged. Things aren't perfect but they are a lot better."

Both parents were ready for the counseling to be over at termination: Mrs. White said "When Nancy first started working with us I thought 4 weeks would not do it. But by the end of 3 weeks I was ready for it to end. It was very intense and we thought about it every day."

Mr. White said "I was glad it was only 4 weeks. It got to be overwhelming and was on my mind every minute." The Homebuilder met with the family 12 times during the intervention and spent 31 hours of face-to-face time with the family and 2.25 hours of telephone time. (Kay McDade)

Staffing

Many family preservation programs use teams. Some use two professionals, and some use a professional and a paraprofessional. At Homebuilders, we use a single worker supported by a team. Although each of our counselors is responsible for conducting the entire intervention for each of his/her clients, he/she has ready access at all times to the larger team for support and backup.

Using a team of two counselors, or of one professional and one paraprofessional, has appeal, especially when one considers the intensity of the service, the 24 hour accessibility of the counselor, the severity of clients' problems, and the emphasis on accountability. A team of two workers probably would be safer going to and from families' homes. Some planning groups worry that they cannot find one worker with the capacity to provide all the desired services. In general, two heads are better than one. Specifically, some kinds of communications exercises are done more effectively with two counselors. Also, many counselors believe they would prefer working as a team and sharing being on call. It is possible that two workers could decrease the length of time needed.

However, holding caseload and duration of intervention constant, using teams costs twice as much. We use single counselors for other reasons as well. What we are trying to do with families is integrate and validate a number of opposing points of view into one resolution. Teams usually split up family members and often end up advocating for "their" person, without as much concern for the whole. If one person is responsible for all family members, she is motivated to get as much information as possible from all family members for a good synthesis. The worker must maintain equally good channels of communication with all family members in order to elicit maximum cooperation. We think this provides better quality information, with a solution that is more tailored to the family as a unit.

Family members may learn to trust and relate to just one person more easily than to two new people. Many families already have a problem with too many different workers, family members, and friends pushing them in different directions. We have had families with as many as 15 other "helpers," many considering themselves to be the primary counselor or case manager. Family members do not usually know what all the different workers are supposed to be doing, or how they relate to each other. Workers often do not know either, and sometimes give the family conflicting demands. When family members become overwhelmed by their situation it can be useful if, even briefly, they only have to think about relating to one service provider who will help them with all their problems, or at least help them to understand and coordinate with all the other helpers who are involved.

A single counselor takes less planning, debriefing, and record-keeping time. No information is lost between team members. The counselor knows that he/she alone is responsible for coalescing information into one big picture. The counselor can do spontaneous interventions; that is, identify an opportunity to teach and take advantage of it without coordinating with someone else. She does not have to worry about control issues, or hard feelings between two workers. Family members know who to call in case of emergency. They know one person has all the information and is able to deal with all their issues.

Using a team to see each family can blur accountability. Therapists often do not feel as much of a sense of accomplishment when things go well because they share credit with another team member. In contrast, when progress is limited, it is difficult to determine whether the problems lie with one worker or the other, or with the interaction between the two.

Our choice to use one worker per family is not intended in any way to minimize the need for counselor safety, support, and training. We have just chosen to deal with those as separate issues from teaming. Rather than workers each having full time bodyguards or consultants, we have addressed worker safety and need for ideas in other ways that will be discussed in other chapters.

Summary

Although Family Preservation Services vary in their interpretations of the details, all involve serving families in crisis. Family Preservation Services value accessibility of workers and service provision in the natural environment. They all provide a wide range of both concrete and clinical services. All programs offer large numbers of hours of service per week, over a short time frame.

II

STAGES OF INTERVENTION

3
Keeping People Safe

Family Preservation Services offer many advantages, but we must stay aware of the risks as well. Programs that keep children in homes where the potential for danger has already come to the attention of the state bear enormous responsibility for accurate assessment of potential violence and prevention of violence. In Chapters 4 and 5 we will discuss more ways to help clients be safe from themselves and each other. Before we can help clients, however, we have to get our counselors into their neighborhoods and homes. Keeping everyone safe must be the top priority, every day, for all programs attempting to serve families in their own homes.

In this section of the book we discuss the stages of the actual intervention with families. The initial stage of that intervention involves the first call to the family and getting to the family's home. Unless those first steps occur effectively and safely, the rest of the intervention cannot occur. In this chapter we will emphasize ways to keep ourselves safe on the way to clients' homes and while we are with them. Many of the precautions we take for ourselves also help to keep the situation safer for clients.

Most Homebuilders clients and most of their neighborhoods have some potential for harm, but few require all the precautions and interventions described in this chapter. Most of us feel we are in more danger from others in client neighborhoods and on the way to their homes than from clients themselves. In Washington State, most Homebuilders feel safe, most of the time. In New York City, most people feel a little uneasy most of the time. The basic level of comfort is as much related to the location of the program as it is to being a Homebuilder. To a large extent, this issue is a dilemma. We balance on a delicate edge between giving distraught families a chance to change, and trying to protect everyone. In 15 years and over 5000 clients, one Homebuilder has been slapped one time. The rate of violence is low partly because most clients and most neighborhoods where we work present a minimal threat and partly, we think, because we are very careful. The precautions

41

and procedures presented here are not intended to imply that being a Homebuilder is the same as being a policeman in a ghetto or a soldier in battle. They are to help you remain as safe as you possibly can even though most situations will not warrant that much wariness.

When we first began, everyone assumed that workers would not enter homes where there was high potential for violence. We learned during the first month that if all those cases were screened out, there would be few left to see. It was difficult to assess the actual danger of clients as described by referring workers. We heard scary stories about particular family members, but when we went out to their homes, the people greeting us seemed a lot like Aunt Sally or Cousin Bob—a little quirky, perhaps, but basically regular folks.

Nevertheless, Aunt Sally and Cousin Bob can do things we might not predict. It's impossible to feel either comfortable or safe in a situation where loaded weapons are within reach, or Aunt Sally's neighbor is threatening to beat you to a pulp, or where one brother has just taken off after another with a butcher knife. It's also difficult to intervene in these situations. Feelings and behavior are out of control. So we spend a lot of time carefully assessing how violent a situation is likely to become, and even more time thinking about how to prevent violence from erupting all around us.

Predicting Violence

No one is nearly as good as any of us would like in predicting violence. Child Protective Services workers have trouble. Police have trouble. Parole Officers have trouble. So do we. Some reports indicate we might all be better off if we just admitted we cannot predict (American Psychiatric Association, 1974; Monahan, 1981). However, others (Gelles, 1987b.) point out some weaknesses in past research and suggest that there are a number of variables that can be taken into consideration if we are predicting violence.

The finding that overshadows all others is that each past incidence of violence increases the current probability of violence. Younger people are more likely to commit violent acts than older people. Also, the younger the person was when he committed his first violent act, the more likely it is that he will commit additional violence. Low socioeconomic status is correlated with violent crime. All major studies have found that drug or alcohol abuse correlates with violence.

Some environmental factors also appear to be important, although the research confirming their correlation with violence is still in its early stages. Ones we consider include the following: Does the family support or discourage violent behavior? Do they use physical punishment? To what degree? Do they think it's okay to hit each other? Do they punish each other when violence occurs? Does the client associate with and plan to continue associating with people who encourage violent behavior or are violent themselves? Are there weapons in the house or readily accessible outside? Careful assessment of all the factors listed above will not eliminate all danger, but it will decrease it, and we need to do everything we can to minimize this danger.

Gathering Information before the Visit

We have several ways to get information pertaining to the potential for violence before we reach the family's home. The information we gather influences other precautions we may take, and the amount of time we spend with family members on the telephone before we set out for the visit. Rarely, the information we get could be so alarming that we would request a teammate or supervisor accompany us.

Talking with the Referring Worker

It's part of our intake worker's job to follow up on any suggestions from the referring worker that a family may be out of control. Our intake worker routinely asks about past violence and assessed potential. If danger seems possible or likely, it's a good idea for the counselor to call the referring worker herself to collect as much information as possible on variables such as those listed above.

Calling the Family

If we are fortunate enough to have a family with a telephone, we can also gather additional information directly from them before the visit. It's good to make the call to set up the appointment at a time when we are not in a hurry. It is not uncommon to spend an hour on the phone with one or more family members before we go to the home. During this conversation, if a family member feels pressured or angry, it is often helpful to actively listen so he will begin expressing his concerns immediately. This can begin to form a positive relationship that will make things easier when we get to the home. If one person talks until he is calm, but is worried that another family member is going to hurt someone before the counselor arrives, we can try to get the other person on the phone and spend some time helping him to deescalate, too. One potential benefit of listening to people before the visit is that it is easier to hear them one at a time than it is to walk into a group of family members all wanting attention at once. If a relationship has begun over the phone, it can reduce the pressure to respond to everyone immediately once we get there.

On the phone, it is often possible to avoid direct questioning by reflecting, with clients, on "How bad it's been to have Joey trying to strangle Susie" or "How scary it's been to have Mike carrying that rifle all the time," or "How concerned everyone is about Tiffany getting beaten up again." An example of beginning to help a client calm herself down over the phone is as follows:

> Abbey (37), the mother of 15-year-old Tammy (the PR), who was in receiving care when we got the referral, was very angry with her daughter and the child welfare system when I called to make our first appointment. We talked for about an hour and a half. Most of that time she was asking "why"—why parents have no power, why kids have all the control, why running away is not a crime, why everybody is blaming the parents. She also told stories about Tammy's past misbehavior, failure to respond to her (and her husband's) efforts to improve the family situation. For about 45 minutes I responded almost entirely by active listening—reflecting frustration, embarrassment, anger, discouragement, confusion. After a time Abbey began to talk more slowly and in a lower tone of voice. She was still asking questions and at that point I occasionally shared with her my understanding of the *intent* of some policies, laws, caseworkers, etc., acknowledging that the system is not perfect, is evolving and sometimes backfires. I shared with her that I was her age and that I also observed generational differences and sometimes found teenagers confusing. By the end of our conversation we had made an appointment and in three or four instances Abbey had laughed at something we had said. She apologized for being so angry and saying so many (according to her culture—Asian) rude things. I assured her that I wanted to hear her real feelings and that I appreciated her candor and her frustration. We hung up looking forward to meeting each other. (Ellen Douthat)

Sometimes, though, reflection fails to comfort. We may then question family members directly after taking the time to get to know them during the phone conversation. A counselor can say, "Mrs. Williams at CPS mentioned that Marty carries a hunting knife all the time. Is that true?" "Does it concern you?" "It concerns me." At this point, we're just trying to gather information about potential for violence, not do anything to prevent it.

If family members are worried, they often have some ideas on keeping control, such as "I won't talk about him coming home drunk again," or

"I could send Janine next door until you got here." If family members are afraid someone will be hurt while waiting for the counselor, it is possible to suggest they stay in different rooms until she arrives. If weapons are an issue, most people are willing to lock them in a car trunk or take them to a neighbor until feelings are less intense and overwhelming. For example:

> My very first case was a distraught father with 5 or 6 kids, one of whom was a baby. His wife left him one night and he called and asked me to come over to help with the children and offer support since he was really shaken. When I got there, he went in a bedroom and I heard a clicking noise. In a couple minutes he emerged with a gun. At first I was very frightened and speechless (I'd never seen a gun up close!). He asked me to keep it for him because he wasn't sure what he'd do if he kept it and he handed it to me. Fortunately, about 2 minutes later there was a knock at the door and a police officer was escorting the wife home. The officer told me about the safekeeping place at the police department and took the gun there--whew—! (Karen Bream)

Getting Consultation from a Supervisor

When a counselor is concerned about the safety of anyone involved in a case, he *must* contact his supervisor and discuss the issues before going to the clients' home. This is not an option; it's mandatory. If the supervisor is unavailable, counselors must call other agency administrative staff or supervisors. With many precarious families, staff arrange to call supervisors at specified times after they have gone to a family's home. If the call does not come, the supervisor knows to get help. Supervisors also carry clients' phone numbers and addresses so they may call or drop by if they are concerned. In some situations a counselor may decide to bring her supervisor or a co-worker on the first visit. On occasion, it may be wise to bring a co-worker for each family member who may have difficulty controlling him or herself. Sometimes the person referring the case will also go along.

Planning to Meet in a Neutral Place.

In some situations, it may be a good idea to meet somewhere other than the family's home. A structured, public environment, such as a restaurant or community center, may make it easier for the family members to retain control. At the least, the counselor may feel safer and find it easier to think clearly. Denny's is great: endless coffee refills, nice people around. Few people get wild at Denny's.

Keeping Ourselves Calm

Once the information about the case has been gathered, and a counselor has ascertained that any necessary precautions have been taken,
the most important factor in precluding violence is the counselor's
own state of mind. We will talk later, in Chapter 13, about ways
counselors learn to keep themselves calm. It helps if workers can fill
their heads with ideas about not having to solve everything immediately, about not having to control everyone, and about having the
time just to listen and watch until appropriate courses of action
reveal themselves. Taking deep breaths helps. Some counselors also
think about any positive qualities/strengths the intake information
indicates.

We emphasize getting focused and organized before leaving for the
visit, whenever possible. Counselors say some of the following things to
themselves on the way to the first and other sessions:

I notice nice things about the drive, neighborhood. I notice where the
nearest fast food places are (are there any *good* ones?). Any parks or good
places to take a walk? Where might I do paperwork near here? Is this a
neighborhood I haven't explored before—haven't visited the library here?
I rehearse and review what resources for the family are near here.
Sometimes I reflect upon other cases with similar features—what worked
and what didn't. What was fun about them. This is the easiest session. All
I have to do is listen, listen, listen. Things never seem as bad when the
people have faces and *are* people as when the situation is presented on
paper. (Ellen Douthat)

I do self-hypnosis, and imagine myself doing a fantastic intake where
I'm "right on" with all my active listening statements, completely charming,
and feeling totally together. Sometimes I imagine something really calm,
like the ocean or an eagle soaring. (Gretel LeVieri)

"Family situations often sound worse on paper than they are in
person. The family sounded agreeable to my coming out over the phone."
"Even though it is not pleasant to listen to people yell at each other,
I can handle it (as I have before) and teach them other ways to interact."
"Pain and discomfort and conflict in a family are to be expected or they
wouldn't need intensive services." "I can always leave if I feel it is
dangerous." "I can't solve or know everything in one night. My job during
the first session is to active listen. I can problem solve later." (Peggy
Mandin)

My job is to active listen, not solve all the problems. The situation may
not be as bad as it appears on the referral sheet. In 3 or 4 hours the session
will probably be over and I will be at home drinking tea. I will survive this.
I can call my supervisor or another counselor for help if I get stuck. (Carol
Mitchell)

Traveling to the Home

Traveling by Car

When we travel by car, we try to park as close to the home as possible. It's a good idea to notice locations of doors. We may want one. It's also a good idea to notice neighbors. We may or may not want one of them, depending on how they look and behave.

Traveling by Subway

Traveling by subway can be a little more exciting than your average drive in the country. It's important to map out the journey carefully and know right where we're going. If the subway is empty or it's late at night or we're going through a particularly rough part of town, we sit by the doors between the cars. If anyone scary comes in, we can go into the next car, or if we need to, pull the red emergency lever hanging down from the ceiling. We encourage workers to move if they feel the least bit uneasy. It's not important to worry about looking foolish. It's important to think about minimizing our risks, all the time.

Again, when we get off the subway, we need to know where we're going. We try to get detailed instructions. If we can't, we see if someone can go with us the first time. It's a good idea to watch carefully for anyone suspicious. If someone may be following us, it is possible to use windows or mirrors to check. We tell our workers to cross the street if they feel nervous, and to stay away from bushes and dark corners. Cars can be good blockades. If someone does come after us, a parked car can keep them at a distance until we can attract attention or run away.

Entering the Home

When we enter apartment buildings, we look for curved mirrors near the ceiling to look in areas we cannot see directly, and listen for sounds of others nearby. If there's an elevator, we send it down to the basement and don't get in until it returns. Unfriendly people can program an elevator to take us to the basement no matter which button we push. When it arrives, they can take us out and mug us, or worse. Don't get in an elevator if someone suspicious is inside. Again, don't worry about looking foolish. Worry about being safe. Once you are in, stand as close as possible to the elevator panel so you can control the stops. If someone in the elevator starts acting strange, push the closest button and get off even if it isn't the floor you want.

When we get to the door of a house or apartment, it's important to listen before we knock. It's good to stand to the side of the door so we won't be close, eye to eye with whoever opens it. When someone does open it, we need to wait to be invited in. We go slowly and let our eyes adjust to the light. Even if the door is ajar, it's not a good idea to just go in.

Meeting the Family

Being Considerate and Careful

Once we're in, we try to sit in a safe place, unless a family member indicates that he wants the worker in a certain seat. If so, we sit where they prefer. Otherwise, we're usually the most comfortable if we leave ourselves an exit and sit near a door. Most of us prefer to have our backs to a wall. Usually, living rooms are the safest places. Guns are often in bedrooms. Kitchens are full of potential weapons.

During this tentative, delicate first meeting, it is critical that we respect clients' personal space and avoid crowding them or doing anything that can be interpreted as pushing them around. It's a good idea to make no assumptions and check out everything we do. We'll talk in detail about ways to engage them in Chapter 4. If the engaging and defusing processes go smoothly, we don't have to worry about further prevention of violence for this session, because people will become engrossed in telling their stories and will be relieved after having done so. Usually, this is the case.

Sometimes, however, people are already fighting with one another, or begin soon after we arrive. They may interrupt and blame each other. We may notice nonverbal signals that precede violence, such as angry facial expressions, clenched fists, rigid body posture, rapid breathing or red faces, as well as verbalizations of intent to fight.

Separating Family Members

If any of the above is occurring, or if family members seem very tense, it is possible to say that we really want to hear everyone's point of view thoroughly and it's easy to get confused with so much going on. Would it be possible for us to talk with people one at a time? An example is:

Nancy, age 13, became extremely angry with her mother, Pam, age 35, because Pam was not believing Nancy's statements regarding her stepfather's sexual abuse toward her. Nancy, who was crying and pacing around the room, finally began lifting up one end of the dining room table (her mother was sitting at the other end) and repeatedly banged it on the floor. Verbal conflict also escalated. Nancy also threw water in her mother's face and pushed over a stack of books so that they slid toward Pam. Pam in turn became angry and threatened to press assault changes against her daughter.

The family lived in a mobile home with little private space. I positioned myself so that Nancy would most likely move in the direction of the front door and suggested we go outside together. After telling Pam I would be back in a minute, I active listened to Nancy and got her to sit in my car. I subsequently went back into the home to active listen to Pam. I continued to go back and forth between Nancy in the car and Pam in the house. I was able to get one of Nancy's books from the home so that she could read to calm down while I was talking with her mother, until they were both calm enough to come together again.

The family did not get back together. The mother called the police—I waited for the officer to arrive (2 hours) and recommended placement in receiving care that night. The mother wanted to press assault charges and refused to have the girl stay home. The girl ended up going to live with her natural father in another state, whom she had not seen since infancy. (Peggy Mandin)

Taking the Hardest One First

Often, one family member may seem particularly upset, pessimistic, or uncooperative. Although it can be difficult, it is often helpful to talk individually with the "hardest" person first, taking as much time as necessary to help him feel important and understood. Once this person has deescalated and his confidence is gained, he can be helpful in supporting us and encouraging other family members to participate. An example of one such case is:

After the first session, the wife told us she wanted to announce her divorce to her husband the next night with us present. (Peggy Mandin and I). We tried to suggest *many* different options, but she was really set on this. The night of the "announcement" we had the husband go first so he would have a chance to have everyone hear his viewpoint/feelings before the details/reactions of the divorce took up the rest of the session. (Karen Bream)

Active Listening

In trying to help clients calm down, *active listening*, discussed in detail in Chapter 4, is our most powerful tool. It's important for us to validate

clients' angry feelings without encouraging angry behavior, with statements such as "It sounds really frustrating," and "You were really at the
end of your rope." Usually the person who is most upset will respond
best if he's treated very gently. People are also often scared or hurt when
they act angry. They may feel much more vulnerable than we would
initially guess from their loud behavior. Sometimes it's very helpful for
us to just sit there and be with angry clients while they vent. It won't go
on forever. We don't point out contradictions or distortions yet. Our
goal now is to understand and to build trust, not to judge or facilitate
change. An example is:

> Chris, a 15-year-old boy, his mother, and stepfather were sitting in their
> living room with me when Chris's younger sister, Amy, walked through
> with a plastic pitcher, which she said she was taking next door to use at a
> birthday party. Chris said loudly that he did not want her to take anything
> that belonged to their family to the neighbor's house. His sister hesitated,
> but left when her mother told her to go ahead. Chris remained sitting, but
> began swearing and making threats toward his sister and the neighbors.
> Chris's mother and father both tried to calm him down, at first by
> reasoning and then by pleading and eventually through commands and
> threats. Chris continued to escalate to the point where it appeared to me
> that he was actually going to go next door and, at the very least, demand
> that his sister bring the pitcher back. Being a new counselor (this was my
> fourth case,) I began mentally reviewing my recent training in search of a
> technique to defuse the situation. Before long, I stumbled upon active
> listening. I made an initial active listening statement about Chris being
> angry about his sister taking the pitcher next door. To my surprise, Chris
> turned toward me and began explaining in a much lower voice that he
> didn't like the neighbors because they had accused him of breaking into
> their house and stealing some things. I then reflected Chris's feelings that
> he was being unfairly accused of something he didn't do. After two or
> three more active listening statements reflecting Chris's disappointment,
> hurt, embarrassment, and anger, Chris became completely deescalated
> and dropped the subject. (Don Miner)

Sharing Our Feelings

If we feel concerned, it's good to share our feelings. "I'm afraid
someone is going to be hurt." "I don't know how I can help you while
you have that knife." "I'm afraid when you scream at me like that." It's
usually a good idea to share feeling if we're overwhelmed too. Family
members can usually tell from our nonverbal behavior (such as our
hands shaking so we can't drink the coffee they gave us) when we're
uncomfortable. We will be more congruent with them, and therefore
more credible if we acknowledge the difficulty we're having. For

example, "I'm getting really overwhelmed by all these issues. Do you think we could go into a little more detail on one at a time, so I can really understand?"

Notifying Family Members of Consequences

If the situation keeps escalating, it is important to let people know that this in unacceptable. We might say, "I'm going to have to leave if you keep squirting that garden hose at your mother," or "I'll have to call the police if you don't let go of Johnny." Another example is:

> The family consisted of 15-year-old Mary and her 36-year old mother, Rita. Mary had been on the run at referral and presenting problems were truancy, alcohol abuse, and sexual involvement. She and her mother had had many conflicts over these issues and sometimes became physical with one another.
>
> During one session Rita and Mary became angry with one another. Their anger quickly escalated to the point of yelling. During this initial stage I fell back on a rule of thumb I had learned in my training ("when in doubt: listen") and made several listening responses. However, Rita and Mary continued to scream at one another. Mary ran upstairs with Rita in close pursuit. I followed them. When they reached the top of the stairs, they began slapping one another, pulling each others hair, and wrestling. I began expressing my concern and fear that one or both of them would be hurt. I made several statements such as "I'm afraid someone is going to get hurt," "I don't want anyone to get hurt," "I'm worried that you will hurt each other," but they continued screaming and fighting.
>
> Next, they headed back downstairs with me close behind expressing my concern. In the living room, Mary knocked everything including the telephone off a table and yelled "I'm going to call the police" to which Rita yelled back "I'm going to call the police." In as calm a voice as I could muster at that point, I said "If you don't stop, I will call the police." They stopped wrestling, hitting and pulling hair but continued yelling. I resumed listening to their feelings and as they began to deescalate. I was able to convince Mary to go out on the front porch. Afterward, I spent time with each of them individually and Mary said "It was weird to hear you say you would call the police." Until then, I didn't know what had made the difference. (Jack Chambers)

Calling Time Out

Sometimes it helps to take a break. It's possible to request this directly: "This is a really difficult topic. Maybe we could take a little break now and get back to it later?" It's also possible to get a break indirectly: "Could I please get a glass of water?" or "I'm getting cramps in my legs from sitting so long. I'd like to get up and move around for a few minutes. Would that be okay?" An example is:

The Anderson family included Carol (39), her husband, Robert (40), and their three daughters, Janice (17), Mary (15), and Sharon (13). I had been working with the Andersons to improve the quality of their communication so that each family member felt increased respect and understanding. Communication difficulties were particularly difficult for Carol and Robert because Carol felt blamed and labeled for past behaviors related to alcoholism. At the time of intervention, Carol had been sober for 3 years and desired greater acceptance and respect from her husband. Because of Robert's long working hours, I was able to meet with all the family members only once each week, though I met with Carol and the girls approximately three times each week. Sessions with all the family members were typically 2–3 hours long, and tended to focus mostly on problems existing between Carol and Robert. Janice, Mary, and Sharon appeared very familiar with their parents' problems, and usually agreed with their mother's complaints about Robert's tendency to focus on the past. During these sessions I felt it was very important to include Robert's concerns, since he was not able to frequently participate in the intervention.

At a session including all family members close to the end of Homebuilders involvement, Robert expressed frustration that household rules and policies had begun changing without his knowledge. Since many of the changes were related to Homebuilders intervention, Robert believed that he should have received more careful explanations from Carol about how the new policies were developed and what they were specifically intended to improve. Carol became very upset by Robert's comments and accused him of not allowing her to grow and change positively. She said the situation was comparable to what had happened 3 years ago when she had become sober and Robert had not trusted her sobriety to be permanent or to positively affect their relationship. Janice supported her mother and said she felt like her father wanted to control the family and not allow anyone to have fun. Mary and Sharon were upset that their father was not more supportive of the changes they had made. As the family members began escalating and raising their voices, I suggested a time-out where we all took a 10 minute break. Afterward I stated that it would probably be helpful to return to Robert's original concern about not having felt included in changes Carol and his daughters had made. I suggested that we use the remainder of our meeting to review the changes and their purposes so that we all could gain greater clarity about the work we had accomplished. Robert expressed having been pleased by the changes, and he wanted to simply understand them better. Carol, Mary, Janice, and Sharon appeared a little surprised by Robert's support, and were very willing to share this information with him. Carol later expressed feeling like her negative expectations of Robert were interfering with their communication because she was fearful of his responses to her. I worked with Carol and Robert to develop a plan for them to call time-outs with each other when either felt misunderstood or were confused about the intent of statements related to the past. I also encouraged them to be careful to separate past from present concerns so that all family members could feel greater permission and support in their desires to change. (Katy Mueller)

Calling Our Supervisor

After active listening, if a situation still feels potentially dangerous and a counselor thinks he doesn't know what to do, he *must* call his supervisor. If there is one thing to remember in times of potential trouble, that's it. Counselors need to memorize supervisors' phone numbers and *use them* whenever they are stymied or afraid. It's almost always possible to call our supervisors without losing credibility with the family. Most families seem flattered and honored that we would reach out for additional information and resources to help them. We can say, "I'm getting bogged down. I'd like to ask my supervisor for some ideas about how to clarify some of this," or, "I bet my supervisor could help us get beyond this. Do you mind if I call her and ask her to come over and help us?"

Reconvening at a Neutral Place

If feelings continue to run high and we're worried about them getting out of control, it is also possible to suggest a shift to a more public setting, like, "Maybe it would be a good idea for us all to walk over to the McDonald's and get a cup of coffee or a soda while we talk."

Leaving

We are not policemen. If people start hitting each other, if we feel scared and out of control, we need to go call the police, or at least our supervisors. Sometimes, the family will give us permission to take one or more persons with us. We recommend that we never touch clients who are about to fight, or try to get between them. That is not our job. That is a police job.

Summary

Although most clients, most visits, and most neighborhoods present minimal threat to workers, some have significant potential for harm to workers and to other clients. There are many precautions workers can take on the way to clients' homes and while they are with clients. Active listening is our most powerful tool in helping people calm down. The first line of defense when we worry that the situation will erupt is to call our supervisor. No tactics, however, are foolproof. We must all continue to develop additional ways to protect ourselves and others, and to remind ourselves to be continually vigilant without forsaking the optimism and desire to help that lead us to the dangerous situations in the first place.

4
Getting Off to a Good Start

The first session with a family is the most delicate one. Family members don't know us. We don't know them. If the family members were referred by Child Protective Services, they are usually defensive and angry about the referral. If the family was referred because an older child is running or being kicked out, family members are usually upset with one another. Many families have not felt good about previous social services involvement. Everyone feels vulnerable and anxious about what might happen. We have already discussed the top initial priority of preventing violence during the first session. In the next chapter we will discuss helping with urgent basic needs that families may have. In this chapter, we will discuss other first-session goals. We want to establish trust between family members and our counselor. We want to begin to understand family members' perceptions about their situations. We want to help them calm down and to reduce their confusion about what is happening to them.

Establishing Trust

Most of our clients are initially unexcited about the prospect of forming a partnership with yet another service provider. They have often had a number of unsuccessful and unpleasant interactions with service providers. They do not expect to like us. They expect to be frustrated by us. They expect to fail us, as they failed others. We have a number of beliefs and behaviors that can help clients feel better about us.

Getting to Know You: Chitchat Therapy on the Phone

In Chapter 3 we discussed using the first phone call to prevent violence. We also use it to begin establishing trust and negotiating to provide services families wish to receive. An example is:

55

I received a phone call one morning from a woman who was crying uncontrollably and who was almost unintelligible. I was open for a new case that day, but had not yet been informed that one had come in. Sandy, 26, mother of Ryan, age 6 months, was upset because she felt that her mother had made reports of domestic violence to the police, implying that Ryan was in danger due to the physical fighting between her and her boyfriend, Roger. CPS had become involved and said they would remove the child unless Sandy and Roger lived separately. Sandy, at the time of the phone call, was staying at her mother's house with Ryan. Her mother was at work for the day. Sandy did not want to stay with her mother, whom she reported was very critical and wanted custody of the baby. Sandy cried that she needed to move as soon as possible; she was also upset because Roger had been put in jail and she wanted to bail him out. He was arrested for an outstanding traffic warrant.

I active listened to Sandy at length, and helped her structure what she would do until I arrived. Mostly this involved caring for Ryan and identifying his schedule between the time of the call and the intake. Sandy agreed to stay at the house to wait for me because her mother was not there. We determined that the family had enough food, diapers, etc. so that none needed to be picked up on the way over. I offered to provide concrete services, to help Sandy find a place to live and move her and this had a calming effect. Sandy requested that I also transport her to the jail where she could post bail for Roger's release, and then transport him to his parents' home. I agreed to consult with a supervisor about this and discuss it further with Sandy at the intake session. By the end of the conversation, Sandy was tearful but able to speak more clearly. I went to see her several (5) hours later, at her request. I spoke to her one more time on the phone before intake. (Peggy Mandin)

Especially during the first visit with families, we consider ourselves guests. We want them to know we appreciate being in their homes and respect their territory. We want to establish that we are not there to order them around. It's probably more helpful for us to imagine ourselves as meeting prospective in-laws at this stage than for us to think of ourselves as physicians meeting patients. We want to be as gracious as we can, and to begin putting family members at ease. The way to do this is the same as the ways we put other people at ease when we first meet them. We smile. We talk about positives like how nice their dog is, or how interesting we find their carving from Puerto Rico. We commiserate with them regarding the weather. We share neutral things about our own lives; I have three sisters myself. I used to live in Brooklyn. We want to communicate that first we are going to relate to them person to person, before we phase into the helper–helpee relationship.

Establishing Trust and Forming a Partnership

The most difficult hurdle in beginning work with families in crisis is that they are vulnerable. Family members are feeling attacked by each other or by the social services system. It is not an easy time for them to reach out and form alliances. They are expecting continued attack from each other or the system or us. At the same time, if we are going to get anywhere (including being asked back the next day), we have to form a partnership with them. Ideally, all family members can consider us as a potential ally; not an easy task when each of their own positions may vary. Change is difficult enough with upset families when the family and the counselor are working together. If we perceive each other as adversaries, it's next to impossible. The relationship is like trying to help someone over a big concrete wall. All to often, we get on opposite sides of the wall and try to drag clients through it. Dragging doesn't work. The clients smash up against the wall. We get frustrated. The way to get over the wall is to be on the same side and give clients a boost up and over it. We respect client decisions at the same time we try to engage them. Some families do not want to see more counselors at all.

> I was assigned a family consisting of a single mother and five children under the age of 8. One child, a 5 year old, had serious behavior problems and was about to be placed in a psychiatric institution. I had been told by the caseworker, the 5 year old's teacher, and a psychologist at his school that the mother was "extremely hostile and paranoid and probably won't let you in her house." When I called her she expressed her frustration that yet another professional would be involved in her life. She stated that she was very tired of having people tell her how terrible her son's behavior was. She said she felt like people were blaming her for his behavior. I responded by saying that it must be difficult to be trying hard to be a good mother and not get any acknowledgment of your efforts. She agreed and said that she felt she did just fine with her son and didn't want another counselor telling her how to manage him. I responded by saying it must be really hard to have people tell her how to be a parent. She agreed, saying she felt she knew him best and knew best how to handle him. I responded by saying it sounded like she didn't feel like others had taken her viewpoints regarding her son seriously. She agreed and added that sometimes it's been frustrating for her to deal with her son. I said I'd like to hear more about all of her frustrations and concerns and she suggested I come to her house and we could talk in person. When I arrived she let me in her house quite willingly. At the end of our fist session she told me that it felt very good to be listened to; in the past she had felt blamed and not taken seriously. From then on we had a very effective partnership as we worked together to help her son. (Susan O'Brien)

Others are initially positive placement is the option they want.

> Alice (38) and her recent husband Richard (24) agreed to talk to me about Homebuilders when I called on the phone, but Alice was adamant that she wanted her son Brian (15) placed in a group home. She stated that she was afraid of him, that she believed he needed treatment, and that the FRS caseworker had as much as promised her Brian could be placed.

We met for about 2 hours and during the session Alice (primarily) talked about all the reasons that having Brian live at home now (he had been in detention and/or on the run for over a year just prior to our meeting; Alice and Richard had married and moved during that time) was impossible. I did a lot of reflecting feelings and tried to frame her concerns as goals and needs for herself and for Brian, very occasionally suggesting that those goals and needs might be met or worked toward with Brian at home. During our meeting Brian and Alice had an argument that resulted in Brian leaving the room for a time. When he returned I expressed appreciation that he had taken care of his feelings without violence or further escalation and that he had returned. While Brian was gone I focused on Alice's concerns for Brian's well-being and reinforced her for her past efforts to get him help. Several times during our session I observed and commented on how well they were able to talk to each other and how much they seemed to care for each other. I also reflected Brian's obvious desire to stay with Alice and Richard. By the end of our session the only barrier Alice was still concerned about was the landlord's two-person, no children restriction on the house they were renting. Alice agreed to talk to the landlord and at least give Brian a month to try and make it work at home. (Ellen Douthat)

Liking Clients.   The families are the heart of our jobs. If we don't like them, how can we like our jobs? If we don't like our jobs, how can we do them well? The more we like the families we see, the more open we will be toward partnership. When we don't like them, they can tell. No matter how we try to hide it, or how sophisticated we are as counselors, our nonverbal cues give us away. We are likely to be tighter. We may find it harder to have warm eye contact. We may not smile as readily. We will be less likely to touch them and to laugh with them. These cues can be demeaning for clients, making them feel smaller, rather than empowering them, helping them feel stronger. Family members will sense our distaste and will find it more difficult to welcome us to their homes. They will feel less comfortable trusting us with information that makes them vulnerable. They will find it more difficult to be open to our suggestions. They will do fewer of the things that refuel us, like telling us how wonderful we are and preparing little treats for us.

It is relatively easy to like clean, articulate, middle class people who come to our offices. When people begin to have serious problems in most areas of their lives, part of what falls by the wayside are many of the characteristics that made them easy to like. Some people are untidy. Some smell bad. Many people have limited social skills. Some are rude. Some homes have lice and cockroaches and rats.

We have some beliefs about people that help us to feel positive about families who initially present a negative image. We believe these beliefs transmit themselves in all sorts of verbal and nonverbal ways that can help or hinder the development of trust and partnerships.

1.   There are more similarities between us than differences. We all need help sometimes. We all get angry. We are all unfair at times. Most of us get dirty. Most of us have living quarters that get messy every once in a while. If there is something a client is doing that we just can't stand, we can usually remember times in our own lives when we or someone we love has done the same or a similar thing. Many of us have had counseling. Some of us have even had Homebuilders services.

2.   Everyone is doing the best they can do. We must see people in their contexts. Within the limits of their skill levels, their intelligence, their histories, their environment, their income, their energy level, the skills of those around them, their health, and their knowledge of their options, everyone is doing exactly as well as they can. Usually if we can stay open to, and make an effort to understand the full complexities of the situations people endure, we will feel compassion. This doesn't mean that clients and their contexts cannot improve, it only means that at any given moment they are doing the best they can in the circumstances they face.

3.   People's motives are generally positive. Most of the time, people don't intend to do each other harm. People are fragile, and we can easily hurt each other without that being our goal. When we are clumsy and impulsive, we can bruise each other, even though we are trying to resolve problems instead of cause more. We may lack skills; tact, self-control, and clear communication are not easy to learn. When we have the skills, we still make mistakes. We may think that if we could just show our son that he really isn't as good as he thinks he is, he will be motivated to do more homework. When our comments crumble his self-esteem and make his grades even worse, we feel rotten. We didn't mean to hurt him. We were trying to motivate him so he would do better work and feel better about himself.

We also misinterpret one another. When a mother tells her daughter to come in early she may be thinking about potential harm from drug pushers on the street. The daughter may interpret her mother's words as "I don't trust you. I know you will get in trouble. You are a rotten kid." There are many ways we can and do hurt and alienate one another. Keeping in touch with their positive intentions rather than the frequent negative results of their attempts to communicate helps us to like clients who are giving and getting a lot of hurt.

4.   Most family members really care about each other. If we listen and observe carefully, through all the layers, we will usually sense a glimmer of yearning for closeness, mutual opportunities, and relief from pain

among family members. The more family members feel safe and understood, the more they will be able to show what might even be called love. The more faith we have in this belief, the more validation for it we will be able to sense and encourage.

Helping Clients Like Us. Clients will be much more likely to form partnerships with us and trust us if they like us. We need to be likable so that they will allow us into their homes and spend time with us and so that they will trust us with information that makes them vulnerable. We need to be likable so they will want to try some of our suggestions and also so that they will support us as we support them. Our clients have done everything from writing us poetry to giving us bananas. The thoughtful, poignant things clients do for workers are probably the biggest factor in keeping us going. We need them.

We hold a number of beliefs and behave in certain ways that can help clients to like us.

1.   It is our job to instill hope. Many of our clients have little interest in forming partnerships because they have little or no hope that anything will improve their situation. Why try if nothing will help? Clients may feel reluctant to work with us on their problems for several reasons. Some believe counseling is irrelevant. Some of our techniques are totally outside their frame of reference. Some think our solutions seen too direct and simplistic to ever affect their overwhelming problems. Many have spent lots of time and money to no avail. Why should it work this time? We use a number of strategies to keep ourselves feeling hopeful and to encourage family members to feel the same way.

The parents of a 14-year-old boy were without hope that he could change. They were also feeling hopeless that their home life would ever improve. They felt miserable and unable to go on living together as a family. The parents struggled for years to get help to improve the boy's behavior. He was adopted by them as an infant. He has been in and out of treatment with numerous psychiatrists, Ph.D. psychologists, and other counselors for 11 years. He has been diagnosed as hyperactive and learning disabled. He has had prescriptions for Ritalin, Haldol, Thorozine, and Melleril at different times over the years. He was placed in a Residential Treatment Center for almost three years and returned home one and one half years prior to Homebuilders involvement. His parents had attended years of family counseling with him. His mother had what she terms a nervous breakdown 12 years prior to Homebuilders involvement. DSHS reported that they were ready to place him immediately. The boy's first statement to me was, "Get out of here, I hate psychiatrists." He had been physically threatening to his parents, pushing his mother to the floor. He also was in the habit of physically stopping his parents from leaving the house at times, i.e., he blocked their exit. He threw things at his parents and kicked doors when angry. His mother reported that he frequently called her vile names. He was accused of hitting a neighbor woman in the arm with a baseball. He frequently yelled at his parents and refused to do most anything requested of him.

I began by active listening extensively with both parents. I listened to how disruptive the boy's behavior was and how hard he was to live with. I listened to how difficult he made their lives and how they felt like giving up because he was so hard to deal with. I listened as the parents reported having tried various behavioral methods of parenting as well as PET. They reported that nothing had worked for very long and that they had no hope that our help would be any different. The mother especially reported feeling overwhelmed and drained. As we discussed her feelings further, she clarified that in part she felt this way because she thought she had to constantly monitor her son's behavior and because her son depended on her to entertain him constantly. As I active listened further, it became apparent that she also felt guilty regarding her unsuccessful parenting efforts. These feelings of guilt resulted in her trying harder to monitor his behavior and keep him entertained. Further active listening elicited Mrs. T.'s feelings of anger, frustration, and helplessness. She was feeling angry at her son for being so difficult to parent, frustrated because he didn't respond positively to most of her parenting efforts, and helpless because she didn't know what else to do.

I worked to help Mr. and Mrs. T. define their problems with the potential removal in behavioral terms—I asked them to describe what he was doing that bothered them the most. As we progressed session to session, I discussed optional parenting strategies with them. I helped them review what they had tried and the outcomes. I gave them information about a few things they hadn't tried too, such as being unpredictable with the PR. We discussed this since they had tried so hard to be consistent with him and he was an expert at getting most any reactions he wanted from them. The referring caseworker reported that "the potential removal had always controlled his parents." An example we used of being unpredictable was for his mother to start singing and looking away absent mindedly whenever he threatened her—she had consistently started crying at these times in the past. I wanted her to have something definite to do for all situations occurring between her and the PR. So, by presenting this as an option worth trying in my opinion doing a little RET with her to help her think differently about these episodes, and by discussing with her the value of taking an experimental approach to parenting, she was able to change her responses to his threats. As mentioned, RET with both parents was a major part of my intervention in regard to the goal of regaining hope. Mrs. T. became quite interested in RET and I explained how she could feel differently (better) even if her son's behavior remained pretty much the same. I also let her know that I had some ideas regarding how we might impact his behavior. Then I taught Mrs. T. how to identify upsetting thoughts, how to challenge them, and how to use replacement calming thoughts. She began practicing immediately and reported a significant decrease in upsetting feelings.

I think that the parents were receptive to what I was presenting because I patiently listened to what they had to say, I active listened, and I took an optimistic (but not overly so) approach to intervening in regard to the problems they reported. I gave them something different to do very early on. I emphasized the value of positive and negative consequences for the PR and helped the parents construct and implement an elaborate point system for the PR to shape more positive behaviors. Mrs. T. was also somewhat encouraged because the boy, in our first attempt to have a counseling session, spent 25 minutes being in the same room with me and answering a few questions. He hadn't been willing to do this with any of the other counselors he'd had and had told his mother he wouldn't talk with me. I used non-threatening "I" statements and active listening to engage him. I talked with him about what he wanted and what he might be able to get out of our counseling.

Why were Mr. and Mrs. T. willing to try RET and an elaborate point system? I presented myself as being very concerned, wanting to help, and as having had experience as a counselor with other adolescents somewhat similar to their son. I didn't use a lot of technical language and I didn't label anyone. I took a positive, optimistic approach to my intervention with them. I let them know I had a few ideas we could try that they hadn't tried yet and ones that had led to success with other adolescents. I let them know that I was aware of the great deal of effort they had already expended regarding parenting. I also explained that I was committed to trying with them and that I would help them, i.e., they wouldn't be doing this alone. They began feeling strong enough to try to change, and they did. (Brewster Johnston)

2.   We cannot know ahead of time if a situation is hopeless. The best way to feel hopeful ourselves is to experience relationships with numerous families whose problems initially seemed serious but were later resolved. It's harder at first. The best thing to do is talk to others and take advantage of their experiences. If we have seen a lot of families and they haven't been able to resolve many of their problems and we feel hopeless, it's time for us to have a checkup. Do we really understand and can we demonstrate all the different skills necessary to help a family through a crisis? Do we have good supervision and teammates who can help us? Do we need more training? If we are hopeless and discouraged, those feelings will be transmitted to our clients. Our own feelings need to be taken care of before we will be able to be helpful.

When we first began Homebuilders we thought we would learn rapidly to identify hopeless families so that we wouldn't waste their time or ours. Now, many years later, we find we still cannot predict ahead of time which families will benefit from our services. Many families whose initial problems seemed totally overwhelming have pulled things together. They may have had discouraging histories, documented failure of previous services, and alarming presenting problems. Some have diagnoses that are scary. On the other hand, families whose problems initially seemed trivial have ended up with their children in placement.

We have come to think it's good that we can't predict success. It means that we have a strong rationale for feeling as hopeful as possible about every family we meet. It means that every family we see has an 88% chance of avoiding the need for out of home placement for the next year. Those are pretty good odds.

When we feel hopeful about families, we can do many things to encourage them. We can validate their reasons for skepticism. We understand that they do have a complicated, difficult situation, yet we feel hope. We can give examples of comparable successful cases. We can explain how we differ from other services they have had; others didn't have as much time as we do and couldn't come to their homes as often. We can point out their strengths along with their problems. We can encourage them to talk about past problems they have solved. We can encourage them to set very small goals so that they will definitely achieve them and we can cheer for them. We can begin providing concrete services for them so they will see that we are different and that even if they are overwhelmed, change can begin. We can disagree when they say it's hopeless. We can watch for faint glimmers of hope in them, and when they appear, we can fan the flames. If we can help families to begin to feel hope, we will already have provided a valuable service for them. They will appreciate it and they will be more likely to ease into a partnership with us for the rest of the intervention.

3.   Clients should have as much power as possible. Clients will want to form partnerships with us if they perceive that we are trying to give them something rather than taking something away. We believe our job is to help clients take control of their lives rather than to take control of their lives for them. This belief, that clients should have the power, is manifested in many ways.

We meet where they want to meet. Although they usually prefer to meet in their homes, some may request to meet in our office. We meet when they want to meet. We talk about what they want to discuss (although we won't leave a situation until issues of safety have been addressed). We don't question their style. We don't care if they are vegetarian or Christian or have five cats or wear purple and orange and plaid and stripes together. We don't even question their inclination to place their children when it exists. It is our job to facilitate their own decision about whether or not they want to stay together. That is not our decision to make. Paradoxically, attempts to influence this decision can put so much pressure on both the counselor and the client that the family becomes less likely to stay together. We want to do everything we can to help them make informed decisions as soon as possible because, after all, that is the whole point: to empower them to handle their problems.

One of the ways we validate client power is by accepting who attends or does not attend sessions, rather than insisting everyone be involved. If one family member wishes another to be involved, we will provide consultation and rationales to help them encourage the other.

At intake Kerry, the stepfather, introduced himself and went to watch TV. Mary, the mother, said she wanted him involved as they disagreed with discipline methods and Kerry would discipline her son, Danny, age 10, without consulting her or override her discipline decisions. Then she wouldn't back him up, and they would argue.

I taught "I" messages and broken record (repeating "I" messages several times in a calm voice to disengage from arguments) to Mary to be more assertive with Kerry. Using these skills, she asked Kerry to participate and he did for one session. He said "I don't have problems with the kids, they listen to me." Basically, he said "do it or else" and saw no reason for other methods. I active listened and gave verbal reinforcement for apparent good relations with the kids, and encouraged him to try the broken record and "I" messages if an opportunity came up.

Kerry backed away after this session and didn't participate. He continued to discipline and complained that Mary didn't back him up. I helped Mary develop "I" statements to ask Kerry to agree to meet again, and he did. The counselor active listened to Kerry's confusion about "why he should do anything differently, Danny's the one with the problem." I active listened and gave rationales as to how it would be to Kerry's benefit to participate, try different things, and to discuss discipline with Mary in advance. I also explained that without his input, I wouldn't be able to come up with the most helpful plan for Danny and it might be something Kerry wouldn't agree with or want to follow. I pointed out that Mary would be more willing to back him up if she had a part in deciding how to discipline. I stressed Kerry's importance in being an active member in planning how to help Danny. I also stressed his importance as a role model for Danny as Danny's natural father was extremely physically abusive and then committed suicide. He has the opportunity to show Danny that men can be different and really make a difference in Danny's life. But he would have to take care not to reinforce Danny's old idea that men are scary and deal with their anger by hitting and yelling. That would mean learning some other alternatives and practicing them and modeling them for Danny. I spent lots of time with Kerry active listening to his interests and ideas.

After that Kerry was very active in developing, monitoring, and revising behavior charts. He developed more realistic expectations for Danny's behavior and saw less need to punish. He was enthusiastic about the concept of natural and logical consequences.

After termination, Kerry and Mary began to fight and Kerry called me for advice rather than reverting to yelling or physical punishment. As he talked to me, he held Danny on his lap and I heard him talk comfortingly and calmly to Danny. Kerry and Mary reported seeing improvement in Danny's behavior, and that they now discuss positive and negative consequences before implementing them. (Christi Lyson)

Often we are pleased at the amount of change and cooperation demonstrated by those who do not attend.

> The father wasn't home during several sessions. During the sessions that he was home, he was usually doing something else, repairs, correcting the kids, going in and out of the room, etc. But . . . he did put stars on the kids charts, he did create a new category on the chart and wrote it in, he did draw up a special chart for one child's school performance and hung it over her desk, he did try "I" statements, he did shampoo the carpet when we got a shampooer donated and delivered it, he did replace a broken window of concern to CPS (which we also had donated), and he did take more notice of the girls appearance (combed their hair, etc.) which was also a CPS concern. (Karen Bream)

4.   Clients are our colleagues. Clients are more apt to like us if we perceive them as colleagues in a joint venture of change for their family. They are, after all, the experts on themselves. They have the information about everything that's happened, everything that was tried, everything that worked and didn't work. Often they also know a lot about why certain things didn't work then, and wouldn't work now. Their information about potential constraints and resources can make our wonderful graduate school ideas sink or swim.

One way family members can tell that we think of them as colleagues is by our lack of professional distance. Most of us are taught to be formal, serious, and objective about our clients. That approach has some advantages. We are not going to become best friends with our clients. We don't want to lose all perspective and think about them night and day. A problem with professional distance, though, is that it may cause clients to feel even more vulnerable and threatened than they already do. As we mentioned before, it's helpful to consider ourselves guests in family's homes. We dress in ways that they will feel are appropriate. We try to "fit in."

We think clients will warm up to us and loosen up much faster if we show we are interested in and sincerely care about them. The relationship we are trying to establish differs from friendship in that help-giving is (usually) nonreciprocal with client families. We won't be telling them our problems. They won't be helping us to get the landlord to fix our apartment. However, the relationship we are trying to establish with them does have many similarities to friendship that is reciprocal. Friends respect and like each other. We have fun with client families. We go out for coffee. We go to McDonald's together. We go with them to doctor's visits. Sometimes we attend family functions, like dance recitals or engagement parties.

5.   Respect is contagious. When clients realize we know how much they have to offer, and how much we need them, they are more likely to

work with us rather than against us. When we treat them with courtesy and respect, they are likely to respond in kind.

6. Not knowing can be valuable. We have talked about how it helps clients build a relationship with us if they know we realize and respect their knowledge and strengths. On the other hand, it also helps if we can admit to them how much we do not know. For one thing, it keeps us more congruent, because it's true. We don't know what's going to help a particular family. We often feel confused and stymied by situations. We haven't solved our lives; we won't solve theirs. Admitting our limitations helps keep the responsibility and power with the clients. We are less intimidating. We can model thinking through issues without being confident. They can view change and problem solving as realistically difficult for everyone. Paradoxically, when we drop the facade of knowing everything, we become more credible to most families.

Eleven-year-old Randy and his mother, Debra, are a case where I didn't know everything. Homebuilders was called in when Randy pointed a rifle at his mother and pulled the trigger. The gun happened not to be loaded, but the family problems certainly were. Following his parents' divorce Randy began to abuse his mother both verbally and physically. Randy stayed in the family home with his father, who would often go off for days at a time, leaving Randy to his own resources. One day Randy returned home to discover his father dead of a heart attack. When Debra moved back home with the two younger daughters in order to clear up the affairs of the estate, the problems between Randy and his mother escalated. He would threaten her with knives and often attack her with his hands and fists or objects thrown. He would wish her dead or threaten to kill her.

Debra and I developed a plan of calling the police every time Randy attacked his mother in these ways. On three different occasions during the intervention this was done and Randy was placed in a receiving home for 3 or 4 days and then returned home, only to have another incident follow within a few more days. Many hours were spent with this family, sometimes late into the night, but nothing seemed to be happening.

Then one night, following still another episode with Randy, Debra called. She was tired and so was I. The conversation went something like this: "Jim, I want to know if you've given up." Debra's question shook me up. I had to stop and think for a moment if she was right. Had I? I *was* thinking lately that I had failed her and the family by not being more effective in my work. But what I said was: "No, I haven't given up, and I won't, but, to tell you the truth, I really don't know what to do anymore."

Thinking about it later, I realized that this admission only helped to bond us closer as counselor and family. We talked on and, as we did, became aware that a lot more had been accomplished than we had realized. For one thing, the physical attacks had at least diminished in number and intensity. There were more good moments in relation to the bad ones than there had been. There were even some indications that Randy was beginning to deal with his grief over the death of his father by talking about it.

By the end of the intervention things had improved, but not much. At this time Randy's mother wrote: "I am more in charge as a parent—a better negotiator and have a clear vision of how I am connected to my family. . . . Jim and I were a team. He mirrored my commitment to me. . . . He was able to share enough of himself with me so that I never felt counseled, but rather in a human relationship where he and I were equals—partners in making things different. . . . He also taught me that crisis means opportunity and that new orientation has helped give me courage."

This was written 4 months ago. The family has since moved and Randy has been doing quite well. He and his mom still have their moments, but overall things have greatly improved. (Jim Poggi)

7. We can do harm. Not only do we not know everything, we can do harm. If all our techniques and strategies and processes really do elicit change, we have to come to terms with the fact that we can make things worse as well as better. Family members already know this. For example, we can teach a woman to be assertive instead of submissive to her husband and then he can beat her up and put her in the hospital. She may have done a great job of being assertive, but it will be difficult for her to see the hospital as real progress. If we are open about risks and if we keep the decision-making power with family members as much as possible, we can reassure people that the potential for danger is minimal in a partnership with us.

Reducing Confusion and Calming People

Family members usually feel calmer as they begin to trust us. They also feel calmer as they grow less confused. Family members are usually partially upset because so many aspects of their lives seem out of control. Nothing seems right. The problems seem bewildering. How do all the problems fit together? Sometimes it seems like the whole world is an enemy. As problems begin to be sorted out they seem less threatening. It usually becomes clear that not everything is wrong. As we help people clarify issues, they begin to feel understood by us. As they feel understood, they feel reassured that they are not alone in facing the problems. This also helps them feel calmer. The main technique we use for helping people clarify their problems is also the main vehicle for their feeling understood.

Active Listening

Carl Rogers (1942) was probably the first counselor to make an art out of listening. One of his students, Thomas Gordon (1975) has done a wonderful job of operationalizing some of the powerful techniques Rogers first described. Gordon's first book, *Parent Effectiveness Training*, describes active listening, a method of eliciting information through activities such as remaining silent, reflecting feelings, reflecting content, and paraphrasing the sender's comments. We recommend Gordon's book for anyone involved with Family Preservation or any type of counseling.

Active listening is especially important when relationships and situations are precarious. We have a rule: *When in doubt, listen.* These delicate times are also the times it can be the most difficult to listen. We tend to get nervous and want to "take charge", fix things, take control. It is ironic that we probably have the best chance of gaining some control if we view our role as supportive facilitators and clarifiers rather than as directors or saviors.

Although active listening seems simple at first, it is a complicated process. We need not only parrot back what people say, we need to *understand*. It can take a lifetime to understand our own family members, much less people we don't even know. It's also much easier to listen to one coherent person than to try to attend to a group of loud, emotional family members all wanting to express their particular point of view.

Sending "I" Messages

Active listening is only half of the communication process. We also need to be able to share our point of view, focus the conversation when it gets too far afield, and set limits when necessary. If a family is orderly and family members are beginning to shift from chitchat to problem areas, we will do nothing but active listening. If family members begin escalating each other or spend more than 20 or 30 minutes sharing picture albums or talking about a child's sweet sixteen party, we begin sending messages to influence their behavior. If family members are screaming and interrupting each other, we might say, "I'd really like to hear each point of view, and it's difficult for me to focus on all of you at the same time." If we have seen family photos for a long time, we might say "I've really enjoyed this chance to see your pictures, but I'm concerned that it's time for us to start talking about some of the concerns you have about your family." We want to send, but we want to send as clearly and gently as possible. Once again, in *Parent Effectiveness Training*, Gordon does a masterful job of operationalizing clear sending in his descriptions of "I" messages. A complete "I" message contains three components: a statement of what the sender is feeling, what the recipient of the message is doing to contribute to that feeling, and a statement of what the sender would like to see happen to improve the situation. For example; "I feel angry when you interrupt me and swear at me. I wish you would be quiet while I talk."

When we send, throughout our involvement with the family, we want to maximize our ability to influence them and minimize any threat they might feel regarding pressure from us. There are a number of fairly subtle differences in messages that can affect how family members respond to us. Lehner (n.d.) has done an excellent job of describing these differences.

Describing behavior, not persons. It helps to say, "I don't like it when you throw things," instead of "You are an evil person."

Using observations, not inferences. It helps to say, "I am disappointed that you hit your sister," more than "I am disappointed that you hate your sister."

Using behavioral descriptions, not judgments. It will be easier for clients to hear if you say, "I was confused when you left the room," rather than "I was confused when you copped out of our session."

Using gradations, not all or none statements. Family members will feel less threatened if we say, "We have been unable to meet three times because you have not been home," instead of "You are never here when I come."

Speaking for now, not always. Family members will be more receptive if we say, "I am uncomfortable with your yelling at me," rather the "You always yell at me."

Sharing ideas, not giving advice. Many clients will be more responsive if we say, "One idea some people find interesting is——" rather than "You should——."

Sending for the receiver, not the sender. It helps if we consider family members' agendas rather than our own in sending messages to them. They may be more willing to respond if we say "I can't hear, and I really want to understand what you're saying," instead of "I get really frightened when people all scream at me."

Sending the amount of information that can be used, not sent. It's helpful to consider how much people can absorb at one time. Frequently there are dozens of messages and pieces of (supposed) wisdom we would like to transmit to family members. It is better to share one or two and congratulate family members for understanding them, than to try to send 15 and feel disappointed and frustrated that they didn't seem to get anything.

Summary

If we can begin to like our clients and to sense that they are beginning to like us, we are off to a good start in establishing the trust necessary for a good partnership. If we can understand what they are saying to us, and share what we have to offer in a way that enhances rather than diminishes them, we have begun the foundation for change.

5

Maintaining Progress between Visits

By the time we are ready to leave the first session, family members have usually calmed down and begun thinking about their situations more clearly. Nevertheless, issues are far from settled and there are many opportunities for the situation to escalate again after we leave. People can hurt one another. Mothers can hit children and big brothers can break little brothers' fingers. People overdose on pills or hang upside down outside their ninth story windows. Family members can do things that will make each other so angry that they refuse to work on their problems any more and demand that one of them live somewhere else.

When we leave sessions we want the family to have a number of ways to keep their feelings and behavior as positive and productive as possible. We stay with the family until all family members are in control at the moment, and we don't leave until they are fairly comfortable about their potential to stay in control until our next visit which is usually the next day, early in the intervention.

We begin by discussing potentially troublesome situations that are likely to arise and by working on ways family members can respond to minimize the potential for the situation disintegrating again. These ways are not aimed at accomplishing major goals or achieving the fundamental changes we would all like. They are stopgaps—short-term measures to help families (and us) get through the night or the next day, not the rest of their lives. Interventions aimed at longer term change are discussed in subsequent chapters.

Monitoring the Situation

When a family has a phone, we often call them every few hours to see how they're doing during times of potential chaos and danger. We want to do everything we can to help them avert violence and carry out the treatment plans we have begun together. We want to do these things without having our own lives totally disrupted.

71

Although family members know that they can always call their counselor or their counselor's supervisor if they are having trouble, sometimes we call them instead of relying on their calling us. For one thing, they don't always call. For another, if they are particularly upset, we may feel vulnerable to being called more often and more unpredictably than we would like. If we call them, even if it is every hour during especially difficult times, we are better able to relax between phone calls than we could if we were sitting around waiting for the phone to ring. Although having families call us when they are upset is a critical and desirable part of our service, it has the potential disadvantage of rewarding clients with our attention and help only when they are upset. If we call them at regular intervals, we can "catch them being good." We can praise them for keeping things together and encourage them to continue trying new strategies. If family members know we will be calling soon, they are better able to keep things under control. They feel supported. They know they will have a chance to ask questions and get advice, so they feel less pressure to "fix" or "take care of" every thing that comes up on their own.

If the situation is beginning to deteriorate, we can talk to all family members on the phone to help them get back on track, or we can go to their home before things have really blown up and work with them in person.

Sometimes a family's relatives or friends can help us monitor the family. We are most likely to need this help in situations where the potential for harm is serious and might continue for several days—for example, when a mother has tried to kill herself before and is afraid she might try again. Involving others to help monitor families is also a good way to facilitate the family's getting along without us. If we can work with a family to set up support from extended family and friends, they are one step closer to being independent from us.

In most cases where we are concerned about someone's safety, we use a combination of strategies to help people stay in control between visits. For example:

Susan was a 40-year-old female nurse. Her 16-year-old son was referred as the PR and things were going ok 2 weeks into the intervention with him. Then Susan and her boyfriend ended their relationship. She was very upset and felt emotionally drained and physically ill. I took her to her family doctor at her request. He was so concerned about her that he was going to admit her to the psychiatric unit at a local hospital, but with my structuring between visits, he agreed not to. Techniques that I used to prevent her hospitalization and keep her from hurting herself included: Contracting not to kill self for short time periods and frequent monitoring (every 4 or so hours for several days).

I also didn't allow her to be alone. Although she was estranged from her husband, she spent one night at his home. She agreed not to hurt herself so I didn't break confidentiality. Because I felt uncomfortable with him not knowing how suicidal she was, I encouraged Susan to spend nights with someone we could talk more openly with about her depression. She then agreed to stay with her sister. Susan and I told the sister of her suicide potential. Her sister was very concerned, especially because Susan had almost successfully killed herself by overdose when her first husband had died. The sister agreed to contact me if Susan seemed despondent or did not return to her house at the agreed upon times.

Sleeping medication was prescribed by her physician. I took the bottle of pills and gave them to Susan one at a time. Susan, meanwhile, continued to work the graveyard shift at a local hospital. Although it was frightening having Susan at work because she had easy access to drugs, she also realized what could happen if she was not successful in committing suicide (i.e., remain in a coma or nonfunctional for years). She had direct exposure where she worked on the neurology ward to patients in such condition.

I also used a crisis card, along with RET calming self-talk card. The self-enhancing ideas related to being alone and the break-up. Examples included: "I've been alone before and I can do well alone again." "I may find another man. Many people say I'm a desirable woman, even if I have my doubts." "This man had many negative qualities. Maybe it's best we're not together." (The court loved this card and called it her "10 Commandments.")

To ensure that I was doing as much as possible in this dangerous situation, I used consultation with supervision frequently. I also gave Susan the book called "Letting Go" by Wanderer and Cabot. It "tells in practical proven terms how to cure a broken heart."

Pleasant events for Susan were also emphasized during the difficult time. We went out to eat because she had lost weight because she couldn't eat when she was so upset. She also enrolled in dance lessons, something she had wanted to do for years. I accompanied her to several lessons and watched her dance at her request. She really enjoyed this activity.

Susan and I also went to the lake where she used to spend time with the boyfriend. It was her idea to do this to put closure on the relationship. (Mary Fischer)

Changing the Environment

In many families, the triggers for major fights are well known. Sometimes it is possible to avert battles by short-term changes in the environment that make it very difficult for a troublesome event to occur. For example, if Mrs. Gonzales commonly hits 2-year-old Maria when Maria breaks knickknacks on the coffee table, maybe the knickknacks could be put away for a while so they will be safe. If Cleon and Robert end up tearing out each other's hair over who gets how much of their bedroom, maybe they could take turns sleeping downstairs or with friends for a few days until they learn better ways of negotiating space. Sometimes it also helps to bring others into the situation. Maybe if Grandma comes for a few days everyone will be on their best behavior. We have already mentioned that encouraging families to put weapons somewhere inaccessible is always a good idea.

Developing a Daily Routine

The more family members are preoccupied with productive pursuits, the less time they will have for getting in trouble. If we help them to establish a daily routine, meals are more likely to get cooked and children are more likely to get to bed on time. The more family members know what they or others should be doing, the less likely they are to explore less desirable options. With some families it is possible early in the intervention to plot out where everyone will be and what they will be doing at any given time. They can follow our recommendations "just until I come again tomorrow," or to discuss it in terms of "what would a day look like if everything were going well? How would people spend their time? What would they be doing?" For some very depressed clients, it helps to plan out each hour—for example, "I will get up at *seven*. I will take a shower and get dressed. I will have cornflakes and milk and bananas. At *eight*, I will wake up Emily. I will feed her cornflakes and milk and bananas. At *eight-forty*, I will send her to school. At *nine* o'clock, I will do exercises with an exercise show on television," etc. Sometimes it is necessary to create some semblance of routine before other progress can be made.

Casey (14) lived with his mother, Suzanne, his 19-year-old brother, John, his mother's 22-year-old boyfriend, and his brother's 16-year-old girlfriend. They had a two-bedroom apartment. Casey slept in the living room. He came and went as he pleased and sometimes would have many friends overnight without asking. His mother said she might find four teenagers she didn't know sleeping in her living room when she awoke. No one was employed. Casey's brother frequently stayed up all night playing video games, keeping others awake as well. Casey and his brother frequently had physical fights that added to the disarray. No one did any chores except the mother.

We discussed the value of routine with Suzanne. We discussed current routines and found none. My visits were the only anchors in their days. We discussed curfews, school attendance, time for chores and sleep. We also discussed rules for overnight guests. I helped Suzanne make charts to encourage Casey to follow rules, and provided coupons from McDonald's to use as reinforcers.

John turned out to be an important resource. He prided himself on being mature and helping his brother. He changed his own behavior to become a better model and encouraged Casey to be more compliant. In return, I helped John and his girlfriend to find an apartment and a job. With Suzanne's contingency management and modeling of a routine by others adults in the household, Casey's behavior changed rapidly. When John and his girlfriend moved out, Casey was able to move back into his bedroom. The privacy helped to decrease pressure. Fighting decreased, chores were being done, and Casey attended school more regularly. (Brewster Johnston)

Assigning Homework

Any assignment that gives family members an alternative to fighting can be helpful. The most common first homework assignment is keeping track of how often certain things occur. If a mother is counting the number of times her teenager swears at her it gives her a different perspective (and behavior). By recording, she distances herself from the situation and begins practicing a new response. She is able to stand back, take a deep breath and plan her eventual response. She is less likely to just react and go back to her old ways, such as yelling, hitting, or pleading.

This type of homework not only gives her an alternative to fighting, it also sharpens the information we all have about the frequency and duration of the problems. Homework also helps the clients become actively involved in the change process and in monitoring their progress right from the beginning. That's what we want: we want them to learn to change themselves.

Contracting

We use contracts with people to effect long-term change, but they can also be helpful in just getting through the next few hours or few days. Clients stay better focused on their plans if they have an explicit agreement to do so. This kind of contract can be written or verbal. Written usually seems stronger. Examples of short-term "structuring" contracts include a teenager promising to call us before he runs away, or a mom calling us before she disciplines a child or if she feels suicidal. We always attempt contracts with people who have indicated they're thinking about hurting themselves and they almost always agree to call us before doing anything.

Developing Crisis Cards

Early on in their intervention, we give most clients something called a *crisis card*. We learned about crisis cards from an excellent program at the University of Washington Department of Psychiatry called the Adult Development Program. Clients learn about developing crisis cards in several stages, which can occur in one visit:

Identifying Feeling Levels

Crisis cards are designed to divert escalating feelings by having clients act before their feelings get out of control. Clients need to be able to monitor their feelings and notice when they are rising before the feelings are so intense that control is impossible. We talk with family members about how feelings vary, and how if we're depressed, we don't always feel exactly the same degree of depression. Sometimes it is worse, sometimes it eases up. Most clients can relate to this concept easily; however, some people have trouble putting names on their feelings. We can give them options. We can listen and help them clarify. What name they put on their state, though, is not nearly as important as their willingness to begin to observe whatever it is that they feel. We talk about needing some way to monitor these feelings so we can catch them before they get out of control. Monitoring these feelings also helps us to determine if the things we're trying do, in fact, make a difference.

We usually begin by helping clients identify "end points." We might say, "0" might be when you *feel fine*. No anger at all. Calm. "10" might be the *most angry you've ever felt*. When do you think you felt more angry than any other time? Do you remember what that felt like? Okay, that's a "10." Then, we help them get a feel for variations by trying to put a number on what they are feeling at the moment. Most clients are usually in the 3–5 ballpark when we first work on crisis cards with them. They feel fairly calm because they've been talking with their worker for a while, but no problem resolution has really begun and they still have a lot of bad feelings about their situation.

Identifying the Danger Point

So a family member will know when she needs a crisis card, we might ask her at what level on a 10-point scale she begins to feel like she is losing control and needs to do something fast. For some it's *four*, for some it's *six*. It's important to go with the number a family member gives us, because, once again, we are trying to help her take charge of her treatment. It's more important that she begins making decisions than that she make the best possible one at this point. A person might say that she feels like she is beginning to lose control when her feelings reach a "5" level. At that point, we discuss the need to try something new. "It might not work the first time, but we'll keep trying until it does." What we need to do is come up with some activities she could do that might help to change or contain those bad feelings and get them down to a more manageable level.

Brainstorming Options

At this point, we encourage family members to come up with as many ideas as they can about what they might do to break the chain of escalating feelings. We usually give them a few examples. Even silly or ridiculous examples can help free family members from the pressure of having to come up with super options. Someone who is angry might do deep knee bends. She might dance with the dog. She might call her mother. Someone who is depressed might go out and buy jewels. She might color her hair green like she's always wanted it. She might clean out the closet. Usually, clients can begin coming up with ideas fairly quickly. Again, it's important to praise all these options. It's more important that clients get the idea that they are capable of taking charge of their lives than that they come up with the best possible crisis card options. We usually encourage clients to write down between six and eight options on a 3×5 inch card. We also encourage them to prioritize these options. "Which would be the most likely to help you feel less angry? Which would be next?" Options should be numbered so that when they are needed clients won't have to think about which to try first, all they will have to do is what is written on the card. A crisis card for *anger* could look like this:

Jody Withers' Anger Crisis Card
Begin if Anger at a "5" or Higher

1. Go in the bathroom for five minutes
2. Pet the cat
3. Take a walk around the block
4. Put on Walkman and listen to Carly Simon
5. Take out old photo albums and look at pictures of happier times.
6. Call a friend (Suzanne, 858-3619)
7. Go to the store and get a magazine and read it
8. Call Karen (Homebuilder, 927-1550)
GOOD JOB JODY FOR TRYING THIS!!!! YOU CAN DO IT!

Summary

We provide structure for families *between* visits as well as *during* visits. It's possible to begin teaching family members right away how to change what they *do* in order to change how they *feel* and begin to take control of their lives. Some of the techniques we use include monitoring the situation by phone, changing the environment, developing a daily routine, assigning homework, contracting, and developing crisis cards.

6

Assessing Strengths and Problems, and Formulating Goals

Our approach to assessment is based on three premises. (1) Problem definitions are constructs. They are ways to conceptualize reality, not reality itself, and we may change them to make them more relevant and effective in the problem resolution process. (2) Families in crisis present unique assessment challenges. Their situations change rapidly. They feel vulnerable because they are not able to manage their problems. They may be tempted to give up even before an assessment process begins. We need to take this into account in the way we approach assessment of families in crisis. (3) Assessment must include descriptions of strengths as well as of problems. We must be alert to families' potential capacities as well as deficits. The way we describe both problems and strengths can facilitate or impede problem resolution.

Once problems and strengths are articulated, we must prioritize problems and formulate goals. Then we may begin to assess if our assessments and our interventions are, indeed, facilitating the necessary changes, or if we must revise them to become more effective.

Problem Definitions are Constructs

Assessments are ways we choose to organize information so that we can affect change. A few years ago, Carlos Casteneda made a big hit with a series of books about an Indian medicine man, or sorcerer, named Don Juan (1968). Don Juan labored to teach Carlos, his apprentice, the importance of *viewing his view*. Power occurs when we realize that we have a choice in defining reality and when we learn to define it in ways that suit our needs. We don't need to be trapped by situations as they "really are," because situations may be interpreted in an almost unlimited number of ways, some helpful, some not so helpful.

79

Our tendency to confuse our assessments with ultimate truth stems from our inclination to believe that truth is *absolute* when, in fact, families and their definitions of their problems change rapidly, especially when they are in crisis. So truth is *relative*. We need an assessment process that is compatible with ongoing change and will not sidetrack us into endless discussions about whether someone really was or was not "inadequate" or "resistant" or "psychotic," but will instead monitor the behaviors that led us to these hypotheses in the first place.

Families in Crisis are Vulnerable and They Change Rapidly

Families in crisis are, by definition, upset. We do not wish to postpone the beginning of our assessment, and it cannot interfere with our being able to engage and defuse family members. Usually, they are bursting with pain, aching to tell their stories. They are not anxious to fill out forms or take tests. Formal procedures and asking questions can easily frustrate the family, distance them from the worker, and impede the flow of information. Families do want to give us information, but they feel most comfortable if they can do it on their terms, in the order and style they prefer. Many questions at this point can seem irrelevant and insensitive to them.

Since our work is occurring in the home or other locations where problems are occurring, we don't have to rely on paper and pencil measures. We are able to see what's going on for ourselves. Because we spend so much time with families, at various times of the day, we may observe patterns that would be unavailable to us through smaller slices of time, especially if those slices occurred in our office, out of context.

Workers can easily feel rushed in this process. Many of us were taught that assessment should be completed in an intake session. Knowing we have only 4 to 6 weeks can pressure us to get on with problem resolution immediately. Since we are involved with the family for only 4 to 6 weeks, we have to work on the assessment rapidly in order to start accomplishing goals as soon as possible. If we had a 4-week assessment period before we began working on goals, we could be finished with the intervention before any systematic change had begun.

We have found, though, if we can take our time now, and make sure that we understand everything family members want us to comprehend, the rest of the intervention will go much more smoothly. If we rush now, we may begin making suggestions about problems that don't exist or are low priority for the family. We may make suggestions to try things the clients have already tried, or push them to work on issues that don't make sense to them. It will not work.

The families have the best data about their situation. We have all been tempted, when confronted by six angry family members, each with differing views on a number of scary problems, to run to our offices and thumb through previous professional reports in hopes of finding the key to understanding and salvation with a particular family. Others' reports do sometimes help. Often, though, the usefulness of reports is limited because previous workers haven't been able to spend much time with families, particularly in the families' natural environments.

This is the time for more active listening. The family members know a lot more than we do about what they want, what has been happening, what they've tried, what helped, what didn't help, and a lot about why all this has been going on. Any solution will have to make sense in terms of their perceptions. If our help doesn't mesh with what they think the problems and solutions are, change will not occur. We need to match our interventions with their values, beliefs about change, reading levels, and religion. If we do not, we will always be slightly out of sync with them and change will be much slower.

We need to stay long enough during the first visit to hear the whole story. If possible, it is best to hear the whole story from everyone's point of view. Frequently we can hear best if we talk with each family member individually at first. Some stories are so inflammatory to other family members that they will never get finished in a group. We want to validate everyone's perspective. Even though each person's story will differ, each person's perception *is* his or her perception and deserves full respect and consideration. This is not the time for grilling and prosecuting. This is not even a time for change, even though clarification can in itself lead to change. The priority now is understanding, withholding judgments on the specifics, trying to feel compassion, and engaging with each family member. This is imperative. The more compassion family members can feel from us, the more they will trust us. The more they trust us, the more information they will give us. The more information we have, the better the assessment we can formulate.

Once the story has been heard, and sometimes reheard, it is important for us to check to see if we really understood what they were trying to say. We can say, "I think I understand what the issues are from your point of view, but I want to check. May I repeat them back to you and see if I have it the way you intended?" This isn't limited to the first few sessions. Assessments have to be updated continually, and checking to see if we got it right is necessary frequently. We need to know if we cut anyone off. Also, when we try to say back what we thought we heard and find ourselves confused, it might mean the family members are still confused, too. More listening and more clarification are necessary.

An assessment is never "done." Especially with families in crisis, all of our definitions of problems and strengths may evolve rapidly. In families where progress occurs smoothly, the assessment is gradually updated until it states that the family is functioning satisfactorily and no further intervention in needed. In families where progress is slow, we need to continually assess our assessment. What effect is problem definition having on motivation of family members? On us? Are the ways the problems are defined generating interventions for change? Are the problem definitions allowing us to set small, obtainable goals? If we are able to view our view, we are more likely to find strategies which fit for particular families, since problem conceptualizations can be revised repeatedly until they are comfortable for family members as well as workers.

Problem and Strength Definition

Problems can be defined in ways that generate options for change or limit them. Descriptions can enlighten family members, relieve them of guilt, free energy, and point the way to change. They can help people feel more hopeful and in charge of their situations. Assessments can also burden, overwhelm, discourage, and alienate family members. They can clarify issues or obscure them. They can generate options for change, or limit them. In this section we wish to discuss ways to maximize the positives of an assessment and minimize potential negatives.

Recognizing Strengths and Potential Resources

As we assess whether a family in crisis can provide a safe, nurturing environment for a child, the family's potential for growth is as important as their current problem. We need to think of ourselves as detectives searching for what is going right in the family. Do they ever joke with each other? Do they show any affection, ever? Do they, even for a moment, listen to one another? Have they had times in the past when they did fun things together? Do they share any common interests? Do they hold any similar views? Do they care what others' opinions are of them? Do they feel good if they are able to please one another, even if it's rare? If we can find these beginnings, and help family members become aware of them too, we can express our own appreciation for these seeds of strength and help them to grow in the process.

We also need to observe families' capacities to learn. Some may initially have overwhelming problems and few strengths because they have never been exposed to alternatives for managing their lives better.

Others may have many strengths, but find it difficult to learn because of beliefs that others should do all the changing.

Other families may have few skills, and, because of developmental disabilities or illness, have less capacity to implement new learnings. With them, we must search for potential resources to supplement and strengthen their situation. Some may have family members or neighbors who could help with child care. Others may require formal social service help such as homemakers or chore services workers. Without those supplements, the family may appear inadequate, but with them, and the monitoring workers could provide, the home may have far more potential than placement settings.

Organizing the Information about Problems

As we listen to families' information and try to understand, we begin encouraging family members to organize the information in certain manageable ways. We focus on minimizing blame and negative labeling, generating options for change, and approaching consensus. We encourage family members to interpret and describe each others' behavior more positively.

Minimizing Blame and Labeling.   Usually family members blame each other for their difficulties. As long as people are being blamed, those people will feel defensive and frightened. They will find it difficult to hear solutions or to want to cooperate. So, the first thing we want to do in assessing problems is to *define them in ways that minimize blaming*.

Most blaming is connected with labeling. Negative labeling can damage the relationship between worker and client and between family members themselves. We try to discourage GLOP (Generalized Labeling of People) whenever we can. General terms are usually negative—e.g., you're a *slut, witch, drunk, lazy, stupid, overreactive, insensitive*. People don't like being described that way. They disagree. They think the situation is being oversimplified and slanted. Often the terms imply some intentionality that the labelee feels is unfair. The general terms mean different things to different people, so little actual information is transmitted.

Labeling can be a big issue between workers and clients, too. It's easy for us to slip into *neurotic, passive aggressive, scapegoat*, rather than defining exactly what we mean. Avoiding labels is difficult, however, because so many of us were taught that the purpose of assessment is to correctly assign diagnostic labels, even though many studies indicate that there is little reliability among professionals in assigning those labels, and that the labels have little predictive value or use in development of treatment plans.

Certain client labels are particularly damaging because they can have such a negative effect on the way we feel about the clients. Labels such as "unmotivated" or "resistant" define clients as adversaries with bad intentions and little common sense or desire to overcome their problems. Labels can position us to demean clients, disagree with them, and pressure them to do things "for their own good" rather than because the courses of action we recommend make sense to them. Labeling makes it harder for us to be warm and supportive, if we're thinking about coping with the negative traits we've assigned to our clients. Instead of calling clients "resistant" or "unmotivated," it's more helpful to describe them as worried about failing again, feeling hopeless, feeling helpless, lacking the skills necessary to begin thinking about the problems, or unable, at the moment, to formulate goals that seem worthwhile and obtainable.

We avoid describing family members in value-laden terms. Once we begin to think of a client as "antagonistic" or "vindictive," we are likely to believe it, and to feel some pressure to justify our initial impressions, hindering us from being open to the whole picture and to more positive interpretations. It will be more helpful to redefine "vindictive" as "focusing on past hurts," and "antagonistic" as "afraid of being disappointed again."

Other labels such as "sociopathic," or "psychotic," can also have a tremendous impact on the client–counselor relationship. Not only do clients not like having these labels, the labels also scare us and make us think the situation is hopeless—much more hopeless than if we stuck to the specifics such as "Jerry took his grandmother's medicine and flushed it down the toilet," or "Sometimes when Susie talks, her sentences don't make sense," or "Theron sometimes hits Judy when they fight." When clients are labeled by referring workers, it is particularly easy for us to look at the referral sheet and say, "Oh, no, a chronic psychopath, nobody can work with those!," rather than remembering that the label resulted from some specific things the client did that are not half as scary as the label might imply.

Labels can also harm our goal of helping clients feel hopeful because they imply an all or nothingness about problems. If someone *is* something, like pathological, or if they *have* something, like low ego strength, the implication is that that is the way they are, and that is the way they always will be. The *have* a condition. We think it's more helpful to define problems in terms of things that people do or do not do. People can stop or start doing some or all of those things if they choose. It is possible to set small goals of changing only one or a few behaviors at a time. The goals begin to seem possible. There is hope.

Clients can be empowered when we accept problem categories they give us, rather than throw in additional abstract ones they didn't know they needed to worry about. If we tell a family that their real problem is that the mother is basically hostile even though she thought she was trying to discipline her children, the mother has a new problem to worry about. She feels even less in control, and even less hopeful about resolving her problems. She is less likely to begin to accept responsibility for change. If the professional is the one who's deciding what the problems are, maybe he can solve them, too. She is more likely to be passive and hope he does something to make her hostility go away.

My second assignment after joining Homebuilders was a particularly difficult one for me. The presenting problems centered around 5-year-old Jason, whose mother complained that he was almost impossible to control—setting fires, destroying property, running through the neighborhood in the middle of the night, pillaging the refrigerator, etc. Jason seemed incapable of sitting still or of following a single request his mother would make of him.

But all this was not what made this family a difficult one. To all appearances Jason had been, from the beginning of his life, a neglected and abused child. As an infant, on three different occasions he had been hospitalized as a failure-to-thrive child. There had been at least eight prior CPS referrals that had faulted the parents as neglectful. Jason had been dismissed from a day-care treatment program on the grounds of noncooperation on the part of his mother.

It was difficult for me in this particular case not to cast blame on Jason's parents for these problems. I got little or no response from his mother, who seemed only to complain of Jason's behaviors, but who did not seem willing to try the suggestions I made. (Jason's dad was not living at home and was for the most part only an occasional and equally passive participant in the sessions.) To top things off, during the first week of our intervention, Jason's maternal grandmother entered the hospital for a serious operation, making it even more difficult for the mother to stay focused.

I remember so clearly the day that things shifted. I was feeling more and more frustrated and was going to confront Jason's mother on what I felt to be her lack of cooperation. What I somehow ended up doing instead was just listening to her as she told me something about her own life as a child in her family, how she had been the one in the family who was always called upon to support her mother and sisters when they had problems. As I listened, I felt touched with compassion and realized how superficial my judgments had been. All of us are just doing the very best we can.

Things changed after that—not all at once and not dramatically. I talked more with Jason's mother about her own life goals and took her one day to the local community college where she was interested in studying—of all things!—early childhood education. Jason ended up in excellent day-care and school programs. His behaviors began to fall more into the normal range. A number of months later I visited Jason's school to see another client and met Jason's teacher. She told me that he was not only doing well, but was showing signs of real leadership in the class. I also learned that Jason's parents were close to getting back together. As Jason's mother wrote in the evaluation: "Jim was very supportive. He brought us back together so that we're very close."

The lesson for me is that we really cannot judge anyone, no matter how bad the evidence looks. (Jim Poggi)

Generating Options for Change.   Few options for change are generated by an assessment that regards Mary to be an "inadequate personality." Aside from suggesting that a personality transplant is needed, this kind of diagnosis doesn't indicate what needs to be changed. The vagueness of the label can prevent us from knowing when that label is no longer deserved or appropriate. It will be difficult for Mary to prove her labelers wrong. If we deal with the specifics of the children being clean, going to the doctor if they have earaches, and receiving proper nutrition, the directions for change become clear. It will also be clear to everyone when the problems are resolved.

Reaching consensus about the facts.   It's always difficult with a number of upset family members whose stories differ, to know what the facts are. Abstractions and inferences usually only escalate disagreements. These are statements like, "Tyrone is always out to get Letitia," or "Tiffany never tries." As long as family members disagree about what is happening, it is difficult to help them work together on their problems. There are two ways to help them to agree on what's happening.

One way to get beyond GLOP is to define the situation very generally. Although people may disagree about others' intentions and the meaning of various events, they can usually reach agreement on broad areas like "things are not going very well here," or "nobody's very happy with the way things are," or "it seems confusing and overwhelming," or "we would all like things to be different," or "sometimes everything just seems hopeless." Most family members can agree about overall statements like these, and the first glimmers of agreement can begin to form the foundation for big changes.

Another way to facilitate family members' agreement is to define the situation very specifically. It can be profitable to try to break down the GLOP and the inferences into some facts. This is a time when it can be helpful to begin asking a few questions gently and kindly, to clarify the issues. There are many excellent books with information about specifying behaviors (Gambrill, 1977; Kazdin, 1980; Herson and Bellack, 1976; Mash and Terdal, 1988), but we'll give a few examples here.

Suppose Mrs. Williams says, "Tyrone is always out to get Letitia." What does she mean by that? What does he do that makes her say that? When does he do it? How often? What happens before he does it? What happens after he does it? Usually questions like this lead to answers like "Tyrone locks her in her room by jamming a stick in the door. He does this when she yells at him and I'm not home." After he does it, Mrs. Williams comes home and screams at him and he runs away. Letitia comes out and cries and says he's always out to get her. Mrs. Williams, Tyrone, and Letitia may still have different interpretations of the meaning of all this, but they can usually agree on these facts. Once they agree about the indicators, we can begin to specify goals such as reducing Letitia's yelling at Tyrone and Tyrone coming up with other options than locking her in her room if she does yell at him.

In another example, we have a disagreement between school personnel and a parent. School personnel believe Mrs. Hughes is "manipulative, rigid and emotionally unstable." Mrs. Hughes believes school personnel are jerking her around for no reason, asking her to jump through hoops other parents can avoid. When we ask school personnel, "What does she do that makes you say that?" "How would we know if things were better?" they begin to talk about Mrs. Hughes being late for meetings, skipping meetings, or writing notes they don't understand. She is "emotionally unstable" because when they said they thought CPS should take her child away, she cried and yelled. When we listen to Mrs. Hughes about her feeling toward school people, she says she doesn't hear about meetings until after they were supposed to occur, or the meetings are scheduled when she has to work. She has not been told the reasons for the meetings. As the facts emerge, we begin to have a basis for beginning negotiations. Ideally, we want a situation where everyone agrees on a number of things it would be good to change.

Shaping toward less negative interpretations. Sometimes it's possible, through active listening, to gradually help people to interpret each other's behavior in less negative ways. It might be possible for us to gradually encourage Mrs. Williams to see that Tyrone may lock Letitia in because he is overwhelmed and hurt by the things she is screaming at him, rather than because he is "out to get her." School personnel may be encouraged to view Mrs. Hughes' "manipulativeness" as related to her lack of direct communications skills and that she is trying to get her needs met in ways even she doesn't always understand. We might suggest she has learned in the past to keep some things hidden in order to keep the peace. She may not trust anyone. She may be terrified of having her child taken away and may say almost anything if she thinks that can be prevented.

Defining problems in terms of skill deficits. Once problems have been specified, we teach families our belief that most problems result from skill deficits. We prefer this view because it is neutral. People usually don't feel put down if they just didn't happen to learn a particular skill. It is also an optimistic view: just because we haven't learned particular skills, doesn't mean we cannot learn them now. Skill building is also fairly easy to define in small steps so family members can feel hopeful and begin to see improvements readily.

Family members usually like this view. They want each other to stop doing some things (screaming, yelling, hitting) and start doing other things (coming home on time, expressing appreciation, home-work). We want family members to see screaming and yelling as lack of communication skills or skills in handling frustration. We want them to begin to identify skills necessary for getting home on time (paying attention to clocks or their watch, mastering the transporta-tion system, saying "no" to friends) and doing homework (keeping track of assignments and work materials, reading, understanding assign-ments, etc.). We give examples, such as a child who throws temper tantrums, exhibits excellent skills in screaming, hits and throws himself around until he gets his way. He has not learned the skills of delaying gratification, taking "no" for an answer, or bargaining.

Personal skills to improve problematic behavior can include anger management, depression management, anxiety and confusion manage-ment, learning positive self-talk, and coping with frustration. Individuals may need to learn job skills, personal grooming, time management, money management, good food habits, leisure time activity skills, and how to use transportation

Interpersonal skills involve social skills, communications skills, asser-tiveness, problem solving and negotiation, giving and accepting feed-back, and appropriate sexual behavior.

Setting goals.   Once the information has been gathered, and family members agree that the worker understands their situation, it is usually possible to begin more formal articulation of problems and goals. We tell family members that we need to set goals so we'll know if we are making any progress. We want to make sure we're really helping them with their problems, not just wasting their time.

Making small steps.   Many problem areas still seem enormous and overwhelming at this point. We tell many families a variation of an old African story: There is a group of explorers in the jungle. They have been there for many months, and their supplies are gone. They have traveled many miles and are exhausted. They have two more miles to go when they encounter a huge, dead elephant blocking their trail. They cannot go around it on either side because the jungle is too dense. They cannot go over it because the way it is lying it is too steep and too tall. It is too heavy for them to move. What can they do?

The (gory) answer is, that they have to cut up the elephant. Many families' problems are enormous, but if we can cut them up into little pieces and begin moving them, one by one, gradually, the path will be clear and the journey can be completed.

We struggle, at this point, to find fairly small changes that will have meaning for family members. We might ask parents, "What one change in your son's behavior, even if it were just a small change, would really mean something to you? What change would let you know that he is trying, and that things are improving?" or, for the son, "What would your father have to do, what one small thing, to show you he's willing to work things out with you?" If we can identify some of these important small changes, we can encourage family members to agree that if the changes do occur, they will remember what they said and give full credit to others for making them, even though they were small items.

Prioritizing Issues. During the information gathering stage, it is usually obvious that the family has more problems than they can begin to tackle in 4 to 6 weeks. It's easy for us, as workers, to begin making decisions about priorities. Some problems seem easy to overcome; others seem difficult. Some, like assault and suicide threats, seem obviously important, while others, like cigarette smoking, seem less so. Except in matters of imminent safety, it is best to help the family members set their own priorities as much as possible. After all, our main purpose is to help them make their own decisions and solve their own problems. We need to encourage them every step of the way. They know better than we do which issues are really bothering them. Their motivation will decrease if we push them to attend to what they may consider low priority items. Still, we can help them to evaluate options. Most counselors help families consider the current annoyance value of the problem to the family, the danger, the potential for success, the probable cost of working on an issue in terms of time, money, energy, and other resources, and the likelihood that the new patterns will be maintained after the worker leaves.

At the same time, taking clients' problems at face value and allowing them to prioritize must be balanced with counselor and referring workers concerns about family members' safety and about ethical matters. A family referred because a 5 year old had marks and bruises from beatings by his mother, will have to deal with that issue. If the mother says it's not a problem, we will strongly express our own concern, and make it clear it is a concern for CPS and CPS concerns must be addressed or the child will be removed. Similarly, a teenager who wanted to earn money through prostitution would not receive support for this goal.

Being Realistic. Many family members want big changes immediately. They want children to attend school 100% of the time, be in by curfew, get rid of unsavory friends, and pick up their rooms. Children want parents to stop yelling, give more spending money, and allow unlimited freedom. Although many of these changes might eventually evolve, they certainly won't happen immediately. One of the ways we can help families be realistic about goals is to make the steps of improvement small. We can also urge them to select only one or two to begin with and to realize that change will occur in increments rather than all at once.

Goal Attainment Scaling. We use Goal Attainment Scaling (Kiresuk and Sherman, 1968) as the basis for our records, as the structure to assess progress on individual goals. Goal Attainment Scaling, as we use it, involves use of a rating scale of two to five potential outcome levels regarding a specific goal. Potential outcome levels look like this:

+2 Best anticipated success
+1 More than expected success
 0 Expected level of success
−1 Less than expected success
−2 Most unfavorable outcome likely

Counselors and family members decide on specific, observable events for each point on the scale, using their best judgment of the possible outcomes. A goal regarding school attendance might look like this:

+2 Gina attends 90% of her classes this week
+1 Gina attends 75% of her classes this week
 0 Gina attends 50% of her classes this week
−1 Gina attends 25% of her classes this week
−2 Gina attends fewer than 25% of her classes this week

Potential outcome levels on a goal attainment scale should be rated weekly in conjunction with a summary of the week's activities related to that goal. The most important thing about Goal Attainment Scaling is that it forces us to select goals, and to monitor them. If progress is not occurring, the expectation is that next week's plan must be different, incorporating new information about the ineffectiveness of the previous plan. Actual problem resolution strategies are discussed in Chapter 9.

Summary

The ways we conceptualize problems are as important as the strategies we have available for problem resolution. We facilitate clients' recognizing their strengths and potential as well as their weaknesses. We encourage them to specify their problems and learn to view them as skill deficits rather than personality traits. Once problems are defined, we help families to prioritize them, set realistic goals, and develop a process for monitoring goal achievement.

7
Helping Clients Learn

We want to do more than teach families. We want them to *learn how to learn*. Ultimately, we hope that they will begin to understand the learning process so well that they will continue to learn productively long after we are gone. Most of our clients have not had positive experiences with learning. Many have had problems in school or have failed at previous social services attempts. Some just do not have enough energy; paying attention is too hard. Before we can begin any systematic teaching, we have to help families accomplish the tasks we have described in previous chapters: calming down, forming a partnership, and clarifying problems and goals. Then we have to help them realize that learning new skills is worth the effort.

Teaching About Learning

We see our jobs as helping families become more aware of the learning process so they can have more influence over what they and others learn. We want them to learn how to get by with less pain, less punishment, more accomplishment, more love (!), and more fun.

Ultimately, we would like people to become *personal scientists*. Scientists observe conditions around them. They systematically vary conditions. They note outcomes. We would like our clients to learn to observe their problems and systematically vary ways of dealing with these problems until they come up with one that fits for them.

We introduce the idea of learning skills as a way of overcoming problems. Many clients believe we should be emphasizing people's pasts and analyzing things that happened to them then. We acknowledge this common approach, but say that although people may have learned to behave the way they do in the past, they can learn to do things differently right *now*.

We talk with families about learning, and help them recognize that we all have particular capacities for it. Some of us are smarter than others.

Some are more sensitive. Some are musically talented. We are not, however, "bad seeds," or "sick personalities" or "evil." We do learn unpleasant, disagreeable behaviors in the same ways we learn the pleasant ones: from our environment, our parents, our siblings, our friends, our enemies, our school teachers, and, more and more, from television.

We are still learning now. Everyone is learning every day as we receive new information and interpret it for ourselves. We cannot help it. Sometimes we learn what we want to learn, like how to swim or fix plumbing; and sometimes we learn what we may not want, like how to smoke, or to feel bitter when we see our mother-in-law.

Even when we are not learning one thing, we are learning another. For example, a child who does not learn addition fails his test. He may learn that he cannot do math, that he is dumb, that he never will do math, and that he is not as good at anything as his sister.

Developing Realistic Expectations

Change is not always smooth and is rarely easy. It will take hard work and involve a lot of trial and error. Sometimes it will seem slow. Nevertheless, small changes can add up to a big difference.

We talk to families about how awkward it can be to learn, especially after a person is grown up and supposed to know how to "do" life. We talk about "stairsteps of competence" as one model for thinking about learning new skills. In this paradigm, we progress through four stages as we gradually master new ways of coping. In the beginning, we may be *unconsciously incompetent* because we do not even know a new skill exists. People who have never heard of active listening are "unconsciously incompetent" for that skill if they do not know how to do it and do not know it exists. Once they learn about it, they become *consciously incompetent*. They know about active listening, but they cannot do it. In this stage, people begin to feel uncomfortable. By opening ourselves to new learning, we come to realize that other options exist, and we may feel guilty, inadequate, or foolish because we did not learn them earlier.

If we work at it, however, we can rise to another level and become *consciously competent*: we begin to demonstrate the new skill, but it is hard. In active listening, for example, we have to think through carefully what we should say. We have to struggle to avoid missing what the sender is trying to communicate. We feel pleased that we can do it at all, but we feel awkward and embarrassed because it is so hard to keep doing it correctly. Finally, if we keep practicing, we reach the level of *unconscious competence*. This is the fun part—where we can demonstrate the skill without even thinking about it. It has finally become a part of us; we have truly mastered it.

We would like our clients to understand these stages so that they will expect to feel awkward and embarrassed sometimes. We want them to realize that learning is complex and does not happen all at once. We do not want these facts to discourage them.

We also talk about how their problems will not all vanish, even though they learn new skills. We point out that some problems cannot be solved; they are *dilemmas* or predicaments.

We discuss ways of viewing counseling. We will not be with them for months or years because we do not think they will need it. We may refer to Betsy Cole, the noted national child welfare expert, who describes our earlier belief in the "inoculation theory of counseling," in which clients had one shot and were then presumed free from problems forever. She observes that we now tend toward the "intravenous theory of counseling," in which a social worker gets hooked up with a client and stays attached for the rest of their lives. We find it more useful to think of counseling as episodic. There are different times in people's lives when they need help, but they usually do not. Though they will learn a lot from our work together, they may later have other problems. This does not mean that they are failures, but only that life's difficulties catch us all from time to time.

They may even notice some new problems while we are with them. As one problem decreases, others may become more apparent and we will work on them. For example, people satiate on rewards. They work for a while and then stop. This does not mean the plan failed, but that we need to try new rewards.

We tell families that we will gradually encourage them to take more responsibility for the change process. Our job is to do for them at the beginning if they are overwhelmed, but we rapidly expect them to feel strong enough to work on problem resolution with us, and eventually to do most of it on their own, while we stand by, cheering them on.

Ways to Facilitate Learning

There are three main ways that we teach clients. (1) *Direct instruction*, in which we present information to clients; (2) *Modeling*, in which we do new activities ourselves, thus showing clients how to do them; and (3) *Contingency management*, in which we teach them to manage contingencies of reinforcement: encouraging learning by rewarding behaviors they want to encourage, and by ignoring or punishing behaviors they want to discourage.

We also encourage clients to learn from others. We want to help them connect with other teachers. We want them to interpret actions of others in ways that will lead to positive instead of negative learning. We do this in the same way we help them to learn to perceive their own problems more positively. For example, if a teenager has a teacher who yells if he is late, it might be helpful to brainstorm with the teenager good reasons the teacher might have for yelling: She may be upset that the child may not learn. She may be upset that if her lesson plan gets interrupted no one will understand the material. Maybe she gets in trouble from the principal if her students are wandering in the halls during class. Of course, we would agree with the teenager that it would be preferable if the teacher didn't yell, but we want to influence him toward a more generous, cooperative interpretation of undesired behavior if we can.

Barriers to Learning

Various life situations and beliefs make learning difficult for clients. They are often preoccupied with basic safety and life maintenance issues like food and housing. Their emotions are often out of control. They find it difficult to form partnerships and to clarify their goals. Many family members believe that learning new skills is irrelevant. They have learned that change is supposed to occur by a counselor "fixing" something. Some of our techniques are totally outside their frame of reference. Who ever heard of "I messages"? (Is it something you do with your eyes?)

To other clients, learning seems impossible. They haven't done well at it in other settings and our concepts seem abstract and obscure. Previous attempts at learning have not only been unsuccessful and unrewarding, they have been downright punishing. People have been ridiculed for failures in school. They have learned to label themselves "stupid." To them, trying to learn again might not only be a waste of time, it might remind them of all the previous times they weren't "good enough." It might be boring and tedious beyond words.

These beliefs are formidable barriers. We need all the optimism, creativity, tenacity, and good humor we can muster to overcome them. We must keep inventing new ways to help families learn to ford rivers themselves rather than our having to carry them over. To do this, we coach them and encourage them to do things that are difficult for them.

We want clients to overcome barriers to learning. Since each family member has different barriers or combinations of barriers, we tailor each approach to the individual. Some of our general strategies, though, are described below.

Overcoming "It's Irrelevant." Many clients find it difficult to see how our wonderful ideas relate to their problems. The first step involves taking care of pressing needs that may be distracting them. If a woman is worried about the roof caving in on her family, she is not going to be interested in active listening. If children are coming in and out of the room crying and threatening each other, she cannot concentrate. If a father has been up all night looking for a runaway, he will be too tired and distracted to learn about contingency management.

We call the times when clients are alert, focused, and interested in learning, "teachable moments." We have a teachable moment when someone we have been listening to for a long time heaves a big sigh and says, "What shall I do?" Other openings sound like: "I just don't know what to do," or "I can't take it any more," or "I'm really sick of this." Once we have a strong relationship with family members, we may observe them getting tangled in their problems and offer suggestions at the time. For example, when a 2 year old is having a tantrum and throwing herself around the living room, one can say to a parent: "This is pretty rough, isn't it? Are you interested in trying something new to see if we can get her calmed down?" When people describe past difficult situations, one can also offer suggestions about what they might have tried. For example, when Carina spilled catsup all over her mother's new blouse after borrowing it without permission: "You wanted to wring her neck? There are disadvantages to that, though, aren't there? Maybe sometime we could talk about other things you might have tried then."

When we have a teachable moment, and when clients are not distracted, we can help family members connect the skill to their problem. When talking about learning, we may be too abstract and our clients cannot make the connection. How is active listening going to help Sara come in on time? Well, it will help, because if we listen, Sara will have more positive feelings about us and her home. She will give us more information about why she does not come home that we can use to resolve some problems. Active listening will also give us a new way of talking that will not hurt Sara as much as the present style.

With direct instruction, there are a number of ways we can help clients realize that what we are teaching is relevant. We can be sensitive to their priorities of the day, focusing on topics that are important to them at the moment, instead of the ones we thought would be relevant when we planned this session 2 days ago. We can present examples of others with the same problems, the same number of children, and the same age children. We can use language that is similar to theirs. We can make sure the material we present is compatible with their values, style, and economic situation. When we enter a family where resources are tight, we might focus on social rewards, such as hugs, or the stickers from "Chiquita" bananas. Some young children will even be delighted by colorful price tags. In wealthier families, parents can reward children with small toys.

Another way of directly instructing clients is to show them rather than telling them about certain principles. One way we demonstrate the negative side effects of continual attempts at control by punishment is to play the Penny Game. Our counselor gives a parent 25 cents. The counselor thinks of a number between one and five. If the parent gets it right, nothing happens. If the parent is wrong, the counselor takes away a penny. Parents feel bad, and they usually don't want to play very long. Then the counselor shifts the rules. She starts with the pennies herself. When a parent guesses wrong, she smiles at him or her and says, "Sorry, you'll do better soon." If the parents guess right, they get a penny. Most parents get the message quickly that positive contingencies make for a better, longer lasting partnership.

When we attempt to help clients learn from others, we can make sure family members see that the other potential teacher has information they need. If they have doubts, we can gather more specific information about what others have to offer, and develop detailed rationales for how this information could help family members solve their problems. For example, in Pierce County, the Juvenile Court offers an excellent course for teenagers on anger management. We can just tell our clients it exists and get them the address, or we can go over the outline and make sure they understand how the skills could help them with their particular issues. We could even take them over and let them talk to young people currently in the group about what they are learning and how the course is helping them.

When we model for clients, we can do it with *their* children in *their* house. We can tell them exactly what we are thinking about doing: "How about next time Jamie refuses to pick up his toys, I try teaching him how, and you watch? Okay? What I'll be doing is: first, just getting him to look at me, stand right in front of him, look directly at him, and tell him to look at me. When he does that, I'll praise him. Then I'll ask him to pick up one toy. If he doesn't, I'll hand it to him and put it in his hand. When he's holding it, I'll praise him again." We keep checking to make sure clients see the relevancy of what we are doing. "It may not seem like holding one toy is going to help much with keeping the whole house cleaner, but it's a start. Remember the elephant story? We've got to take one step at a time."

Modeling can be a big help in getting clients to see how principles can be relevant. Active listening can sound awfully phony, but if a mother watches the counselor use it smoothly and successfully with her daughter, she will be more interested in trying it herself.

When we model new skills, we need to choose examples that fit clients' situations. For example, in assertiveness training we often talk about sending back bad food in restaurants. For many clients in impoverished environments, being assertive with landlords and "friends" trying to steal food is much more relevant.

When we help families arrange reinforcement contingencies, we take care to focus on the specific behaviors that are the most important to each family member. If we use rewards, we make sure they are things a person really wants, rather than something we think they ought to want. We can also make certain the rewards are compatible with parents' values and budgets.

Overcoming "It's Impossible." Many of our clients are discouraged. Some are in despair of ever having their families be happy. We have previously discussed ways to give hope to clients in Chapters 4 and 6. We want to remember these strategies throughout the intervention and continue to use them as we move into the teaching phase.

We point out differences between FPS and other services families have had. We have lots of time to help them. We can work with them individually or as a group. We can provide concrete help if they need it. If they are too overwhelmed to do anything but tell us what they need, change can still begin to occur. If a mother sees bunk beds arriving after she had totally given up on getting her house in order, she will begin to perk up. If a child gets to go to the zoo for being willing to spend time with a counselor even if he has not talked about his problem, next time he will be more open to all subjects.

Essentially, as we teach people who are very discouraged, we want to make failure impossible and make certain they notice this. We do this by helping them set goals that are so small that they cannot help but achieve them. In the example above, regarding a child picking up his toys, the child was rewarded for eye contact, and then for touching one toy, even if we had to put it in his hand. If all a depressed mother has to do to reach her first goal is get out of bed and comb her hair in the morning, chances are she will succeed. When we fuss over her, she will begin to realize that she is able to do *something*—life is not over. As tasks become more difficult, we can continue to make failure impossible through our close involvement and supervision. At the beginning, the mother's only job may be to tell us what she needs. If she needs a bed, we get it, and she sees success. She sees that she was able to influence her situation. She cannot fail to get food at a food bank we know of if we go with her and all she has to do is give her name at the desk. She cannot fail calling the landlord if we sit beside her and rest our hand on her shoulder while she reads a script we prepared together. With any one family member, this concept of small steps might be expressed in a number of ways.

> The potential removal was a 17-year-old gifted boy, Brad, living with his 14-year-old brother, his mother, and father. Brad was from a family of 7 children. His five older siblings were living independently. Brad was referred to Homebuilders by the mental health center where he had been seen for 1 year. A counselor had been making twice weekly home visits for this length of time. Before the referral to Homebuilders, Brad had been seen by the Office of Involuntary Commitment because there was a fear that his continued withdrawal would lead to psychiatric hospitalization. Brad hadn't gone out of the house for the last several months and he had refused to go to school for 2½ years. He had not been to school except for a few days in the ninth grade.
>
> The school district was extremely concerned. Although they had tried to set up a group home placement, Brad refused to go. School staff agreed that the placement may have been too overwhelming.
>
> At intake Brad's father was an inpatient at an alcoholism treatment center. Apparently he had been abusing alcohol for years and agreed to go for help because of the encouragement of one of Brad's sisters. The primary goals of the intervention included:
>
> 1. Brad learns anxiety management techniques.
> 2. School options are considered for Brad.
> 3. Family members improve communication skills.
>
> At first it was very hard for Brad to spend time with me. Although he was extremely quiet, he was willing to talk to me because he wanted to remain at home.
>
> I did the intake with the four family members, followed by daily sessions with Brad during week #1. I began staying just 15 minutes for individual sessions, then added time as I began to engage Brad. To achieve goal #1, I used systematic desensitization. With an anxiety hierarchy and relaxation training I began with imagery and moved to in vivo situations. This went fairly fast, since Brad had had relaxation training from the mental health center. This counselor went out twice a week, while I continued to go out 7 days a week, sometimes staying for hours when working on the anxiety management goal.
>
> Accompanying the systematic desensitization to achieve goal #1, I also used RET with Brad. This was designed to help him decrease his expectations of himself. We also worked on instructions for what to do in a panic attack. Along with the above described strategies, the telephone was used to increase Brad's social skills and for relationship building. At first he was anxious about this, but he was able to calm his fears about talking on the phone. Using these strategies, Brad was going outside within about two and one-half weeks.
>
> After accomplishing the first goal, we considered school options for Brad. He decided that a local alternative school would be the most comfortable educational setting for him. Another anxiety hierarchy regard-

ing school was, therefore, established. We began by driving around the school, followed by sitting in the parking lot, and then walking around the building. We ultimately met with the director of the school and Brad began attending 2 hours per day. When this became too much for Brad, an in-home tutor was assigned for him with the option of returning to alternative school that year.

To address the third goal of improving family members' communication skills, we had weekly family meetings. I taught communication skills including active listening and "I" messages to both parents, Brad, and his brother. Brad began to talk some with his parents, but his father wanted more. To continue work on this goal, I made a referral for individual and family counseling at Catholic Community Services. Going to the office where my program was housed was on Brad's original hierarchy. I saw the ongoing counselor with Brad for his first visit. Meanwhile, other members continued to participate in alcohol-related counseling.

At termination Brad was at home. He was able to leave his home with less anxiety and his parents felt better about his improved behavior. He had stopped going to school, but had the option to return. He was going out (to the library, to a local variety store, riding the bus, playing basketball). (Mary Fischer)

When we instruct directly, we make failure almost impossible by doling out small bits of information at a time. We can be prepared for variations in our clients' energy. We can have videotapes to watch if they are tired, and save the role playing for a more energetic day. If a whole book is overwhelming, we can abstract the most important sections.

When we model, we can begin with very simple tasks. We can also model failing. For example, we may respond to a teenager with a perfect "I message" about feeling hurt when he says counselors are jerks; but the teenager may say "Yeah, well, that's tough. You are all jerks," and walk out of the apartment, slamming the door behind him. We do not usually plan to fail, but there are advantages when it happens. We can reinforce the idea that we do not have all the answers and that we are all in this together. We can confirm the fact that change is not easy. If we handle the failure cheerfully, without punishing ourselves, we model that one does not have to succeed the first time. Failure is not awful. We will just try something else. We can also model relentless optimism. We can keep our eyes on the tiny sparks of progress instead of on the ashes of past failures.

When we arrange contingencies, we stay with the idea of small steps. Even though parents want their children "fixed" immediately, we have to encourage them to work on few goals and small steps. We have to be constantly on the lookout to "catch people being good" whether they are on a formal behavior management program or not. When we see parents or children productively working toward problem resolution or cooperation, we need to comment on it: "Hey, Johnny, that's great that you're helping Billy with his jacket." "Mrs. Gould, I noticed you really making an effort to say positive things to Janey in the other room. That's great. Good job." All clients already engage in many strong, appropriate, functional behaviors. We need to keep ourselves aware of this, and we need to help them to become aware of it. This awareness will help us all realize that positive learning is possible and, indeed, has already occurred.

Overcoming "It's Punishing."   To work hard at something and never catch on is no fun. Nor is it fun to have a life full of problems and drudgery and then be faced with more boring tasks. When working with families, we need to acknowledge that learning has the potential to be a real drag; it was in the past and probably will be sometimes in the future. We also need to state our intention to make learning not only relevant and possible, but even (heaven forbid) fun. We do this from the beginning by being open to humor whenever possible. Sometimes family members will begin to poke fun at themselves and their situations. Sometimes we can get a few laughs out of them right from the first session. Just because their situations are often deadly serious does not mean that the process of change has to be that way as well. Anything we can do to make the process fun will encourage people to hang in there with us, will relax them so they will be better able to listen and try new options, and will make our job more rewarding, and give us all more energy. We do not make fun of people (except maybe ourselves), and we do not fail to validate the pain of the situation. We do seek whimsy and materials that arouse people's sense of humor as well as their curiosity.

With direct instruction, we use materials with clients' names on them, or with pictures of them included. We explain concepts by drawing funny pictures on big pieces of paper. We post reminders of new behaviors on the walls "Don't forget about hugs!" and big rewards "Good Job Jerry. Keep It Up."

With modeling, we may use silly examples when the going gets heavy. If a family is having trouble communicating anything but hatred, model giving "I messages" to the dog, or pretend to give them over the phone to your own spouse.

When arranging contingencies, the key is to keep the focus on desirable behavior, and on rewards instead of on punishments. That may be difficult at the beginning. When family members are angry with one another they do not always like to see each other get rewards. They will be more receptive to others having nice things happen to them if they are being rewarded themselves. Adults like stickers too. Parents feel better about keeping reward charts for doing chores if, at the end of the week, they get an ice cream sundae for their supervision and monitoring efforts. (The counselor can always have one, too. It is important to keep things positive for us.)

Rewarding Attempts

We need to be eternally vigilant for any signs that family members are considering new options or beginning to try them. We need to acknowledge, validate, and reward even the smallest of steps. When family members' first attempts are ineffective or clumsy we need to praise their efforts and intentions. Later, we will be able to applaud their successes. If we assign homework, we must remember to check on it. If a family is working on chore charts, we need to reward the parents for filling in the chart as well as the children for doing the chores. Mothers like ice cream sundaes almost as well as children do. Some adults will beam if they can get a sticker. We all need recognition and appreciation. The more ways and times we can find to express our positive feelings about how family members are trying to learn, the faster they will learn.

Try, Try, Again

Helping clients learn is not a smooth process. Teaching is not a nice, neat phase that gets accomplished somewhere between assessment and referral to other services. Learning occurs during and in between deescalation, forming relationships, assessment, crisis, reassessment, referral, uprisings, encouragement, and discouragement.

Expect to continually revise teaching strategies and to try, try, again when they fail. In the revision process, first listen some more to what the client wants and what he or she thinks is the reason the intervention is not going as smoothly as you both would like. Is the goal one she really believes in? Are the steps too big for success? If some behavior needs to be decreased, has the replacement behavior been clearly defined? Have we really taught the parent and child all the tiny little skills needed to add up to a behavior change that will make a difference, or are we taking too much for granted? Can they demonstrate the skills for us?

Teaching can fail in dozens of ways, but it can also succeed in dozens of ways. The most important thing is to recognize the flexibility and options we have in facilitating learning. If we are not succeeding, we must look to our friends for help and to our own creativity for new ideas. Try, try, again.

Summary

Many families referred to Family Preservation Services are difficult to teach because they have not learned how to learn. We must become aware of the barriers they experience in processing, accepting, and acting on new information and help them to overcome those barriers.

8

Helping Clients Learn to Meet
Their Basic Needs

People need survival skills to stay alive. They don't need communications skills if they're starving to death, or freezing from the cold. Having appropriate clothing, being free from rats and insects, and having wires properly insulated are higher priorities than assertiveness training or parenting skills. We call services aimed at helping clients learn to meet their basic needs "concrete services" because they are not abstract processes. Concrete services might include helping make the beds, washing the sweaters and the diapers, or helping a family move.

Clients need help with basic needs because they will not be able to concentrate on anything else until those needs are met. Abraham Maslow's (1954) hierarchy of needs specifies that needs for security, food, and shelter must be met before one moves on to developing human potential and creativity. Mothers are unlikely to reward their children for good behavior when they are preoccupied with finding food for those children. Children can't concentrate in school if they are being jeered by their classmates because they wear inadequate, smelly clothing.

Clients need help from us in many communities because no one else is available to spend the necessary amount of time to help with basic needs. Public agencies' caseloads may allow workers to point clients toward food banks or emergency shelters, but they do not allow them time to teach clients budgeting, negotiating, and self-advocacy skills that may be necessary if the client is to develop independence.

In emergency situations, or situations where clients are overwhelmed, we may end up providing these services ourselves. If other resources are available, we will use them, but other agencies may not exist, or they may feel they have already given too much to some of the families we see. We must also go beyond "doing for" clients, to teaching them to "do for themselves." This task requires constant vigilance, because it's usually *easier* in the short run for everyone involved to have those with the skills (presumably our counselors) do the job, rather than going the *more productive route—taking the time to teach those skills to the family members.*

We try to "do for" only when the family members are unable to do even a piece of the work themselves. Any bit of their involvement is productive in their learning the skills to continue meeting their needs and in reinforcing the idea that they do have the capacity to affect their lives. If a mother can't do the dishes, she can put the soap in the sink. If she can't call the food bank maybe she can step up to the counter and ask for food if you take her there. No matter how small some first steps may be, they *are* the first steps and we need to validate and encourage them as such.

Concrete services we frequently provide, and the percentage of clients receiving those services and the average number of hours spent are shown in Table 3.

Counselors themselves help clients with basic needs rather than delegating this task to a paraprofessional or a volunteer partially to engage them. Many of the families we see initially believe that a counselor either cannot or will not really help. They may resent interference from one more worker. When we offer concrete assistance, such as providing a bed or helping to get the plumbing fixed, families may be surprised and grateful to see that the worker can actually *do something.* Family members are then more willing to begin sharing information and to accept workers' suggestions.

Clients are often the most willing to share information when the two of us are involved in concrete tasks, such as washing dishes or waiting in line at the welfare office. Teenagers are famous for opening up while being driven in a car. It's important that when family members are in the mood to share, we are there to hear them and incorporate the new information into the overall treatment plan.

We can also learn about clients from watching them trying to negotiate with landlords, or food banks, or exterminators. We can see what they try and where processes break down. We can gather quality information that would be lost if they, or a volunteer, tried to tell us about the experience. Often, we can take adavantage of teachable moments that occur when we're waiting in line or traveling home from an adventure. We reduce compartmentalization of problems, and learn how various problems interact and fit together.

Probably the best reason for having professionals help clients with basic needs is that while it may be fairly simple to obtain food for clients, or get them a bus pass, it is not so simple to teach them to get food or bus passes for themselves. Doing for them can involve a few phone calls. Teaching them to do for themselves can involve all the issues and skills discussed in the previous chapters.

Table 3. Concrete Services Ranked by Number of Cases Where Provided and Average Hours Served[a] (N = 86)

Rank	Number of cases	Percent	Service category	Average number of hours[b] X	(SD)
1	48	56	Provide transportation (e.g., you drove a client to Job Service)	6.12	(4.46)
2	18	21	Help client find a job	7.46	(2.96)
3	16	19	Provide recreational activities	7.94	(2.68)
4.5	15	17	Help client get transportation	7.58	(3.01)
4.5	15	17	Do housework/cleaning with the client	8.17	(2.86)
6	14	16	Give financial assistance to client	7.62	(3.03)
7	11	13	Help client obtain financial assistance (e.g., AFDC, SSI)	8.09	(2.42)
9	10	12	Help client obtain utility benefits or services	8.34	(3.46)
9	10	12	Help client obtain medical or dental services (e.g., visiting nurses)	8.62	(2.76)
9	10	12	Provide toys or recreational equipment	7.93	(27.1)
12	9	10.5	Help client get food	8.10	(2.50)
12	9	10.5	Help client obtain legal aid	9.22	(8.86)
12	9	10.5	Arrange for lifeskill classes (e.g., driver education classes, other education programs)	8.16	(2.39)
14.5	8	9	Help client obtain housing	8.72	(2.97)
14.5	8	9	Provide food	8.41	(1.97)
16	7	8	Help client obtain childcare/babysitting	8.37	(2.02)
17	6	7	Arrange for recreational activities (e.g., YMCA, Boy/Girl Scouts)	8.38	(2.09)
18	5	6	Move client to new dwelling	8.78	(0.96)
19.5	4	5	Help client obtain clothing	8.71	(1.79)
19.5	4	5	Provide childcare/babysitting	8.62	(1.62)
22	3	3.5	Provide a job	8.69	(1.46)
22	3	3.5	Provide clothing	8.64	(1.65)
22	3	3.5	Provide furniture or other household goods	8.63	(1.70)
24.5	2	2	Help arrange homemaker/cleaning services	8.72	(1.48)
24.5	2	2	Help client obtain furniture or other household goods	8.72	(1.48)

[a] Tied scores are arranged alphabetically.
[b] Average amount of worker time spent providing the service for each case.

Basic Strategies with Common Problems

No Food or Inadequate Food

As stated above, if clients are totally overwhelmed, we may tap our own personal and professional contacts for donations, or we may use funds we have earmarked for client needs to bring them some food until things begin to get a little more under control. These funds are not extensive—less than $20 per family in Washington State and around $100 per family in New York—but they allow us a necessary flexibility of response in emergency situations. In some situations, children are hungry, and their hunger has to take priority over other concerns.

> Loretta and I spent the better part of a week working to get enough food for her family of five. She was receiving AFDC and Food Stamps, but paying over 50% of her income in rent. She had a list of all the food banks in the area (she had been to them several times before). We planned out which ones we would go to on what days. One day we spent all morning and most of the afternoon going to four different food banks, and were able to get food at three of them (the fourth one ran out before we got there). At the first one, it became apparent that Pat, Loretta's 8-year-old son who was with us, had not eaten breakfast yet that morning. He took a tub of butter and a yogurt container and was eating them as fast as he could with his fingers. It was hard for me to watch him eat that way, especially the butter. I knew he was hungry, and one of our goals was working on developing his impulse control skills, but my sense of decorum (such a minor thing compared to hunger!) was revolting inside of me. I was able to say to Pat that when he closed up the butter and yogurt, then he could get in my car and I would take him home for breakfast. That worked pretty well. Loretta had to convince Pat that his tub of butter would be saved for him in order to get him to let go of it when we got back to the house.
>
> We went to the other food pantries, and made quite a haul. We even were able to get dog food for the family dog. One thing that is always interesting to me is how, in these situations, the food bank workers assume I'm a client too. It can feel a little awkward sometimes—I have to challenge my own prejudices about what people who go to food banks look like. Of course, they don't look different than me. But I really think it says a lot, that I don't stick out as a professional, that I'm there waiting in endless lines, keeping an eye on the kid, and going the whole nine yards with the family. I'm not above it, and I respect the planning, waiting, and tolerance it takes for a parent to go through the enormous hassle. (Gretel LaVieri)

In establishing a long-term plan, we need to determine whether the lack of food is a chronic problem, or a short-term issue. If the shortage is one of many problems that have converged to render the parent(s) incapacitated, but they are likely to recuperate to the point where it is not an issue again, all we may need to do is help them find a food bank. If food is probably a one time only problem, it is easiest to take them, if we have a car. We don't need to spend a lot of time on this issue, because once others, like returning to a job are resolved, the food issue will be as well.

Other families run out of food every month. We need to work with them to decide if the problem is lack of financial resources or poor budgeting. If there are not enough resources, or if they are inadequately managed, we use strategies listed under "financial resources" later in this chapter. Some families don't have food because "friends" and extended family members come in and steal it for themselves, or more commonly, to sell for drug money. Here, we teach them to be more assertive. Families have taught us to prevent stealing by opening all packages immediately, to prevent resale.

Some families need basic education about nutrition and meal planning. Some almost never have nutritious food. We had one family with a friend who was a trucker, hauling Hostess Twinkies. Their entire refrigerator was filled with Twinkies. Some have never heard of four food groups, or have no idea that a steady diet of Kool-Aid is not appropriate for a baby. Here we have to be sensitive to helping parents maintain their self-esteem as they learn. We have to present information in a way that acknowledges lack of information—rather than stupidity, maliciousness, or lack of caring—as the reason they may not have been feeding their children in the best possible way.

No Shelter or Inadequate Shelter

Emergency Shelter   We will take families to shelters if they are over-whelmed. In a few cases, with public agency permission, clients have stayed with us in our own homes for one or two nights when emergency shelter was not available. Some of these situations are among the most poignant we see.

Kelly and her three small children were evicted from her apartment. My first face-to-face session with the family was to see them on the final day of their eviction. BSI made an exception to policy and provided emergency funding so that I could pay for one night's lodging at a motel. Kelly abandoned most of her family's belongings because of her inability to transport or store her things. On that first day, on one of our trips back and forth between the motel and her old apartment, we saw that her belongings had been dumped on the side of the road. We passed strangers picking through Kelly's belongings. The children recognized toys they had forgotten to take with them. I asked her if she'd like to stop and squeeze more items into my already full station wagon. "No, just go on." I got the feeling that she didn't want to stop, didn't want to be recognized as the owner of those things, now strewn into the dirt alongside the road.

Kelly had exhausted all of her resources. She had difficulty finding reliable day-care so she missed work and because she had missed work she fell behind with rent, etc. I contacted all the local agencies that worked with the homeless. The answer I got was there were no vacancies in emergency housing. The CPS referring worker was able to get home-based moneys from her department and pay for a first months rent and deposit. I assisted Kelly in looking for a place to rent, negotiating terms with the landlord, and moving. I contacted the various churches that donated furniture and helped Kelly take the furniture home. CPS provided Kelly and her family with a clothing voucher at the Goodwill store and I provided transportation. We frequently made the rounds to the food banks to ensure her family had food. I assisted Kelly in signing up for welfare benefits, arrange a payment plan with the utility company, and going to the bank to inquire how she might be able to open up a savings account. CPS offered to provide her with subsidized day-care.

At termination Kelly and her three children had food, clothing, and shelter and the promise of a welfare check coming soon. Kelly selected a trailer in a low income housing project notorious in the community for being a rough neighborhood. She had other options but this was the place she felt most comfortable in. I thought to myself . . . that I would have chosen a different neighborhood to live in. In the days and weeks to come, I realized that Kelly was skilled at knowing how to make a comeback after a setback. Neighbors who were leaving the project donated a bed, TV set, and table to the family. Kelly was already beginning to barter for services. "I'll watch your kids if you give me a ride to the store." I later concluded to myself that perhaps Kelly knew how to pick a neighborhood where people of limited means sometimes helped each other out. A kind of neighborhood where people would offer their friendship quickly as opposed to neighborhoods where you pass a trial period before you are cautiously approached. (Colleen Cline)

Long-Term Housing.   We are not a housing program. In large cities, such as New York and Seattle, waiting for housing takes far longer than the 4 to 6 weeks we have available to work with our clients. For fairly arbitrary reasons (our referring workers do not see them), we don't normally get referrals of clients who are living in emergency shelters. But once in a while, a family we are already seeing loses their home and has to enter an emergency shelter. In these cases we do advocate for entry, and continue to work with them on other problems for the 4- to 6-week period. We do not continue with them until long-term housing is obtained, but refer that task to housing coordinators and advocates for follow-up. With some of the families we see, housing can be a major focus for the whole intervention.

I received this referral from FRS on a Tuesday evening at approximately 4:15. The details were sketchy: a 43-year-old single mom with a 16-year-old son (the PR), mom requesting placement of son. Before contacting Homebuilders, the referring caseworker had contacted the Salvation Army who provided an emergency housing voucher for one night. The information given to the Homebuilder was that the family was staying at a local motel but the caseworker was not sure which one. The caseworker also was not sure of all the reasons for Mom wanting to place the kid. I called several motels before finding the right one (a somewhat complicated task since the motel managers spoke very little English), and arranged to go out to meet the mother at the motel room. The intake interview took place at 7:45 PM. The mother was extremely anxious and angry. She reported that she had been staying with friends and they were asked to leave due to her son's inappropriate behavior—he had recently been arrested for stealing from a local store, had stolen money from her friends, and was argumentative and refused to comply with their rules. She stated she felt she wouldn't be in this homeless situation if it were not for her son.

Although there were obviously several goals with this family, the most immediate one was finding more permanent shelter. The voucher from Salvation Army was only for one day which meant that the family had to be out of the motel by 11:00 the following morning after intake. I was on the phone bright and early calling every agency I could think of to help. The Salvation Army office that issued the voucher had closed for the week while the staff attended a seminar and no one could be reached for an extension of the voucher. FRS did not pay for the motel stating they wanted to save their money for assisting her with the move-in costs once she found permanent housing. While I was on the phone trying to find resources the mom called me crying and angry because the motel manager (who spoke very little English!) was hassling her about whether or not she was going to pay for another day. I finally ended up going over to the motel and paying for one more day myself. We spent the rest of the day continuing to search for resources, begging and pleading with agency personnel until finally getting assistance from World for Women who provided a voucher for 21 days.

During the next few weeks focusing on rebuilding the relationship between the mom and son was difficult because they were stuck in one room together with no transportation and no money. They had limited use of the telephone in the room because the motel charged 25 cents per call, and there were constant arguments between the mother and the motel manager over various issues. We dealt with this by getting them out of the room as much as possible, taking them out to the mall or to a coffee shop for our sessions. I took mom to the office to make calls on possible apartments because of the expense of calling from the room. It was difficult for her to focus her energies toward even looking for a place unless I was with her, so I provided coffee and donuts and we split the list, each making calls, then I drove her around to look at apartments. I provided concrete services such as money for laundry, newspapers, and even purchased a pair of shoes for the son. I drove her to the food banks for food and to the DSHS office to pick up her check when it finally arrived.

As a new Homebuilder, it was the greatest challenge I had had yet, doing homebuilding without a home. I mostly did it in the car. Sometimes I felt more like a caseworker than a homebuilder. Because mom was so anxious about so many things I had to make the most of "teachable moments" and sometimes subtly create them myself. I think one of the most important things I did with this family was to model calmness and hopefulness, even though it was not always what I was feeling at the moment. I was so worried that we wouldn't find any affordable housing before my time with them ended, but we did. About 6 days before termination we found her a wonderful situation sharing a house with another person, the price was right, the neighborhood was good, and best of all both mom and son would each have their own room (in their previous situation the son had slept on the floor in a cold basement). I helped her move and helped her unpack and put away her things. I also was able to get the son into an alternative high school program. Although there were still issues to be dealt with, it seemed like a happy ending to me. Both mom and son were thrilled with their new home, both were pleased with the school situation for the son, their relationship was closer, and mom was calmer. I think they even learned a few new communication skills.

A lot of hard work and some frustration but it was worth it! (Marilyn LaMascus)

Inadequate Housing. Many of the families we see have inadequate housing—bare wires, ceilings falling in, rodents, poor locks, other unsanitary conditions. If there are other agencies who can help, we use them. We encourage clients to call for themselves, but if that is too big a step, we will encourage them to observe while we call. In some cases, agencies will no longer serve Homebuilders clients because workers have been to their houses and despair of ever making any lasting changes. For these families, we have to rely on our program funds or our own elbow grease to facilitate changes. If a client has a landlord, and it is appropriate for him to fix certain items, she may need to assert herself with that landlord in order to motivate him. We may work with her ahead of time for days to clarify issues, rationales, and to role play sending clear messages and, if necessary, threats. Usually in these circumstances, we accompany clients for moral support and, if necessary, on-site coaching. Sometimes we may have to make a number of visits to landlords. Some times we need to enlist legal advocates to help us.

Moving. It is not uncommon for us to help clients move. Usually a whole team will take that on, rather than leaving it all to one of our workers. For example:

I've helped move several of my clients or other counselor's clients, but probably the most taxing move was a family of three—Mother, Edna, who was disabled, daughter Mary, 15, and son Ethan, 15. The family did not want to move—had lived in their house for 6 or 7 years. CPS thought the house too small (the children shared a bedroom) and unsanitary (the plumbing was unreliable and there had been a fire in the kitchen that made it difficult to clean) and were insisting that the family move into public housing (it had been arranged on an emergency basis). This meant giving up their dog, Bozo. I spent a week working with Edna trying to find something they could afford instead of public housing, but it became obvious to her that a decent rental house could not be had for what she could afford to pay. So we tried to find a home for the dog—without success. I took Bozo home (foster care) while we continued to try and find a place for him. Then we moved the family into public housing. I borrowed another Homebuilder's truck and on the President's Day holiday we (the kids and I and Mary's boyfriend) moved them lock, stock, and waterbed. It took from about 9:30 AM until 8:30 that night. At one point we were gone a long time on one of the runs and Edna began fantasizing she'd been abandoned or there'd been an accident or she would be attacked and robbed while she was alone. She was in tears when we got back. After we fixed her something to eat she felt better; we got her dressed and got her and the wheel chair moved as well. Mary was excited about the new house and was already putting things away. Edna was homesick for the old house and Ethan was homesick for Bozo. The next time I called (2 days later) Edna had gone to the hospital with appendicitis and had to stay about 10 days. But eventually she did get home and got her knick-knacks up and was feeling better about the house. A relative agreed to take Bozo just in time to keep my dogs from chewing him up. (Ellen Douthat)

House-Cleaning. The goal with house-cleaning is to improve clients' ability to take care of it themselves. But we will help with housework, both to get the cleaning started, and to help establish our relationship with the family. In encouraging family members to take it on themselves, it's important to start with small goals, to reward accomplishment of those goals, and to divide work among all family members. Often, the more specific we can be, the easier the chores will be to accomplish. For example, success is more likely with "Cherie will wash all dishes in the sink before 8:30 AM" than "Cherie will clean up in the morning."

With heavy housework, such as a room filled with three feet of garbage, we negotiate with the public agency and other groups for help, but if they cannot, our whole team will probably take it on. In cases like these, it is important to discuss how the room got so dirty and rehearse skills to prevent it from filling up again.

Money

Obviously, in most cases involving lack of food, shelter, and clothing, money is a major issue, and no long-lasting changes will occur unless families find better ways to become self-sufficient or to tap into adequate public support mechanisms. In helping families get money, we sometimes coach them through the process of identifying and approaching state agencies that could allocate emergency or on-going financial resources. If clients are too incapacitated, we use a wide range of personal contacts throughout the system to advocate for resources. In addition, we may use our client fund.

Once clients have some money, we may spend considerable time helping them to learn budgeting, financial management, and payment of large debts, and to plan and implement ways to meet basic needs in the future.

Employment

We also help clients find employment. We work as coaches, tutors, and advocates for parents and youth in almost all phases of seeking employment and training for employment. We help family members identify their work interests, gather information about the local job market, and match their interests to opportunities. We model, shape, encourage, and cajole to help clients learn how to locate potential employers. We may serve as client advocates with employers or job placement agencies. With many clients, strategies involve hours of prepping, encouraging, and rehearsing what to say about a spotty work history, how to sell yourself, how to introduce yourself, and how to answer specific questions regarding the job.

We can also help clients make appointments for interviews. Once appointments are secured, we help them consider what to wear, obtain appropriate clothes, and get specific information about the organization so they are prepared to ask and answer questions. We also encourage clients to call for feedback following interviews and applications for jobs they did not receive. We would like them to be able to learn from failures as well as successes. If clients simply cannot find a job, we will encourage them to focus on training, or on volunteer opportunities to help them become more marketable.

When clients already have jobs, we help them identify potential problem areas and begin planning to overcome them. We also do tutoring in time management, assertiveness, and mood management around potential job problems.

Medical Services

In emergency situations, we can provide transportation and accompany family members to emergency rooms. We can encourage clients to set up long-term health plans, but there are many barriers to their carrying out these plans and we are not always as successful as we would like. We can help clients identify medical resources and apply for funds to pay for the services, and we can provide baby-sitting or transportation, but we cannot always help clients to take advantage of the services, or to overcome their fear of what they might find out if they see a doctor. Especially in the Bronx, long waits for treatment and family members' feelings of intimidation by medical staff add to their reluctance to go to the doctor.

Transportation

Emergency Transportation. Most Homebuilders counselors have cars, so we can provide emergency transportation when necessary. If our workers do not have cars, they can use our client fund for taxis.

Routine Transportation. Clients' lack of skills regarding transportation can contribute significantly to their inability to obtain food, shelter, medical care, and other services. We can teach those who don't know how to use public transportation. We can help them get bus passes if they don't have money, we can help them figure out maps and stops and procedures, and we can go along with them until they know their way around on buses or trains.

Some families have cars that don't work. Sometimes it's possible to find vocational schools that will fix cars free. In other situations, the money we have in our client fund might be enough to get the car fixed.

Others do not use public transportation and do not even venture out of their apartments because they are afraid of muggers and rapists and drug dealers. We are less successful with these clients. Some areas are very dangerous these days; maybe they are smart to remain inside. What we can do is help find companions to walk children to school. We can help mothers plot the safest way to get to the food bank. We can walk with them and discuss their fears, hoping they will feel safer after successfully covering these routes. We can encourage them to think of others who could accompany them. We can link people with classes in self-protection, or we can share our own training in self-defense. Some families need help with a variety of concrete services and social support. For example:

A 20-year-old mother had three children under 5 years old. All three had severe ear infections and had not been seen by a physician. The mother hadn't been away from her 2-year-old son for more than 2 hours since he had been born. They had recently moved and didn't know anyone in their new neighborhood. The mother had the flu. She was constantly shrieking at her children. She had caught the 5 year old trying to strangle the 3 year old. There was no food in the house. The family had been reported to CPS by the 5 year old's kindergarten teacher who was concerned about his lack of health care.

I helped the family find a doctor on a bus route near them, and accompanied them the first time. We brought food, and then I helped the mother to locate a food bank near her. I went with her the first time. I baby-sat to give the mother time to recuperate from the flu. I worked with her on budgeting so that food money would be more likely to last the whole month.

Since she could think of no one who could help her with her children or her life, I encouraged her to brainstorm about people who had been helpful to her in the past. She began to remember one particular friend. She talked about a disagreement with her sister that had ruined a once-pleasant relationship. She said the children's father had been interested in them, but that she had lost track of him when he moved to another city. I helped her to track down these people. We discussed the problems with her sister and we role played an apology, which she felt her sister deserved. The past friend was receptive to resuming their relationship and they made plans to spend the day together on the weekend. The sister remained unapproachable, but the children's father had been trying to find her, and wanted to take the children some weekends. I went with her to approach two of her friendlier-looking neighbors. One invited us in for coffee. We encouraged the other to come over for cookies that evening.

I went with the mother to the public assistance office and met with a counselor to discuss possible work training programs. She enrolled in a child care course that met three mornings a week. We worked together to find a cooperative day-care program and she arranged to volunteer one day a week in exchange for some child care. I also, of course, spent some time helping this mother with parenting skills, and to unravel some of her confusion and discouragement, but the bulk of the intervention was spent on helping her to rearrange her life, so the medical care, food, child care transportation, and money were more possible for her to obtain. (Jill Kinney)

Other Goods

Procedures for obtaining furniture, clothing, and toys are similar to these we use to help clients get food. We work first on identifying resources, then on gaining access to those resources, then on setting up long-term plans for continued access or maintenance. If we cannot find any other resources, we will use our small client fund to obtain necessary items. Sometimes the processes of getting the goods can have other positive effects as well. For example:

I was working with a multigenerational family: Mother/grandmother Elaine (42), her daughter Sally (20), and Sally's son Jason (2), and Sally's four teenage siblings—one girl, three boys—all very close in age and very close in size. They *all* needed clothing. We took Sally to a food bank that had a clothing bank attached. John and I were helping Sally hunt through clothing barrels—no sorting had been done at all. We decided since everything *I* came up with would be totally unacceptable to the teens, that the wisest thing would be to go get the teens and let them look through the clothes themselves. We were able to get the girl and two of the boys and spent about an hour looking through all the barrels. One of the boys also found a huge stuffed drum major's hat (about 2–1/2 feet tall). We took the clothes and the hat home and later that week I took pictures of all the kids in the hat—including Jason, who could barely walk with it on. All Jason's uncles were extremely pleased with Jason in the hat and with the Hard Rock Cafe sweatshirts we found. John and I found out sometime later that we'd been misdirected by the food bank volunteer and had actually taken things from a retail thrift store's warehouse (which was in the same building). By that time all we could do was hope that the retail thrift store would think the clothes got where they most needed to go. (Ellen Douthat)

Summary

We help families with basic needs because they will not be able to care adequately for their children without mastering these areas. They will not be able to concentrate on more abstract skills such as parenting and communications unless basic needs have been met. As we provide help, we must continually press for clients to learn the skills that we use ourselves to help them, rather than continuing to provide help for them, so that, as rapidly as possible, they no longer need our assistance.

9
Solving Problems

Describing problem resolution strategies out of context is risky because the success of any strategy depends on what has come before: a particular and sufficient foundation must be established. Some readers may be disappointed if a technique they read about here does not work with their families. Possibly they will have neglected earlier stages of laying the foundation, but even if these stages have been accomplished, most people cannot learn these techniques by reading alone. Like swimming, problem resolution strategies cannot be learned from a book. Reading might speed up the process, but one has to get in the water and thrash around a bit before one can really swim.

Our counselors receive 7 days of training in problem resolution strategies. New staff are accompanied by their supervisor on their first case, and receive individual tutoring for the next several months. New counselors work intensively to master these techniques during the first year of their employment, but we all continue to learn for as long as we are Homebuilders. True mastery involves self-discipline, hard work, training, and many hours of supervised practice. It is not for those seeking easy answers or magical solutions.

In this chapter, we have not listed all the problem resolution strategies we use. Most of the techniques we rely on have been written about by others. We will cite references so that readers may further explore areas of interest beyond the scope of this book. We have divided client problems into major areas in order to highlight strategies. This is an arbitrary division with many limitations. Client problems do not fall nicely into categories. Problem resolution strategies may be combined and revised into an infinite number of resolution plans. The distinctions drawn in this chapter serve to facilitate the reader's understanding of the breadth of options available for helping troubled families, not suggest that problems and treatment options are easily classified in reality. Given these caveats, we are going to suggest some ways to overcome specific barriers to learning that clients present as we teach certain skills.

Intrapersonal Problems: Helping Clients Learn to
Change Their Feelings

Members of families in crisis have substantial problems just coping with themselves, let alone with other family members, school, jobs, and the community at large. In most seriously disorganized families, uncontrollable anger is a problem for at least one family member. In child abuse cases, parents lash out at children and in some families, all members may become involved in physical confrontations with one another. Usually, these clients would like to be able to control their tempers. They are afraid of harming the ones they love, and are confused and anxious about being out of control. Obviously, helping clients who have severe problems with anger has many ramifications regarding service delivery in the clients' homes. Counselors must take every precaution to make sure that clients' feelings do not lead to harm (methods used to preclude client assault are discussed in Chapter 4).

One client was so depressed that he had not been out of his basement for 2 years. Many have attempted suicide. Some clients are immobilized by high levels of anxiety. Some seem to function only through heavy use of alcohol or drugs. Many teenagers run away to avoid situations that raise their anxiety beyond their ability to control it. We rely on a variety of techniques to help clients learn to manage their feelings and to discover new ways of interacting with their environment.

Suicide Prevention

Programs attempting to help depressed clients without locking them up or relying heavily on medication must take any suicide potential very seriously. Nonjudgmental reflective listening and support are crucial. We make every effort to understand sincerely how and why the client is perceiving his situation the way he does. We do not dismiss or undervalue client statements.

Sometimes a client may mention suicide during the initial phase of our intervention. Direct questioning about suicidal thoughts, done tactfully and with appropriate timing, can give a client permission to discuss issues and feelings he had previously considered taboo. However, we must be wary of clients' initial relief after talking. Suicidal thinking may recur. We keep the topic open in order to evaluate continuously the potential for suicide.

We stay with someone who may be suicidal, or arrange for friends to stay with them. We call depressed clients frequently to make sure they are okay. If they are beginning to lose control, we immediately go to their home.

Whenever we are concerned about a client's potential for suicide, we get a verbal promise from the client that he will call us when he begins thinking about suicide, or that he will absolutely not kill himself for a certain agreed on time period. We obtain daily case consultation from supervisors when we have potentially suicidal clients. In a few cases, referral for psychiatric hospitalization may be the wisest course of action. We must not get so caught up in our desire to prevent out of home placement that we take undue risks with our clients' lives.

Changing Feelings

The procedures described above are designed to prevent tragedy. Subsequently, we begin to teach clients a variety of ways to better control their emotions. As in other phases of the intervention, we listen at length, often at the beginning of each session, to help clients calm down and to clarify what is causing them the most discomfort. We want to know everything clients have tried before, and all the reasons previous counselors' strategies did not work for particular family members.

Direct Interventions

If a person considers his depression to be due to lack of food and shelter, we begin to help with those issues. If clients are angry at landlords for unfair treatment, we begin to advocate. If a client is anxious that her ex-husband will beat her up, we help with legal proceedings.

We sometimes work directly on feelings by teaching clients relaxation skills or meditation or by using systematic desensitization. Other clients may be encouraged to exercise and eat properly. In some cases, family members are encouraged to receive medical examinations or reevaluate their diets.

Cognitive Strategies

Often, however, clients need more complex interventions to accomplish any long-term change in feelings. Many people have had difficulty with certain emotions for years, and those emotions seem to be connected to a wide range of outside events. Many people benefit from cognitive intervention strategies. We frequently use Rational Emotive Therapy (RET) (Ellis, 1973). The basic premise of RET is that people have the feelings they do, not merely because of events which occur, but because of the way people interpret those events. More specifically, people feel the way they do because they say things to themselves that are irrational, illogical, and escalate their emotions. Common self-defeating beliefs related to anger are: "He shouldn't be doing this to me"; "I shouldn't have to put up with this"; "I must have my own way"; or "People should be punished for their mistakes." We use RET to challenge these beliefs and to encourage people to substitute more comfortable ways of viewing reality such as: "People don't have to do what I want"; "I can function okay and be reasonably happy even if I don't have many things exactly the way I want them"; "There's no way I'm going to control the whole world"; "Nobody's perfect"; "People have a right to be wrong"; "Punishing people for their mistakes rarely achieves the long-term goals we would like"; "My life will be much easier and more pleasant if I learn to ease up a little on my demands for others, and myself."

Among depressed people, common problematic beliefs may be: "Everything is horrible." "I am an awful person." "Nothing will ever change." "My life is over." "I can't stand it." Therapists challenge these beliefs and attempt to induce clients to consider alternative ways of thinking, such as: "Many thing are happening in ways I don't like, but not everything is bad"; "Although I am far from perfect, so is everyone else"; and "I also have many desirable qualities"; "Most things will change—there are specific changes likely for most of the problems that currently seem overwhelming"; "There are still many possibilities for a new and meaningful life"; "I am standing it—I may not be standing it too well, but I am, indeed getting through this period of my life."

RET and most cognitive approaches usually need some modification in order to be effective with out clients because the techniques are too technical and too abstract. It is important to form a strong relationship with people before challenging their beliefs or introducing RET. We usually talk about it as a way "not to hurt so much," even if the situation should remain the same. RET is a way for a person to do something on his own, even if no one will cooperate with him. It will give him more energy just trying to hold himself together. We help people recognize that they do talk to themselves, and that this self-talk affects their feelings.

We try to avoid harsh challenges that may antagonize clients. For example, instead of saying, "where's your evidence" or ridiculing a client by saying "don't you see how stupid your thinking is on this point," we try to be tactful, and polite, using a warm style and humor wherever possible. We are more likely to ask a person if there might be another way of viewing the situation, and to speak in terms of "helpful" and "unhelpful" ways of thinking, rather than "rational" and "irrational." Some clients, however, are cognitively oriented and can be taught RET in a straightforward manner. Many can make use of simple and well written books such as *A Rational Counseling Primer* (Young, 1974), *The Anger Trap and How to Spring It* (Waters, 1980), and *Overcoming Frustration and Anger* (Hauck, 1974). Some children's books are *I Can't Wait* (Crary, 1982a), *I Want It* (Crary, 1982b), *I Want to Play* (1982c), *I'm Lost* (1985), *My Name Is Not Dummy* (Crary, 1983), and *Without Spanking or Spoiling* (Crary, 1979).

Often, however, we use no written materials, and help people examine their interpretation of the world by saying simple things like "Yes, that's one way of looking at it. Another way might be . . ." or "Could someone else possibly see the situation this way. . . ." Clients usually need lots of help generating self-statements that are more useful to them. We often write out, with the client, a list of calming self-statements related to the specific issue that are most upsetting.

Values Clarification

We also encourage family members to clarify some of their values and attitudes. Values clarification exercises that prioritize concerns are particularly helpful in helping people to reevaluate punishment as a long-range tool. Is it more important that the parents have some channels of communication with their teenager, or that she not have blue hair? Parents can consider whether or not they are concerned about their daughter's becoming more angry than she already is and withdrawing. Is being able to dictate her behavior worth paying that price, or are they interested in considering other alternatives for influencing their daughter's behavior?

We also ask some depressed clients to spell out exactly what events could give them hope. How would they know that they were worthwhile? Who are some people who have cared for them in the past? How would they feel about someone else who is as unhappy as they are? Would they condemn that person or would they feel compassion?

Behavioral Strategies for Coping with Feelings

We help people to identify what happens before they start to have certain feelings, as well as what happens after they start to have those feelings. Once the conditions are identified, we can specify new behaviors that will compete with the old, ineffective means of coping.

Sometimes we have the family member define what he would be doing if he were not suffering from a particular feeling. Is fear keeping him from trying? Does he need new skills to play a new role? Other methods for replacing ineffective behaviors with more productive responses involve fairly direct efforts. When clients begin to get angry, they might try telling it all to a tape recorder or writing it down. Rather than letting depressed clients stay home alone all day, we work hard to get them out and active, involved in happier pursuits. For many families, structuring a daily routine helps family members know what they will be doing all day long. Routines can minimize decision making and maximize activity.

Crisis Cards have been described previously as a tool for preventing violence, but they are helpful in other situations as well. A sample card for someone who is depressed might include the following: stand up; walk into another room; try to touch the ceiling; call the dog in; brush the dog; take the dog for a walk around the block; call Sally (753-8495); call Homebuilders (878-3630).

A sample card for someone who is anxious might include the following: start deep breathing exercises; do muscle relaxation exercises; read a list of calming statements; read poetry; go for a walk; listen to music; call my Homebuilder (927-7547).

We emphasize small steps in teaching, and positive attention for trying. Sometimes we ask people to record the intensity of their moods and feelings so that they can measure their improvement. We teach people specific ways to think about and interpret outbursts or other disappointments after they occur, so that they can view these episodes as opportunities for further learning of a difficult skill, rather than as overwhelming failures. Clients need to realize that no one copes with emotions perfectly and be less demanding of themselves.

We often role play new ways of coping, practicing specific behaviors such as how to respond if someone says "no," or how to graciously refuse invitations that might be dangerous, such as taking drugs. Sometimes a counselor will bring a co-worker to the home and, as a team, they will practice a modified fair-fight strategy (Bach and Wyden, 1969). Here, two counselors play the roles of two family members and model new ways of handling conflict, gradually phasing family members into their own roles.

Resolving Interpersonal Problems

Most clients need help controlling and clarifying their own emotions, but even after they have gained some skill in this area, they may need help dealing with others. Other people are upset with them, or they are frustrated by others. We help people deal with their interpersonal relationships and the problems in those relationships.

Some of our family members lack relationships or adequate support systems. Some single parents have not been out of the house for months; some have not had positive contacts with other adults for years. Some teenagers have never had friendships with others. We work directly on improving and increasing clients' support networks. In many cases, Homebuilders' success is defined by its having been a real turning point in clients' lives, rather than merely a band-aid solution.

Some family members lack even the most basic social skills, reacting to others almost entirely with aggression, or not reacting at all, avoiding people whenever possible. With such people, we sometimes use a social skills checklist to pinpoint areas requiring support and tutoring. Common examples of client problem areas include lack of eye contact; no greeting skills; speech too loud or too soft; self-stimulatory behavior, such as scratching or rocking; interrupting frequently; extreme profanity; or failure to sit on furniture appropriately. Once these areas are identified, we spend time constructing individualized treatment plans. Frequently, plans involve modeling, shaping, role-playing, and large doses of reinforcement for more functional social behavior.

Some clients are so poorly groomed that they have little chance of success with others until they make their appearance more appealing. We help these people with clothing, hair styles, make-up, and routines for cleanliness.

Other people have basic social skills, but do not have conversational skills. They do not know how to begin and end conversations. They do not know how to greet people or say good-bye. They cannot resist interrupting. They tell inappropriate jokes or disclose intimate information too early in a relationship. We help them work on these skills, too.

Once these social behaviors are established, we help clients to connect with outside resources. These resources could include single parents groups, churches, old friends, volunteer organizations and neighborhood centers, and the bus system. Here again, it is important for counselors and clients to think in small steps. Often clients will not be able merely to get the address of a church and go. Usually we need to cajole them, go with them, do everything we can to make the outing pleasant, including engaging others at the church to help clients meet some friendly people. Sometimes we need to go along several times.

Communications Skills

Most of our families have trouble communicating. Some resources that we have found useful for our own communications with families we can also recommend to our clients: Thomas Gordon's *Parent Effectiveness Training* (1975) is a valuable resource for families. We also recommend *Systematic Training for Effective Parenting* (Dinkmeyer and McKay, 1976). Family members can benefit from learning how to actively listen and send "I" messages.

Teaching these skills requires patience and tact. Many parents do not see why they should change the way that they talk to their child: "He's the one who needs to change." We point out that one does not have to be part of the problem in order to be part of the solution. We emphasize that parents *do not* have to change the way they talk, but that we have found that it is one of the fastest ways to change a child's behavior. We point out that it is one way for parents to be more influential with their kids. We help parents to evaluate their expectations of themselves: do they believe that teaching their children is part of their job?

We also talk about the reality of changing others. Changing our behavior with others is usually effective because they find it difficult to continue to do the same old thing. We ask parents if they have tried anything else that worked. Most have not. We try to present communications skills as a kind of game, something that could even be fun to try. What's there to lose? It might not work, but, who knows, it might.

We teach communication skills in a variety of ways. We explain concepts. We demonstrate active listening and its antithesis, called "active hassling." Sometimes we play the role of someone who has a problem while the client tries to listen. We make sure that the desired responses are clear by telling the client *exactly* what to say at the beginning so that she will have a successful experience. Sometimes we sit beside the parent and whisper listening responses to her as she begins trying to listen to her kids. We provide lavish praise for approximations.

Sometimes we use simple homework sheets so that people can practice labeling feelings: for example, What is the person likely to be feeling when he says the following? "My grandma is gone for the next month. Nothing is going right for me now. I wish she were here"; (a) Happy, (b) Angry, (c) Confused, or (d) Lonely.

Some family members can use lists of feeling words to help them communicate. Sometimes it helps to use cassette recorders to play and then discuss tapes of people listening or hassling. We may use a game in which we tell a story and family members take turns trying to identify what we are feeling. Other times, we might bring a list of "you" messages for the family to change into "I" messages.

Some of us put cute, funny posters up around the house reminding people to "Listen Up!" or "Really Try to Understand," or "How do You Feel?" Others encourage people to keep track of the times they try to listen and then bring little rewards at the end of the week. Sometimes it helps to have a person write down situations in which they did not understand another family member, and then to discuss or role play these situations during the next session.

Assertiveness

People who are angry can learn to get their needs met without the anger. Other people can learn not to give in and reinforce angry family members' outbursts. Depressed or anxious clients can begin to develop a sense of control over their environment. We use a "territorial approach" to assertiveness, as discussed by Bakker and Bakker-Rabdau (1973). Some of the elements of this approach involve people keeping logs to identify incidents and situations that incite or increase anger; learning to identify angry feelings at lower levels of arousal where feelings will be easier to influence; learning specific ways to calm down and to express feelings. Family members usually need support and practice in order to break long-standing habits of aggressive or submissive behavior. We cannot just talk about assertive responses; we must rehearse these responses with clients, coaching and encouraging them as they refine these new skills.

Problem Solving

Once people understand each other, they can begin to work out their differences. We teach a variety of strategies for negotiation and problem solving. Jeff Gold, a Seattle practitioner, has developed a process in which family members define the problem through paraphrasing each other until all feel heard. They then brainstorm as many solutions as possible. Then, each participant judges the overall quality and practicality of each possible solution. In the next step, family members list variations on the solution that is rated highest, trying to fine-tune it to meet as many family members' needs as possible. After a compromise is reached, family members write down the solution, decide who will do what and how, and set a date for evaluating the success of the solution.

In another problem-solving model, family members brainstorm all possible solutions to a problem and then systematicaly list all the pros and cons for each option. This process can be time consuming and tedious, but solutions frequently become obvious when evaluated in this way. An example of this process is presented in Chapter 10.

Parenting Skills

We use and teach most of the standard behavioral parenting techniques such as shaping, modeling, and managing contingencies. These are described in detail in books such as *Behavior Modification in the Natural Environment* (1969) by Tharp and Wetzel, *Behavior Modification Handbook of Assessment, Intervention and Evaluation* (1977) by Gambrill, and *Behavior Modification Approaches to Parenting* (1974) by Mash, Handy, and Hammerlynch. Behavioral books that can be understood by some families include Becker's *Parents are Teachers: A Child Management Program* (1971), and Patterson's *Living with Children: New Methods for Parents and Children* (1968).

We introduce behavioral strategies as realistically as possible. Clients are told that these interventions will not always work. In fact, we would be lucky to develop a strategy that worked perfectly the first time. Possibly, the situation might get temporarily worse as the child tests out the new limits. But we will never know if these methods will work unless we try them. We will keep fine-tuning the approach until we do get the results we would like. Clients are warned that as one problem behavior decreases, other behaviors may become more annoying and apparent, so that it may seem that one "bad" behavior is replacing another. Parents are also told that the same behavior may arise again in the future. That does not mean the intervention did not work, or will not work again. It only means that situations and people change—they can change again.

Parents have a number of common concerns about behavioral methods. We counteract some of these reservations before they occur. Some families will see reinforcers or rewards as bribery: we use terms such as "incentives" and "motivators" instead of "rewards." We might ask the parents what incentives maintain their work? Would they go to work without a paycheck? Sometimes it helps to look up "bribery" in the dictionary. In most, the definition describes bribery as a gift or favor promised to prevent good judgment or corrupt someone's conduct. Our intentions are quite the contrary. We are using rewards to improve judgment and conduct.

Other parents feel uncomfortable rewarding children because they "should be doing it anyway, as part of the family." We agree that it would be very desirable if the child had already learned about contributing, cooperating, and reciprocity. Many children appear to do so automatically. This child, however, has not, and apparently will have to be taught in a structured manner.

To counteract the concern that "it will take too much time," we point out that parents are currently spending a great deal of time worrying, calling the police, and tearing their hair trying to correct their children's behavior. Probably the new techniques will take less time than parents are already spending. The time spent worrying and calling the police has not yielded positive results. Maybe it's time to take a different tack.

Examples

In reality, problem-solving strategies are combined in infinite ways. Examples are the best way to demonstrate how they actually work.

Example of an ADD child with a learning disability. Anthony was 11 years old. He had been diagnosed as Attentional Disorder Deficit and was on medication. Homebuilders became involved with his family after his mother contacted FRS requesting placement.

Tony: Assault and Property Damage

Tony's mother stated that she was unable to maintain her son in their home because of his assaultive behavior, threatening family members with knives, throwing objects, destroying property. Tony was also difficult to contain and supervise in the school environment. One month prior to Homebuilder involvement, Tony had been assigned to a part-time school program for children with behavior management problems. A few hours after my first face-to-face intake with the family, Tony threatened to stab his mother with a finger nail file. That incident resulted in a police intervention. Tony was placed into protective custody for 3 days.

During the 5 week intervention the family and I developed two goals. Goal number one was to teach Tony cognitive and behavioral skills that would help him cope better with his disappointments. Throughout the intervention I observed that Tony had a habit of comparing things. His final evaluation of most situations seemed to be that he was on the losing end of things. He became upset easily and the way he expressed his anger was extreme.

Tony's mom was instructed on how to chart and reinforce desired behaviors. Over time Charmaine had become so discouraged by Tony's acting out behaviors, it's all that she seemed to notice. The charting format used was one that involved internal reinforcement. At certain times of the day his mother would check to see how Tony was doing on the identified behaviors on his chart and reward him with a ticket. X amount of tickets earned Tony a fun, recreational adventure. Point goals were established every week, so Tony always had something to look forward to and something to strive for.

Tony and his family members were instructed in anger management, Rational Emotive Therapy, and problem-solving skills. I observed Tony in his two school programs. Charmaine, his teachers, and I worked to establish common responses to Tony's acting out behaviors. The school sent home a daily progress note and his mom reinforced his school efforts with praise and tickets. Tony and his sister made a video tape on what bugs them about each other and what they can do about it. I coached them on alternatives to their usual "fight until someone gets real mad or hurt method." They got to keep the video so that they can look at it from time to time. I also wrote Tony his own individualized teaching story, a story about his past and present life. The story depicted Tony, the hero, learning how to master certain skills to make better outcomes for himself. His teachers at both schools kept a copy of the story for those days Tony might need a reminder on how to do things more successfully.

At termination Tony had no more incidents of hitting or threatening behaviors. He was still getting mad, but not as often. Family members also learned not to get as upset. His sister reported less fighting and didn't complain as much that Tony was going into her room and taking things.

Goal two was to provide Charmaine with support and help her develop coping strategies. Active listening, pointing out how well she had coped in previous situations, challenging her statements of "I feel guilty because——," or "I can't stand it when Tony does——," helping her to realize that the same applause and hurrays she gave to Tony were good to give to herself, teaching her assertiveness skills, in addition to the ongoing support and consultation she received from Tony's behavior management teacher helped Charmaine decide YES she could cope. At termination her son was still a handful but she was convinced that home was the best place for him.

Four months later, at the local roller skating rink, I ran into Tony. Tony said, "Hey Colleen, I'm not as bad as I used to be. I'm improving!" Just then two boys tapped him on the shoulder and angrily complained that he had been bugging them and trying to trip them on the rink. I was waiting for Tony to get mad back but he didn't! His sister came up and Tony hugged her. She said with a blush, please don't do that in public.

It was good for me to accidentally run into Tony and his sister. I enjoyed seeing Tony out having a good time. It pleased me to think that he wanted to spontaneously give his sister a hug and she told him not to hug her in public. She didn't say *don't ever*, just not here. I could see by the encounter with the other boys that Tony still had a knack for getting into trouble but it didn't become an EXPLOSION of angry threats, words, and actions. Charmaine was still hanging in there. I bet she was enjoying a quiet Friday night at home. Most of all, I felt gratified by Tony's exuberant hello and goodbye hugs. It was an ahhhhhh moment. You know, the kind of moment that makes you love being a Homebuilder. (Colleen Cline)

In the Bronx, one of the referral sources for the Homebuilders program is a Persons in Need of Supervision (PINS) Diversion Program. The Family Court refers children to the PINS Program rather than commit them to the Division of Juvenile Justice. The PINS Program may refer the family for counseling, placement, or other services.

Destria: Persons in Need of Supervision

Destria DeLago was one of the first cases referred to the Bronx Project. Destria (14), her sister, Maria (12), and their mother had moved from Puerto Rico to New York City 5 years earlier. At the time of referral, Destria had not attended school for 1 year. She had frequent verbal confrontations with her sister and her mother. She frequently stayed out all night on the streets in a very undesirable and dangerous area of Manhattan. Mrs. DeLago was frightened for her daughter's safety and opposed to the friends Destria sometimes brought home from Manhattan. Mrs. DeLago and the PINS referring worker agreed that unless Destria's Manhattan involvement could be minimized, she would have to be placed in a group home for her own safety.

The referral of Destria's family came to Homebuilders at 10:00 AM. I called the family immediately and was able to set up an appointment for later that same afternoon. When I arrived, all three DeLagos were slumped around a television in their living room in a crowded tenement house in the Bronx. Mrs. DeLago immediately began reciting a litany of Destria's misdeeds and misadventures. Destria and her sister continued watching the television. That afternoon, I listened to Mrs. DeLago for two and a half hours. My goal was to begin to build a relationship between them and to begin helping Mrs. DeLago clarify her thoughts, feelings, and goals. At the end of the time spent listening to Mrs. DeLago, I asked both girls if they had anything they would like to say to that time. Both declined. I suggested that I return the next day and take both of them out for a hamburger at McDonald's. They agreed.

The next day, I listened to the girls' side of the story. Destria seemed very, very angry, but had few specific complaints. Maria felt that her mother was too strict, but that Destria brought on a lot of her problems herself. After the hamburgers, Maria had some friends to meet and I suggested that Destria and I go sit in the park and continue talking. The more she talked, the more angry Destria became. She talked about hating school, and hating her mother and sister. I happened to have with me a large framed picture of Pinocchio for another family I was seeing. At one point Destria picked up the picture and acted like she was going to throw it on the ground. She told me I would be an easy mark for a mugger, that I looked like someone who would have some money and that I wouldn't fight back. Destria also talked about wanting to take me to a secret spot up on a nearby rooftop. I declined, feeling afraid that Destria was so angry that she might try to push me off.

During the first week I met with Destria and her mother and sister, alone and together, for six sessions for a total of 12 hours. Together, we found out what school Destria was supposed to be attending and set up a reinforcement program for Destria's attendance, with the school counselor and her homeroom teacher. Destria and I discussed Destria's feelings of boredom and restrictedness and worked on other cognitions about classroom activities, such as interpreting teacher's speeches as indications of their concern, rather than as premeditated torture for their students.

Mrs. DeLago and Maria discussed ways they would change the home environment to make it more attractive to Destria so that Destria might want to spend more time at home and less in Manhattan. Mrs. DeLago was willing to stop calling Destria a "slut" and "whore" in exchange for Destria obeying her curfew. Maria was willing to stop going through Destria's drawers if Destria would stop cuffing her on the shoulder and head.

These activities were seen as important components to a more pleasant, safe life for Destria and her family, but her anger was still a mystery. She seemed to be going along with the program, but I still felt that she was like a stick of dynamite, ready to explode. During the second week, I took Destria to a community center in hopes of enticing her to take part in some activities that could eventually substitute for part of Destria's time in Manhattan. Destria played ping pong and talked with several other teenagers. Standing in line at McDonald's with me afterward, Destria started talking about what was really on her mind. Three months ago in Manhattan she had been "hanging out" with two of her friends who were prostituting. Their pimp had grabbed her, dragged her in an alley and raped her. Destria had initially felt devasted, but as she thought about the incident, and discussed it with her friends, she became furious. It was a horrible act that the pimp had committed and he was known to commit it several times a week, often with girls younger and more helpless than Destria. She and her friends had developed a plan to murder this man. The night before, someone had loaned them a Uzzi automatic machine gun. They were going to wait until late at night and blow the man's head off. Destria was excited about obtaining revenge, but tortured about the pain inflicted on her and other girls and ambivalent about committing such a dastardly deed as murder, realizing it would result in her going to prison.

I was stunned and surprised by this revelation, but relieved to understand Destria's anger. Many long discussions followed regarding Destria's feelings of vulnerability and confusion and betrayal by her friends who did not protect her, as well as her feelings of rage. We discussed many possible consequences of different courses of action and gradually Destria's feelings of anger decreased. I attempted to interest Destria in a group for rape victims at that time, but Destria did not want to discuss the matter in front of strangers.

During the third and fourth week, I continued to monitor and reinforce Destria's school attendance. I also continued to support Destria in dealing with her feelings, and to teach her appropriate ways to express and cope with her anger. I worked with all family members to improve communications skills and to negotiate equitable distribution of responsibilities for chores. I also reinforced Mrs. DeLago socially and with ice cream sundaes for monitoring the girls fights and reinforcing peaceful negotiations.

By the end of the intervention all family members were saying that their fighting had greatly decreased and their communication had increased. Destria was attending school 75% of the time. She had had one incident of inappropriate behavior that had been resolved with school staff. Other than this report, Destria'a teachers noted comments of "excellent" and "good" on the attendance sheets. Destria had discarded her thoughts of murdering the pimp. She was involved with several activities, including ongoing counseling at the Community Center, and had not been to

Manhattan for 2 weeks. Destria also was matched with an "Amiga" (Big Sister) to help support her progress and to provide companionship and structure that were alternatives to Manhattan hangouts. All family members reported feeling more positive about themselves and each other. The PINS referring worker was pleased with the family's progress and closed the case, assessing that placement was no longer an issue and planned follow-up services should suffice to maintain the more desirable behaviors. (Nella Yelenovich)

The Clark Family: Child Abuse

The family was referred to Homebuilders from a public health nurse. The reason the nurse requested Homebuilders intervention centered around the release of the family's premature daughter from the hospital. The infant had spent the first 3 months after birth in the hospital to make sure she was strong enough to deal with the world outside.

The nurse was also concerned about the family situation because their 3-year-old boy had recently been diagnosed as hyperactive with some brain damage. Children's Protective Services and the nurse were suspicious about the boy's three concussions over the past year. Another child had died not long ago from Sudden Infant Death Syndrome. The nurse wondered if the 3 year old and baby shouldn't be placed in foster care.

The nurse discussed her fears with the parents and they consented to having a Homebuilder counselor come to their home. Since they had no phone, the Homebuilder counselor had to visit the family unannounced. Upon arrival, I clarified who I was and asked to stay a while and talk. The father was not at home.

After I sat down, the first thing I noticed was the smell of gas leaking from the furnace. The mother said she thought she had smelled gas but hadn't felt up to walking to a public phone to call for help. Her pediatrician had ordered her to get a telephone installed due to the uncertain condition of the baby, yet since her husband was out of work, they couldn't pay the installation fee. I suggested that the woman dress herself and her children warmly, open the window a little and turn down the furnace. While she did that, I went to a telephone and called the landlord to send out a repairman.

When I returned, the woman talked about her situation. She said she had been very depressed since the baby's birth, and had often felt the child did not belong to her. She was also extremely upset about her son's "wild" behavior. She wondered if he, like an uncle in prison, didn't have a "bad seed" in him. She had been thinking that she would rather kill him now rather than see him grow up to be a murderer like his uncle.

She was very thin, pale, and weak. She had a chronic cold, and had lost her front teeth due to poor health. Now 22, she had had three children and four miscarriages in 5 years of marriage. She said she was very lonely. Her husband was usually away from the house from mid-morning to late at night unsuccessfully trying to sell insurance. He had not sold a policy in 5 months. The woman told me that every counselor they had ever seen had told her that her husband was "rotten" and she should leave him. But she said she loved him and that he didn't beat her. They had moved to Washington from another state last June so that they could stay married and still be able to get help from the state. They were now in the WIN program.

The next day we approached a local charitable organization and got the $25.00 needed to have a telephone installed. We also got two old bedsheets that could be nailed up as curtains, since the woman had expressed fears about sitting alone at night with no curtains for privacy. She had told me that one recent night a strange man had been peering in her window. She had been raped once before and was very scared it might happen again.

On my next visit to the family, we focused a lot on the 3-year-old son. The woman said that she did not love him, and described a variety of what she labeled self-destructive and wild behaviors that he engaged in. She reported incidents such as him throwing himself backward off of furniture, touching the hot stove and laughing, turning on the kitchen burners, banging his head against the wall until unconscious, biting, scratching, and hitting other people. Although he was 3, he still was not talking at all. She was concerned that Children's Protective Services would think she was abusing him because he hurt himself so much, and because they locked him in his room at night. They did this because he only slept 2 or 3 hours at a stretch. When awake, he would go into the kitchen at night and eat until he vomited. She said they thought she should put him in an institution because she couldn't handle him. He would not kiss or show any affection to people. She said he had been removed from the home by Children's Protective Services in the state from which they had moved the previous year when she had a "nervous breakdown" and was hospitalized. Since their move, the parents had already voluntarily placed the boy once for 72 hours because the mother felt she "couldn't cope" with him. She was also afraid she might harm him because he made her so angry sometimes.

Before leaving, we made a list of what the mother could do if she felt her son's behavior was so bad that she would want to place him again. I let her know I thought it was a good idea to put him in his room sometimes, and explained the concept of time out. The list also included calling me (their phone was to be installed the next day). We then made an appointment to take the son to a local children's hospital learning center to see about enrolling him in a special school program. Finally, we talked about the mother getting some free time for herself. I volunteered to baby-sit for several hours later that week. The mother accepted my offer.

During the baby-sitting, the Homebuilder was alone with the children for 5 hours. She was able to learn a lot about the little boy. She observed him engage in some of the behaviors the mom had reported. However, by the end of the day she had determined that he would respond to positive reinforcement and time out. She taught him to play a kissing game. Information gathered that day was invaluable. It was proof for both the counselor and mother that the little boy could change, and did care about people. The mother cried the first time she and her son played the kissing game.

During our second week of intervention, the mother began to talk more about her discontent in the marriage. She said that she knew her husband wasn't really working all the times he was gone. She expressed resentment over the fact that he dressed nicely while she had only one outfit, that he was free to play all day and night while she sat in their apartment, that he would not let her get a driver's license but also would not drive her places. Feeling she had reached a teachable moment, I began to talk about territoriality and assertiveness training. I also called the woman's DSHS caseworker and got authorization to get her front teeth replaced.

The father began to be curious about what was happening, and decided to stay home to meet me one day. While his wife was at the dentist, he and I spent several hours talking. He shared his own frustrations with having to be on welfare. I told him how I wanted him to be a part of the counseling process and he agreed to attend the next session. After that discussion he seemed more willing to participate.

During the last weeks of intervention, we focused primarily on some behavioral child-management skills. The son had begun attending the school program, and the mother rode the bus with him every day. I was pleased to see this, as it gave the mother a chance to watch the teachers, and to make friends with the staff there. She began to report having some positive feelings about her son, and no longer felt she should send him away. She also began to feel much better about herself. She had temporary caps on her teeth, and began to smile more. She was also beginning to gain a little weight.

As the end of the intervention approached, I explored with the woman ways she could continue counseling. She decided that she wanted to go back to a counselor at the mental health center. She had seen the counselor a couple of times right after the baby was born last summer, and thought she could trust her. She made an appointment. During the last week I helped the family move to a better apartment in a neighborhood where they felt safer. It wasn't until after the move that the family found out the school bus would no longer be able to transport the boy to school. The mom became very upset, but quickly deescalated herself and began to problem solve. She talked with the counselors at the learning center and followed their suggestion to see if the boy could be transferred to a child study and treatment center's day-care program. He was put on the waiting list.

A follow-up call from this family several months later revealed that although there had been many upsetting events that had happened after I left, they were still together as a family. The woman had been seeing her counselor and had continued to work on being more assertive. She and her husband were also going for marital counseling. The father had quit insurance and was in a job training program. The son was attending the new school, and the mother was participating in a parent education program required by the school. They reported that the son was starting to talk and did not seem as "wild." The infant daughter was doing well.

If the mother had been placed in a psychiatric hospital, the cost of hospitalization would have been $5,926. If the two children had been removed by Children's Protective Services, the cost of their placement would have been $15,000, or $7,500 each. Total costs would have been $20,926. Homebuilder costs were $2,937. (Charlotte Booth)

Gary: Mental Health

This case was referred by the Office of Involuntary Commitment. In addition to his being a severe behavior problem, a 15-year-old boy was suspected of being prepsychotic or having a severe character disorder. There were several major problem areas.

The boy had daily violent temper outbursts; he would scream obscenities and end up on the floor sobbing that he should be killed or that he would kill someone else. He had punched dozens of holes in the walls and doors of their house. Once, he put all his bedroom furniture in a pile and chopped it into little pieces. His 12-year-old sister was in a body cast from a spinal operation. He would spit in her face and hit her. One time, a baby-sitter had locked herself in the parents bedroom during a fight with the boy. He had taken a pellet gun and shot it through the door.

When I went to the home it became evident that it was a violent family instead of just a violent boy. During one disagreement, the stepfather put a gun to the boy's head and marched him out to the car, tied one of the boy's legs to the bumper, and threatened to drag him if he didn't shape up. The stepfather had said, "I'm going to kill him or me if this doesn't get better." At other times, the stepfather had hit the boy with pieces of wood and scratched his face with his fingernails. The mother spit at the boy.

Many fights centered around the boy's not doing chores, even though he was around home all day. He had been expelled from school. Teachers said, "Everybody hates him. You can't trust him for a minute. The only emotion he feels is anger." The parent's relationship was quite strained due to family problems; the stepfather had walked out twice in the last 6 months. Both parents told the counselor that a divorce seemed imminent.

I spent several days just listening to let everyone make sure their version of the problem had been fully understood. All expressed relief and all expressed interest in learning different ways to cope. The mother was the first to make a major change, she learned active listening so that when the boy started to yell at her, instead of yelling back, she was able to help him calm himself down. This resulted in a rapid reduction of his outbursts. The boy was also trying to notice what triggered his anger. He began to learn Rational Emotive Therapy to tell himself calming statements. The stepfather also began working on other ways of expressing his frustration. All family members learned to recognize when their frustration and anger were beginning to build and to construct "I" messages before the situation got out of control.

The stepfather began leaving lists of chores for the boy to do each day. Allowance was contingent on task completion. The schools were not willing to give the boy another chance, so I arranged for a tutor to come to the home.

At the end of 5 weeks, there had been only two major outbursts. The boy was doing 80% of his chores and getting almost straight A's with the tutor. The mother said, "I don't feel afraid anymore." On one occasion I provided child care while the parents took a weekend vacation; they had renewed their commitment to their marriage. The relationship between the boy and the stepfather was still strained. Since the family lived in a remote area of the county and it would be difficult for them to find on-going services, they decided instead of having one more intensive week with me they would rather have once a week follow-up sessions with me. Two years later, I ran into the boy at the county fair. He was still living at home. Out of home placement was no longer an option. Homebuilder cost was $4,200. Hospitalization would have been over $36,000. (Charlotte Booth)

10

Completing the Intervention

Most counseling services continue until either clients feel they have accomplished all they can or until counselors feel they have offered all they can. Since there in no preconceived notion of how long this should take, clients and counselors are free to continue as long as they wish. The goals of our family preservation service are much narrower. We continue only until the threat of out of home placement has been averted. Ours is a highly specialized service aimed only at the most disorganized families during the specific period when out of home placement is imminent. We do not have the funds to continue until a family's goals are all accomplished. Other services in the community may have resources and families should be referred to them if they need additional help.

Setting Realistic Expectations for FPS.   Although Family Preservation Services (FPS) are an exciting, promising, and encouraging alternative to unnecessary out of home placement of children, we must create expectations that will allow their potential to be realized without crushing them with expectations for magic. FPS are time limited and only one small piece of a continuum of care that is needed for adequate services to families. Family preservation programs will not eliminate poverty, drugs, racism, or AIDS, nor will they make up for the enormous gaps in our services and for the vast underfunding of social-service programs in our society.

We are not making perfect families. We do not even know what perfect families should look like. Our job is to help the family function safely and more positively together. If we were a garage, we would be getting cars back on the road again by fixing the steering and the brakes, not by fixing the chipped paint or dented fenders. When the car is back on the road safely, we have done our job.

Not all problems of families' are solvable. A mother, for example, bound to a wheel chair, on welfare with four children is going to have a rough time. Her options are limited and the demands of her life are great. Life for families in large urban areas these days is a *dilemma*: people are terrified by drugs and crime, but have no money to move. Besides, where would they move? What would happen to their friends and extended families? FPS will help us learn to solve as many problems as we can. For some predicaments, however, the best we can do is to learn to endure some pain and frustration as gracefully as possible.

For many families who can benefit from Family Preservation, other services will still be needed. FPS does not enable families to live out their lives without ever needing help again. Success for us means that the level of help a family may need after our services will not be intensive nor will placement be necessary. Some may need ongoing counseling. Some may need neighborhood centers. Others may only need their next door neighbor. Other problems require time or specialized skills and knowledge beyond what FPS workers can provide. The amount of time and the particular expertise necessary to find housing for families, for example, are best delegated to an appropriate Social Service agency.

The Continuum of Care

Family Preservation Services work most effectively when they are a part of a whole continuum of services. Families all have their ups and downs. Many are able to continue functioning without formal agency help. Others need fairly limited services available from clergy, Boys and Girls Clubs, or outpatient counseling. Some require more intensive involvement such as special school programs, day treatment, or drug treatment programs. Sometimes none of these services or combinations of services is effective enough to stabilize families at a level where they and their communities feel secure about their ability to coexist safely and to provide adequate nurturance and control of children. Those are the families that need Family Preservation Services, an intensive intervention that will combine many other services during a short period, until less intensive services will suffice.

Many families are involved with other service providers at the same time we are with them. We work as closely with referring workers as they would like and the family situation necessitates. Sometimes we go on intakes together, sometimes on other joint ventures. With some particularly dangerous or unusual cases, we may talk every day. Sometimes partnerships with CPS workers can allow changes to occur that we would never be able to accomplish without them.

Carmela, in her mid-twenties, lived with her two daughters, Kim (age 11) and Tonisha (age 7). The girls had reported being sexually abused by

Carmela's (former) live-in boyfriend. They also reported to CPS that their mom and her boyfriend used pot and cocaine. CPS was concerned about Carmela's ability to protect the kids, and to provide for them. There were many times when she didn't have food for them. Carmela was receiving AFDC, SSI for Kim, and Food Stamps, and was living in public housing, so while her money was tight, she had enough coming in and low enough rent that food should not have been that much of a problem.

I spent a lot of time with Carmela, helping her to get her kids back from receiving care, helping her find furniture, and a lot of basic necessities (toilet paper, transportation, household items). Carmela told me a lot about herself—she grew up in Newark and had Kim when she was 15 to get away from her stepfather who was sexually abusing her, and left the state to get away from Kim's father, who was physically abusing her. She had been using pot for several years, and had been using it daily for at least the last few years. She told me that she couldn't imagine getting through a day without it. She also used coke when she could get it. I talked with her about cutting down her use to weekends, getting it and her pipe out of the house so it wasn't as easy to use, building her support system to include people who were clean so she wouldn't be tempted to use it when she was with them, and finding pleasant events (she reported feeling depressed, and said she used more when she was down, and felt more down the more she used . . .). Sounds great, but we made little progress. We were talking, but nothing was happening. Carmela kept coming back to saying that she didn't really have a drug problem, that she'd been able to manage this long, and she could take care of herself and her kids.

Carmela did schedule a drug evaluation (a condition of her keeping her kids), and, with prompting from a counselor she had been working with for the past 2 years at a job skills development program, attended a drug treatment fair and came home loaded with info. I went with Carmela to her drug evaluation (not by plan, but because it snowed and our plans to pick up furniture that day fell through). The whole process freaked her out—she was *very* angry that it took 2 hours, and was furious with CPS that they were making her do this. The drug evaluator recommended that Carmela enter intensive (3–4 day/week) outpatient treatment, as she was in the mid-stage of addiction. Carmela cried and yelled and swore, and said she would rather leave the state than enter treatment. I active listened to her, of course, and went over what her options were, the pros and cons of each choice, etc. I really stressed to Carmela that she can take back power in this situation by researching what treatment programs were available, checking them out, and negotiate with CPS what program she would enter. I encouraged her to advocate for herself, and offered to back her up. And I also let her know that I had real concerns about her ability to care for her kids while she continued using pot at the rate she did, since I had seen that the kids were lacking warm clothes, regular meals, and prompt medical attention during the intervention.

I arranged a meeting with Carmela and the CPS caseworker, who was fantastic, to negotiate a new CPS contract related to goals for drug treatment. Carmela wanted to include Lee, the counselor from the jobs skill program, because she felt Lee was totally on her side. I encouraged her to invite her. We all met together for a very moving meeting. Lee talked about her own recovery from drugs, and encouraged Carmela to seek treatment. She offered to help Carmela through the process by making referrals and providing support. The CPS worker stated that if Carmela entered treatment, she could close the case out in less than 3 months; if she didn't, she would seek custody. She stressed that she was really pleased with Carmela's progress in working with me, and was actually quite gentle about something that was hard for Carmela to hear. I provided support for Carmela, and helped to advocate for her to make her own choices about where she would seek treatment. It ended positively, with Carmela agreeing to treatment after a teary but strong declaration that she was ready to continue making positive changes in her life, and felt that, with Lee's continued support, she could. (She was getting close to having her GED, and had completed 30 credit hours at a local community college.) It's important that Carmela could say that she felt she was making her own decisions about her life, and not just being backed into a corner by CPS. Having Lee involved helped tremendously—I'm so glad Carmela has her. I feel much better knowing that Carmela will be getting help, and that the kids will no doubt benefit. And placement was avoided. (Gretel LaVieri)

We also work closely with other agencies such as schools, that will be involved with families long after we are gone. We want to make sure that our goals and procedures are coordinated with theirs and, wherever possible, we want to be helpful to them so their job will be easier after we leave.

Eight-year-old Sharrie Williams lived with her 49-year-old mother from a western European country, her 15-year-old sister, and her 14-year-old brother. Her parents were divorced. Sharrie was referred in October because her mother threatened to kill herself unless Sharrie was removed from the home. Sharrie had not attended school since the previous May. Because she would not attend school, Mrs. Williams had to take Sharrie to the homes she cleaned for a living. She expressed feeling discouraged and out of control as a parent.

Sharrie had stopped attending school after she and another girl reported seeing a man expose himself on the perimeter of the school playground. They reported this to the playground supervisor, but apparently were not believed. Sharrie developed a cough. Although her doctor found Sharrie to be medically healthy and labeled the cough psychosomatic, school personnel said that Sharrie could remain at home for the remainder of the school year.

Sharrie was healthy all summer, but again refused to attend school when it resumed in the fall. School personnel worked with Mrs. Williams to get Sharrie to school, but she attended for only 1 day when she was accompanied by her sister, Cami.

Although Mrs. Williams was very skeptical about whether counseling would be helpful, she agreed to participate in the Homebuilders intervention. The school principal, on the other hand, opposed Homebuilders, stating that Sharrie was seriously disturbed and needed to be institutionalized.

The first goal was to help Sharrie increase her school attendance. At first, Mrs. Williams and I brainstormed a list of options to influence Sharrie's school attendance. These included enrolling Sharrie in another school, using short-term foster placement as an experiment, providing incentives for Sharrie's small steps toward attending school, and physically taking Sharrie to school. I encouraged Mrs. Williams to try a reinforcement plan, where if Sharrie went to school accompanied by her mother on the following Friday, she would receive a prize and a trip to McDonald's with her sister. This plan worked very well, but when similar reinforcements were not successful in getting Sharrie to go to school the following Monday, Mrs. Williams decided to try the option of physically taking Sharrie to school. I helped with this venture, but it was apparent that Sharrie had intense feeling about school. They stopped short of carrying her into the building. The plan was abandoned, but Sharrie returned home with some school assignments, which I helped her to complete, while Mrs. Williams went to work. Although I tried to encourage Sharrie to talk about reasons she had for not attending school, Sharrie was reluctant to address this issue.

Mrs. Williams and I then formulated a new game plan. Emphasizing how successful the reinforcement system using Cami had been, Mrs. Williams set up a chart where Sharrie could earn stickers and other prizes for attending school for smaller amounts of time. They discussed how Sharrie's increasing her school attendance was like encouraging a child to eat something she didn't like; you simply kept putting small bites on the plate until the food is consumed. The plan was effective, although Mrs. Williams had to attend school with Sharrie. During the times when Mrs. Williams had to work and could not attend school, I remained at home with Sharrie and helped her to complete her school assignments.

When some school personnel expressed concern about Mrs. Williams school attendance, a meeting was held with them, and several plans were discussed. The school social worker said that Cami could earn some high school credits for serving as an aide in Sharrie's classroom in the late afternoon so that Mrs. Williams could leave school early. I recommended that the teacher give Mrs. Williams some tasks to complete outside of the classroom in order to phase herself out of the classroom in the morning and early afternoon.

A month later, Sharrie was attending school almost all of the time, and without her mother. School personnel continued to reward her attendance. When we had a snowstorm near Thanksgiving and school was closed, Mrs. Williams reported that Sharrie had gotten bored and wanted to get back to her classroom. In a client satisfaction survey, Mrs. Williams rated Homebuilders a 5 on a scale of 1 to 5 in terms of helpfulness. She said she especially appreciated me for not blaming her for Sharrie's reluctance to attend school. (Mary Fischer)

We have a firm idea of how long this Family Preservation Service should take. From crisis intervention theory as well as our own years of experience, we know most families can prevent placement within 4 to 6 weeks. At the same time it must be said that the termination process is not always comfortable for everyone. Families referred to us frequently have multiple, long-standing problems and all their goals cannot be reached within the time limits. This lack of closure may leave us and the family members feeling frustrated. Clients usually have come to like their worker and enjoyed the process and they fear that they will backslide when the counselor leaves. Many do not wish to seek additional services from other agencies, though they would feel comfortable if their current worker remained to help them. On our part, we see that more could be done for any family. We also fear placement will occur after we leave unless we can cover every possible base. Referring workers are pleased with progress and would like to see even more. They also worry about families backsliding.

Although we sometimes allow extensions, they must be accompanied by clear rationales and goals. With most families, extensions do not increase the chances for success. Our data show that if progress had not occurred within 4 to 6 weeks and we do extend, the probability that the family will stabilize decreases rapidly during the time of the extended involvement. In other words, if families are not able to respond within the short time frame, it may be that a Homebuilders intervention is unlikely to be successful, even over a substantially longer time. We also find in these cases that our counselors become more frustrated, tired, and discouraged than they would have been had we allowed placement to occur earlier, at the regular 4 to 6 week limit.

When to Terminate

We consider a number of issues in deciding when to terminate. The most important is client safety, but other factors are also considered.

The Situation Is Too Dangerous to Continue

Although uncommon, some situations and some family members are too dangerous to have a child or a worker with them while we help them improve their skills. These examples are extreme: a mother begins to hallucinate and threatens to kill her child; someone notices a 9 year old hanging by a window ledge on the twelfth floor of a building. In such situations, we recommend to the referring worker to seek placement as soon as possible. Although we press for placement immediately, we will stay involved to support a family if the placement process must take a few days.

Sometimes the situations are dangerous for workers as well as children.

Sylvia, a single mother, her daughters, ages 8 and 9, and a son, 12, lived in the most dangerous part of town. The son actually was living with friends of the family and only came home occasionally.

The family lived in a large old house with four other adults (two men, two women) and two other children. Many strangers were frequently in and out of the house, staying there temporarily. Some drug use was admitted to by some of the adults and drug use was often talked about. On one occasion I observed the mother making arrangements with two unknown adults to steal $100 worth of meat for the household. Sylvia was on probation for cocaine use. CPS was concerned about the children living in an environment where drug use was suspected, and parenting efforts were unpredictable and often minimal.

During the third day of the intervention I took Sylvia to visit her sister to collect money she had loaned her. In the parking lot of her sister's apartment Sylvia saw her boyfriend washing a car. She was angry at him for supposedly being unfaithful. Sylvia attacked him with a tool he had been using to work on the car. They struggled for control of the hose and sprayed each other. Sylvia subsequently got in the car and pulled out wires from under the dash. She then found a metal table leg leaning up against the apartment building and used it to smash out the car's headlights and windows. All of this time they were arguing. I stayed in the car with one of the children, observing and waiting for an opportunity to intervene. When Sylvia came near my car, I rolled down the window to try to talk to her, but she ignored me and the fight continued to escalate.

Sylvia's boyfriend tried to go into one of the apartments but the door was locked. Sylvia, thinking that this was the girlfriend's apartment, broke out several of the windows with the table leg. She also kept threatening to hit her boyfriend with it. A crowd had gathered and several people tried to calm Sylvia down. Then the suspected girlfriend drove up with others and a long argument ensued.

After Sylvia calmed down enough to get in my car (with the table legs), she discovered that her hand was bleeding. She refused my offer to help her get medical treatment. I drove her and the child home. There was much story telling by Sylvia told to her roommates about the incident and they all laughed about it. After I left, Sylvia gathered up her boyfriend's clothes, cut them up, and placed them by the front door in case he came to get them.

On the next visit I saw what appeared to be a gun on the dining room table. I asked Sylvia about this and she said it was a toy gun belonging to one of the children. I did not get up to go look at the gun to make sure it was a toy, thinking this would upset Sylvia. I consulted with my supervisor and my team and we all decided it was too violent and unpredictable a situation for me to keep working in, based on observation. We felt that there was a high probability that I would continue to be in situations where violence might occur, and inadvertently be in danger or in situations where someone else, such as Sylvia's children, would be in danger. We relayed this information to the CPS worker and CPS supervisor. The CPS supervisor was upset that we were withdrawing from the case, but the CPS worker was very understanding about it.

Later contact with the CPS worker revealed that adults living in the client's house were members of a nationally known gang and that drug use was occurring there frequently. I found out some weeks later that CPS paid to move the family to a safer neighborhood. Apparently CPS felt it was appropriate to move the family as a last try at keeping them together—hoping this would eliminate issues of danger and concern. (Peggy Mandin)

Threat of Placement Has Passed

Most commonly, termination occurs when everyone agrees that the need for placement is passed. In most of these situations, other, less intensive resources will suffice to maintain the family stability. Some families resolve the problems that led to threat of removal sooner than 4 weeks. For them, termination occurs as soon as they are stabilized, with a follow-up plan for maintaining that stability.

None of the families who terminate routinely is problem free. They still have their communications difficulties and individually they all have things they would like changed. They do, however, want to stay together and are able to function as a family group enough to meet at least the minimum expectations of their community regarding nurturance and protection of children. With a fair number of families, some of their severest problems have been resolved. They have learned new strategies for coping with life and with each other and they feel optimistic about going on.

The Family Refuses Further Services

A few families choose to stop working with us even when out of home placement is still an issue. This is their prerogative. When this happens, the referring worker decides either to place a child or decides that the family can now remain safely together.

Placement Occurs

Termination also usually occurs when a child is placed outside the home, or a firm decision is made by the family and/or the referring worker to place the child outside the home in the future. Once this decision has been made, our job is done. We have failed to prevent placement, and we must move on to a new family. If two or more children in a family are in danger of placement, and only one is placed, we continue working to prevent placement of the others.

The family consists of Tom, age 33, his wife, Debbie, age 28; Debbie's natural son, Jimmy, age 9 (the potential removal); and Tom and Debbie's natural children, Tommy, age 4, and Jerry, age 3. At the time of referral, I was informed by the caseworker that Tom and Debbie had been heavily involved in drugs in the past, and that they currently had friends/contacts in the drug community. Debbie reported having quit using drugs and alcohol "five years ago." From the very first session, Debbie exhibited extreme mood swings where she would cry, laugh, yell, and swear in rapid succession. I saw no other evidence of drug use, so I felt these emotions might be brought on by stress due to the family's situation (being evicted, little money, unreliable transportation, child behavior problems).

During the first 2 weeks of the intervention, Debbie's thinking became more and more distorted and she threatened Jimmy with a knife at his back.

She thought she was one of the babies in the Bible and the Virgin Mary was her mother.

She thought her husband was having affairs and involved in a conspiracy with the police department, medical personnel, and drug dealers to have her involuntarily committed to Western State.

She said she knew Homebuilders Co-Director, David Haapala, and had been to his house because he had worked on her car. She stated she was angry at David because he had sold her car without permission.

She read magazine articles that she was sure were referring to her husband and his affairs/illegal activities.

She was found wandering the streets with her three children. She was incoherent.

The mental health professionals were finally called to evaluate Debbie and she was placed in a local hospital where drugs were discovered in her purse. During Debbie's 5-day stay in the hospital, I met with the hospital social worker to work on a discharge plan for Debbie. Before a referral to community resources could be made, Debbie's psychiatrist unexpectedly released her from the hospital without the knowledge of the social worker or me.

After Debbie returned home, as she was stabilizing on prescribed medication and withdrawing from street drugs, I spent time at the home helping her make arrangements for bills to be paid, helping with child care, helping her contact possible day-care providers, and locate other resources for the family. As the hospital social worker could no longer work with Debbie because of her release, I helped Debbie connect with a dual program at the local mental health center, which addressed both mental health and drug addiction issues.

Jimmy was removed from the home (on the last day of the intervention) to give Debbie a chance to heal without having the added stress of dealing with his behaviors. Three weeks after termination, Debbie had just begun her program at the mental health center, had stabilized on her prescribed medications, and Jimmy had been coming home regularly for extended visits—up to 5 days at a time. The plan was for Jimmy to return home permanently in 1 to 2 months after Debbie felt comfortable with her new program. Both Debbie and Tom reported looking forward to beneficial results from the mental health center program, and Debbie stated that she felt "more like myself again." (Peggy Mandin)

We All Give Up

Most placements occur after we have tried everything we can think of and still have not been able to help family members and/or referring workers feel more comfortable about the situation. These are the most difficult decisions. In some situations, counselors and family members begin to wonder if there is any hope, or counselors, supervisors, and referring workers begin to wonder if enough progress can ever be made that they will feel safe leaving a child in a family. In other cases, parents remain angry at their children even when, in fact, progress is being made. These cases are often upsetting for counselors because they see that a child might be placed unnecessarily or unwisely. Knowing when to give up is difficult. If the situation either remains the same or deteriorates more, most participants agree that everything has, indeed, been tried, and that it is time to go ahead and place the child. We do have some strategies we use when families seem to be stuck. Frequently these procedures help to mobilize families and workers so that routine procedures will be more effective.

When Cases Are Stuck

Checking the Basics. Usually progress is slow or absent when we have not adequately prepared the family for change: we have not helped them to calm down; we have not helped with basic needs; we have not formed a partnership; we have not defined problems in a way that gives hope; we have not overcome their barriers to learning. It is never too late to go back and attend to these basic issues.

We need to check all areas. Are we doing what the family wants? Are we following *their* agenda? Do we have the priorities right? Are the goals realistic? Are the steps small enough? Is this a teachable moment? Are we up against dilemmas instead of problems? Have family members really learned to apply the skills we thought we taught them, or have they just learned to say the right words? Can they demonstrate new behaviors?

Getting Consultation.   With some discouraged and discouraging families, we may ask the family members' permission to bring a supervisor or another counselor along on the next visit. Supervisors have more experience and another person can provide a different perspective. Adding another person also gives the message that what is happening is important, especially, the decision to place a child because it will have implications for the future of all family members.

Involving Everyone.   Getting all the people who are involved with a family together can sometimes be helpful. Many of our clients are involved with other workers: certainly the public agency worker who referred them, often the schools, and sometimes the juvenile court. Informal supporters can also be helpful. A large meeting can help to emphasize the seriousness and importance of key decisions. The discussions may also produce effective treatment plans that would have been impossible without such a coordinated effort.

Evaluating All Options.   When progress is slow or absent, acknowledge it and share the pros and cons of continuing to try. Some families find it helpful to list all the different courses of action currently available to them, along with all the pros and cons of each. In this process, we listen actively for all expressions of frustration and pain. Family members digressing and talking once again about family problems is a hopeful sign: they are not finished with that issue and are still trying to figure out how to cope with it.

We encourage family members to consider all the pros and cons of all the options they (and we) can think of. This process itself often raises some hope and releases some frustration. Many alternatives are still left to try. We strive for perspective in this exercise and may use a certain degree of humor. It is a time when clients may polarize each other. A calm counselor with a light touch can take some of the pressure off everyone and inspire them to come up with more creative ideas. A sample list of options and consequences follows:

1.   I (the worker) could just see Mary (the child) alone and see if we can get anywhere in working on her school problems or her problems with her temper.

Pros	*Cons*
Doesn't waste any more of parent's time	Mary might feel she is being pressured to move faster than she is able—might backfire
Mary might like additional time	

Counselor could put 100% of effort in these two areas	Parents may have some other areas of concern that they would like time to work on
Gives parents time out to think of other things they might like to try	Doesn't give us structure to work on everyone learning new ways of problem resolution that they'll be able to continue when the counselor is gone
School personnel would like more time spent in this area	
Might work	Might not work

2.   We could spend more time working on ways for Mrs. Smith to get more positive things going in her life so that she'll have some space that's refueling her instead of having everything drain her like it is now.

Pros	Cons
She deserves it	Would take effort to come up with ideas of what she could do
She might be stronger in dealing with other areas if she could get more perspective	Would take effort to carry them out
Might force Mary to take more responsibility for her own problems instead of relying so much on her mom to take care of everything	Mary might backslide initially if her mom weren't continuing to watch her so closely
Mrs. Smith might have some fun	It's usually scary to try new things—Mrs. Smith might feel some anxiety at the beginning
Mrs. Smith might meet new people who could have other ideas about dealing with similar issues	
Mr. Smith might get involved and have some fun too	

3.   Work on assertiveness training with Mr. Smith to see if we can get his blood pressure down as a result of having new ways to deal with things when he feels like blowing up.

Pros	Cons
Blood pressure might go down	Would take time
Could model constructive stuff	Would take energy
It's interesting subject matter	Might not work, might make things worse
Mr. Smith may have to deal with fewer negative consequences of his anger	

4. Place Mary in a foster home or group home.

Pros	*Cons*
Give everybody time out	Everyone might miss each other and be lonely
Parents no longer have to deal with school, curfew, sassing	Sometimes families find it harder to reunite than they might wish
Mary no longer has to deal with her parents	Costs a lot of money for parents
Everyone might be relieved	Can't be sure what foster parents will be like—might make things worse
	Other kids in group home might teach Mary to do even more self-destructive things
	Parent's friends, relatives, and neighbors may disapprove
	Parents may feel guilty or feel like failures
	Mary's friends may disapprove; she may lose some friends
	Mary may feel like a failure or very rejected and down on herself
	Might give everyone more problems they'll have to work on later

5. Whole family work on learning no-lose problem solving.

Pros	*Cons*
Good way to deal with lots of problems—family learns to cope without counselor	Takes time
	Takes energy
Might come up with a truly elegant idea for this situation	Might not work; everyone might feel even more like a failure afterward
Practice doing something cooperative while counselor is there to help	
It's interesting; sometimes fun	

6. Whole family work on values clarification—trying to figure out what's behind some of the conflicting beliefs they have. (Give examples.)

Pros	*Cons*
Usually everyone feels less helpless if they feel less confused about themselves	Takes time
	Takes energy
	Might find out things are even worse than we thought
Usually everyone feels less defensive if they feel more understanding of the other guy	
Usually people find out they have more common values than they thought and find room to negotiate how they act them out	
Good technique for family to use in the future	

7. Mary goes to temporary foster home—pros, cons, etc.

8. We all go to circus, zoo, movies, something fun together three times a week instead of having therapy sessions—pros, cons, etc.

9. Counselor says good-bye now and family works out next options on their own—pros, cons, etc.

Using Multiple Impact Therapy. Another strategy we use when every-thing else seems to have failed is Multiple Impact Therapy (MIT). This strategy combines many of the advantages of the techniques described above into one big infusion of time, perspective, support, and creativity. MIT is described in detail by its founders in *Multiple Impact Therapy with Families* by MacGregor (1964).

Homebuilders use a six-step adapted version of MIT to bring many resources to bear on especially difficult problem situations. The method involves one counselor for each family member. To introduce the process to the family, the primary counselor explains that it is sometimes helpful for each family member to have his or her own counselor, and for each counselor to do a certain amount of negotiating for "their person" in a lengthy, structured exercise to see if there is any possible way for family members to agree on a course of action. They are told that sometimes family members hurt each other so badly that it becomes difficult for them to communicate. If other people speak for and represent each member, they can frequently begin to hear and under-stand each other in new ways that heal some of the hurt and lead to new problem resolution strategies.

If the family members agree, the counselor then arranges for help from co-workers: one for each family member. In *Step 1*, there is a brief meeting with the whole family on arrival at the home to explain the process and goals. Discussion is lead by a "Master of Ceremonies" who may or may not be the family's primary counselor. Advocates are assigned to each family member. In *Step 2*, counselors and clients meet individually for about one and one-half hours. The main goal is gathering information. The counselors emphasize that when this phase of MIT is over, the counselor must be able to truly represent the family member with whom he has been working. What is the problem? What are wants and concerns related to the problem? The counselor and client try to come up with possible short-term solutions or indicators that the family is heading in the right direction. What could each family member do to make things better? How might they show they are trying? What are their expectations? Counselors try to elicit small and observable criteria so that everyone will be able to acknowledge them. Counselors also attempt to elicit clients' perspectives of the positive aspects of their family. Before returning to the larger group, counselors rehearse what they plan to say to the family, revising it as necessary, and taking care to delete information that the client does not want shared.

As each pair finishes, they return to the central meeting place to socialize and try to keep things light until all counselor–client pairs are finished. If any pair is late getting back, the Master of Ceremonies has the responsibility for interrupting and calling "time."

In *Step 3*, the Master of Ceremonies explains to the family that the counselors will now leave to share the information they have gathered. Counselors usually go eat together, meeting for an hour or an hour and a half to share each family member's viewpoint, and to discuss strategy. They decide who will speak first, what each counselor will say, what small behavior changes will be requested by each person, and what overall problem resolution strategies might work best for the entire family. Usually, the family also uses this break to eat and relax.

Counselors then return to the home for the last steps of MIT, a large group session that usually lasts 1–2 hours. The Master of Ceremonies explains more ground rules. There will be no interrupting. If a counselor is misrepresenting a client or if a client is having trouble not reacting to what is being said, the client should tap the counselor on the shoulder. Then, the two of them take time out to talk privately. Family members are asked to hold reactions and comments until each person has a chance to present.

In *Step 4*, each counselor takes 5–10 minutes to speak for his/her family member, using "I" language, stating the most important issue, what could be done to make it better, and any positive comments about the family.

In *Step 5*, each pair goes off alone to prepare a response to what other members have said through their advocates. Advocates then present these responses to the large group.

In *Step 6*, the Master of Ceremonies leads a group discussion: "Where do we go from here?" What behavioral change will each person agree to try for the next few days, as a sign that the situation can and will improve? In this round, clients can speak for themselves, although if emotions begin to escalate, advocates can step in again and present their clients' points of view in less hurtful language. MIT is not foolproof, but it does provide a unique in-depth consultation to families. MIT also helps families hear old information in new ways and observe good models of communication. Even if the family does not decide to remain together, they may part with less rancor and more compassion; a worthwhile goal in itself.

Postponing Termination

The 4 to 6 week end point is a guideline rather than a commandment. If a family has not stabilized within 4 to 6 weeks and placement has not occurred, we consider extensions. An extension can also be requested when placement appears to have been averted momentarily, but we agree with the family that the threat of an immediate crisis is high if termination occurs. These decisions are taken seriously because we are always balancing the need to help each family against serving as many families as possible. We try to assess whether more time will make a difference. Precisely what will we do during the extension? What are the goals? What new techniques will be tried? Is there any other agency that could accomplish the same amount during this time?

How to Terminate

We begin the termination process during the first session. As soon as family members begin to calm down, we tell them that our involvement is limited to a short period. If additional services are needed after that time we will help connect them with other community agencies. Each week we review progress toward family goals. This helps to keep us all on track, and it focuses attention on the time-limited nature of the intervention. "Counting down" the weeks as they go helps the family keep focused of the length of the intervention, so the final week does not arrive unexpectedly.

We also talk frequently about how family members can continue, after we are gone, to use the skills they have learned, and about who will provide emotional support for them when they need it. We prefer to help families identify and nurture informal support networks because they do not cost money and they do not involve the stigma of having to ask for formal agency help.

If informal supports are not sufficient, we begin early to discuss agency programs that might be helpful and begin procedures for entering clients into them. Many family members are not initially enthusiastic about starting with new agencies or resuming contacts with agencies they have known before. The largest proportion of our clients needs only minimal access to counseling resources by the end of their time with us. We listen to their expectations for the future and concerns about past experiences. Sometimes it is helpful to identify the family member who seems most interested in ongoing programs. For a few, all that is necessary is a phone number and an address. With most clients, however, it is helpful to be with them when they make the first appointment and to attend at least the first session with them. After the first session we discuss family members' feelings about it. Did it meet their expectations? Do they think it will help in the future? If they did not like it, why not? Are there any ways to eliminate their concerns?

The format of the final Homebuilders session varies according to the particular worker and the particular family. Some workers celebrate with their families over pizza. Many review skills learned and do final rehearsals about what to try when problems recur or when new ones arise. We want to reward them for all their hard work. We want to do as much last minute preparation for the future as we can. We also want them to know that although we will not see them routinely, we are not abandoning them.

Follow-Up from Homebuilders

We do not want families to feel that their ties have been severed. We make it clear that we still care about them and can be called after termination.

Booster Shots

For a fairly small percentage of families, "booster shots" are part of the follow-up plan. For example, we may have helped a family get on a waiting list for ongoing counseling, but their first appointment is a month away. We will go with them if they like. A child who has school problems may need someone to check in at the change of classes after winter break. With some families who are feeling precarious, a visit a week can occur for a few weeks after termination.

Informal Contacts

With most families, follow-up contacts are not formally planned. During the final sessions we tell family members that although the formal part of the intervention is over, they may call us any time if they have problems. It is not uncommon for us to maintain minimal and informal contact with clients for years. Most of these clients are brief phone conversations about good news as well as sad. Sometimes a situation requires a long problem-solving telephone conversation. Sometimes it warrants a home visit. Sometimes it involves referral to another agency. Rarely does it require another referral to Homebuilders for a complete intervention.

We also ask the family's permission for our research staff to phone or write immediately after termination, at 3 months following termination, and 1 year after intake to see how they are doing. If families are having trouble, their counselor or the counselor's supervisor will contact them.

Summary

We help clients view termination and their independence from us as a process of growth that begins the first day of our involvement and continues long afterward. We begin preparing clients to do without us as soon as we meet them. The bulk of our efforts throughout our intervention is aimed at leaving them with skills or other resources to sustain them when we go. The tie is never completely severed. They may always call us if they need additional help.

III

ORGANIZATIONAL ISSUES

11

Administering Family Preservation Services

Social service agencies face enormous challenges today. Problems such as crack, AIDS, poverty, and violence appear overwhelming and terrifying. The resources our society is willing to allocate to fighting the problems seem pitiful, like fighting an elephant with a pea shooter. We may easily become daunted and discouraged. This context makes the challenge of agency management all the more formidable.

When we began in 1974 in Tacoma, Washington, we were part of Catholic Community Services. Partially in order to overcome catchment area restrictions of the parent organization and partially because Homebuilders was getting complicated enough to need its own board, we moved to our own private nonprofit agency, Behavioral Sciences Institute, in 1982. Seventeen staff chose nine Board members, wrote their own personnel policies, and developed their own salary schedule for approval by the Board. Three of us got second mortgages on our houses so the agency could have some operating funds.

Now, 11 of the original staff and 5 of the original Board members are still together. We operate programs in Pierce, King, Spokane, Whitman, Kitsap, Yakima, Snohomish, Kititas, and Thurston counties in Washington State, and in the Bronx in New York City. We have a Training Division and a Research Division. The staff total is 80.

We have eight Board members from Washington State, one from New York City, one from Tuscon, one from San Francisco, one from Santa Fe, and one from Atlanta. They include two psychologists, three social workers, one sociologist, a financial consultant, a lawyer, an organizational consultant, a program developer, an accountant, and a property manager.

Our annual budget is about $3,200,000. We receive funds from Washington State Department of Social and Health Services for our Washington programs. Special Services for Children, the public agency in New York City, funds our Bronx Project. Our training and research activities are funded by fees for services and grants from the Edna McConnell Clark, MONY, and Northwest Foundations.

In administering Homebuilders we utilize the same values about the specialness of individuals and the technology of social learning with staff as we use with clients. Throughout the development of Homebuilders and Behavioral Sciences Institute five beliefs have been, and remain central in preventing staff turnover and helping the program to run smoothly. (1) Helping severely troubled families in debilitating conditions is difficult. We want to set up conditions for the counselors that make doing their job as easy as possible. (2) We can't expect staff to do what we want unless they know what that is. We must clarify our goals, values, and expectations for them and with them. (3) Decisions are made most effectively if those who will be affected by them have input into them. (4) Internal communication and teamwork form the machinery that allows the organization to function. (5) People work best when they are supported and validated. We do our best on all these issues but have learned that as soon as we master one area, the agency grows and we are beginners again. This is another area where realistic goals are important.

Making Counselors Jobs as Easy as Possible

Just as we try to remove barriers to clients receiving services, we try to remove barriers to counselors providing it. Although they need to let their secretary know where they are, counselors have to be in the office only for weekly staff meetings and case consultation. They are free to do paperwork, prep for client sessions, and make phone calls at home if they wish. Since we want them to visit clients often, we reimburse for mileage at a high rate. If they go out for a snack or a meal with clients or visitors, BSI will pay for counselors' food under some conditions.

We also try to see that staff get some time off. If they work over 40 hours in a week, they accumulate the overtime as compensatory time. They may take up to 3 days of comp time in any month, more with permission of their supervisors. Counselors also receive 20 days of vacation, 12 days of sick leave, and 11 holidays per year.

We continually emphasize counselors helping families as the agency priority, and the rewards that come from these relationships are what counselors mention if they are asked about the high points of the job.

Often when I go to work in the morning I know I'm going to get to do something fun with a client. There are lots of good reasons to do fun things with clients like to cheer them up when things are not going so well and to encourage them to do this for themselves; to engage with them; to reward them for working on goals; to provide a pleasant environment to work on goals; to make teaching sessions a pleasure. I'm not always going to get to do fun things when I work, of course. So many of the people I see are experiencing very difficult times. It's very pleasant for me though to go off to see these people knowing that someone in that house I'm headed for will be glad to see me, thinks of me as friendly and helpful, caring and resourceful. Today I helped a family get food, took an isolated mother of a 10-month-old baby out for coffee and helped her think of alternative ways to deal with her anger—ways besides hitting someone or getting stoned. It was nice to know things were a little better for this family at the end of the day.

Some other days I like are ones I spend working with my team. I get reinforcements for being up on paperwork; encouragement for my efforts; friendly greetings; helpful suggestions for working with client problems I'm stuck on; and support when it seems too much to do alone. (Dawn James)

High point of job:

When I closed with one of my first families I felt like the single mom had no better relationship with her teenage son than when I had started. She didn't seem to have learned communication skills nor had she learned to cope better with her son doing poorly in school and her son not showing responsibility at home. I visited weeks later and mom was joking and being affectionate with son. She reported listening more to him and had figured out that "I" messages did work. She was using RET skills at home and at work and was feeling much better about her home and work life. The son had enrolled in Tae Kwan Do and was excited and motivated about it.

It was heart-warming to see and for the first time, I got a sense that these families really could be helped to make positive changes. (Joanne Swanson)

The focus on contributing to client welfare makes support staff jobs meaningful too.

It's energizing to me to know that I'm a part of such a helpful organization that is changing the future. Hopefully families are learning skills now that will be handed down for generations. My teammates also make work seem more fun and interesting and purposeful. All the office-based staff are so helpful and supportive. I know there is always someone I can call if I need help. I know that my being here is making a difference. My support is helping staff so their job is easier and more pleasant. We're all working together for a great cause. Staff relationships and support are a real "high." (Merri Hyatt)

Some ideas and beliefs form the foundation for the organization and they are not negotiable. Our primary commitment is to client and staff safety. We will not make any changes that increase anyone's chances of being hurt. We wish to provide a service where clients are respected. We want staff to feel that same respect within the agency. We will not trick people and we will avoid procedures that demean them. We try to maximize people's control over their own destinies, both so that they will be comfortable implementing decisions that are made, and so that they will learn to be better decision makers and take on greater responsibilities as the agency grows. We are committed to teamwork. We are also committed to accountability. We want to be able to measure what we do, both with clients and with each other, so that we can gain as much information as possible to help us continue to learn and to improve.

As the organization grows, we all have to keep evolving along with it. We must learn by doing, and in doing, we will make mistakes. If we are afraid of making mistakes, we may become paralyzed, mired in past patterns of behavior that are now outdated and ineffective. Thus one of our biggest continuing challenges is to find the courage and the compassion to allow ourselves and others permission and support for making mistakes so that we may all learn together to manage a larger, more complex organization. As we review mistakes we try to focus on what we learned rather than on how stupid we were to make the mistake.

> As Homebuilder counselors we are encouraged to make mistakes. Not on purpose, of course, but since we all make mistakes anyway, it is best if we can learn something from them. And if we can train ourselves to be acutely conscious of even our smaller errors, then perhaps we can avoid making more serious, if not tragic, ones.
>
> Such was the case with James, Arthur, and Casey, three beautiful and quite lovely children—ages 6, 5, and 3, respectively—whom I invited for an outing to a science center. I had seen these three in action with their mother and should have known better. My mistake was in thinking that taking charge of them by myself would be no problem.
>
> Before we set out I made it very clear to them that they were to stay by my side at all times. It was in going from the car to the center that I first became aware of my grave miscalculation. James, Arthur, and Casey scampered off in all directions intrigued by the ducks that up to then had been calmly swimming in the flat, wide ponds that graced the entrance. I did manage to get the boys inside to the exhibits, but there things did not go any better. I could not possibly keep track of all three of them as they ran from game to game in such a beehive of buzzing children. At one point an attendant delivered James to me; he had somehow gotten lost and was in tears.
>
> On the way out my goal was to get all three safely to the car and back home again as soon as possible. The ducks, however, called and off they went trying to scare them away. As I was managing James and Casey up the steps I heard behind me an unmistakable splash. There was Arthur thrashing around in the water, yelling for dear life. I rushed to fish him out, pretending to the concerned passer-by that I too was only happening by. Arthur, soaking wet, screamed all the way to the car, which was about

four blocks away. I kept wondering what Arthur's mom and my supervisors would say when he contracted double pneumonia. Once at the car I wrapped him in a blanket and sped off to my own house, since Arthur's mother was not yet at home. I peeled off Arthur's soaked clothes, threw them in the dryer, piled the boys back into the car to fetch a Burger King lunch, and then returned home to try to put all the pieces back together.

Later, when I called Arthur's mom to let her know what had happened, she just laughed and asked me if I had felt embarrassed. I lied when I said I hadn't, but she just laughed again and said, "Well, maybe *you* weren't, but *I* sure would be!"

I learned not to take so many small children out at once. (Jim Poggi)

We would like to facilitate development of an atmosphere that is pleasant, positive, and even *fun*. We want staff to stay for long periods of time. Since we all spend so much time working, we want that portion of our lives to be friendly and supportive. We would like the work to be more than "a job."

We try to make the organization's underlying rules and assumptions open to all. We strive to make the unspoken rules explicit so that they may be understood and challenged. We have lists of the advantages and disadvantages of the Homebuilders counselor job. We list ways in which working with Homebuilders might lead to conflict with peers (such as ridicule for low salaries and long hours). We articulate what we think enables staff to get promoted at BSI and ways staff might examine their own values and goals to decide if they do, indeed, want to get promoted.

Staff training (see Chapter 13) involves specification of expectations for all. Currently we are heavily involved in developing standards for programs, supervisors, and counselors. We hope this project, called QUEST (Quality Enhancement Systems and Training), will be a major step in further clarifying goals and expectations. As we define desired outcomes, we will then be able to assess how well we are doing in meeting them. In areas where we do poorly, we will know to develop new supports and training.

Maximizing Communication, Connectedness, and Teamwork

As the organization has grown, our "Mom and Pop" style of management, with informal communications and decision-making processes, has become more difficult to maintain successfully. Mom and Pop don't have the time to get to know 70 employees in the same way they could know 17. Seventy employees can't get to know each other as well as 17, especially when some of them are thousands of miles apart.

Keeping everyone up to date in a rapidly changing environment sometimes feels like a losing battle, but we continue to try new ways to connect and reconnect as we grow.

We hold yearly retreats with all staff, and miniteam retreats whenever we wish. At some retreats we give out "T" shirts or mugs with "Homebuilders" and "BSI" on them. We regularly send out anonymous "How's It Going?" questionnaires that are then collated and given to the staff and Board. We experiment with fax machines and electronic mail. We have a newsletter (The BSEye).

We encourage interaction among all levels of the organization. Directors try to take each new employee to lunch to establish the beginnings of the direct channel we would like to make possible. We have joint staff–Board parties. Board members are encouraged to attend staff retreats. Visitors, funding agents, and evaluators are encouraged to talk with staff at all levels. Staff report this emphasis is helpful.

> I feel connected with the rest of the organization by getting staff meeting minutes from the other offices and by being encouraged to talk with anyone in the agency if I have a question. If I wonder how Kitsap runs the office, I know I could call Barb and I know she would be happy to share information with me. People often call me asking for suggestions and help and I feel that helps the different offices feel connected. Staff retreats also enable us to put faces and names together. I also enjoy the newsletter which lets me see another, more social side of the staff.
>
> Five heads are better than four is the general feeling at BSI, which encourages staff to express their views and allows for open communication. Electronic mail has made it a lot easier to get up-to-the-minute news passed between offices. (Merri Hyatt)
>
> With our team we are encouraged to communicate in various ways. We have weekly (sometimes biweekly) consultation time with the other team members and supervisors. During these times we are asked how things with our clients are *really* going, and given a lot of support if we are feeling overwhelmed, or have run out of ideas. We talk with each other between times, and encouraged to call our supervisor is we ever feel need for support or advise with clients.
>
> We call in to the office daily, to let our secretary know our schedule, and are able to hear sympathy at that time too, if our days seem unbearably long!
>
> Within the organization itself, communication is encouraged. From the directors, to the program manager, to the supervisors and counselor there is always an invitation to call whenever need be, and a direct line for consultation. Weekly minutes for meetings in each office are printed and available for reference. (Sarah Butler-Wills)

We structure positive interactions among employees by developing traditions such as "Pixies" where staff draw each others' names and secretly leave surprises around various holidays, or "gift fights" where staff bring gifts and can choose to select an unopened present or steal from someone who has already opened theirs.

We talk openly about the advantages and disadvantages of teamwork. For all the advantages gained by more brainpower and support, there *is* a concurrent loss of autonomy. We discuss which aspects of our current teamwork are working and which are not. We conceptualize our ideal of teamwork and discuss how we might get from where we are now to where we would like to be. We brainstorm ways to maximize the positives of teamwork and minimize the negatives. We encourage new staff to join existing efforts such as a "Paperwork Anonymous" group that meets when members are having trouble doing their paperwork on time. We reinforce the idea of mutual accountability by having agency co-directors anonymously evaluated through an annual questionnaire sent to all employees, with the results going to the Board. Administrators and supervisors are evaluated by team members, as well as evaluate those they supervise. Team members also have considerable input into the hiring of new members. Staff feel the teamwork is a critical part of their job.

> Hanging over my desk at the office is a full-color poster of the Blue Angels Navy Air Acrobatic Team flying in tight formation. I keep it there as a reminder to myself that good work as a Homebuilder means equally tight teamwork. I don't know about other counselors, but I have had my temptations to be a lone ranger. Sometimes I like to think I know best what needs to be done and that others are less smart or experienced than I am. This attitude, I know, can be counterproductive at best—I always learn something from consulting others—and dangerous at worst, especially in a job such as ours that is so open to risks.
>
> I have been told that the Blue Angels need to be very sensitively attuned to one another if they want to survive as aeroacrobats. One slip of the stick and all of them can be "goners," as actually happened one time with their Air Force counterparts, all of whom followed the leader into the ground.
>
> There is a double lesson here: One is that we do not play follow-the-leader, for the reason just given. We are encouraged to express our views and "control" our own cases. Still, we are urged, especially in tight spots, to call no matter what time of day or night. At 1:00 AM recently I found myself in mid-crisis connected by wire to four different supervisors, who guided the family and myself safely through the night to a successful landing.
>
> The other lesson is that knowing you have a team behind you is tremendously supportive, uplifting, and even exciting. It is a true love experience to know that others support you—and you, them— in what is at best a difficult job. (Jim Poggi)

We assume that all of our staff know basic communications skills because we emphasize these skills in our training. We also assume that we all can fail in using these skills, because we might be afraid of saying something someone else is not going to like. When communication begins to break down, we often reintroduce training in Rational Emotive Therapy to decrease staff members' fear of reprisals. We update assertiveness training to stress the points that people cannot do anything about problems that aren't expressed, and that the way messages are delivered will help in encouraging a positive response from the recipient. If relationships get too tense, we can hold mini-Multiple Impact Therapy sessions with each other (described in Chapter 10.)

Maximizing Involvement in Decision Making

When the organization was fairly small and focused, all staff could have input on almost all decisions. Most decisions could be made by consensus. Now, many more decisions must be made, in many more specialized areas. We still have to decide how many dollars to allocate for staff training, but we also need to decide how we will cope with highly technical data collection problems and recruitment materials. We are unable to provide all staff with enough information about each issue to allow them to make well-informed decisions about the entire agency.

On the other hand, agency administrators used to be accessible and informed enough to be involved in decision making at the line level. As responsibilities in other areas grow, top administrators find it impossible to keep up with current family issues and community resources. We have always believed that two heads are better than one, and five heads are better than two. Obviously, in the formation of BSI, we were committed to allowing all staff input regarding their working conditions and futures. We believe that time spent in reaching consensus diminishes time needed for effective implementation of decisions. We try to help all staff become aware that there are very few perfect decisions. Many issues are not problems, but dilemmas. Just because we eventually revise decisions doesn't mean that they weren't the best decisions possible when they were made.

We think of ourselves as using participatory management. BSI never could have begun without the participation of all staff. We were able to develop a sense of group spirit and camaraderie that made being together fun and supportive. We still believe that involving staff with organizational issues increases the likelihood that the best ideas will surface and bad choices will be minimized. Staff develop progressively more experience and understanding of the organizational life of BSI so that they feel more a part of it. The interactions that occur with participatory management teach all of us how to function within a group and to develop as potential leaders.

Participatory management in the way we use it is not a one person/ one vote democracy. We attempt to reach consensus on major issues, and are committed to listening to input, but administrators retain the ultimate decision-making power. Administrators are responsible for keeping staff informed of important issues facing the agency, and for providing them with information necessary to make wise decisions on issues that directly influence them. We constantly try to shift power and decision making down to the point closest to implementation. In situations where administrators and some staff differ regarding desirability of certain options, or where decisions must be made rapidly without staff input, staff have a right to explanations from those who did make the decisions.

Maximizing Support and Validation

We work hard on rewarding good work and recognizing the uniqueness of each person in the organization.

We type snippets of good feedback from clients and trainees onto paper hearts and stars and post them on bulletin boards. We also give hearts and stars to those who do not work directly with clients and trainees. We have huge bulletin boards in our offices, each with pictures of and some funny personal information about individual staff members. We have annual awards ceremonies where each staff members receives at least one award acknowledging his or her unique contribution to the organization.

We encourage staff to bring families and friends to agency parties, and even to invite them to visit now and then during work hours. We allow new mothers to bring their babies to the agency, until the babies get old enough to be disruptive. We celebrate personal milestones with birthday cakes at staff meetings. We attempt to adapt to personal situations whenever possible by allowing staff to take leaves to accommodate personal goals.

We utilize people's skills and resources outside of their particular job descriptions. For example, several new counselors had requested a meeting with agency co-directors to discuss agency finances. As they discussed financial dilemmas and constraints, it became obvious that these new staff had substantial experience and contacts regarding fund raising. They decided they would like to work on development of a fund-raising mechanism in their county, and are developing a proposal to present at the next Board meeting. During our transition from one organization to the other, we relied heavily on a concept called the "Clown Army." Anyone can volunteer to be part of the Clown Army and it can tackle any problem it wants. The group has been most impressive during funding crises when they could mobilize 30 people immediately to go to the capitol to meet with Legislators.

The sense of individual importance helps tie people to the organization when time are difficult as well as during easier periods.

> I like coming to work because of a sense of "family" and history. It's a positive environment. There's a feeling that the people at BSI are friends, and that there's never a dull moment, something exciting is usually going on.
>
> There's a chance to catch up on new news—cases, training, people, legislative stuff.
>
> There is very little to no backstabbing/negative interactions. The people there have been with me in many life changes—single, married, baby— there are lots of years of memories.
>
> There is always something to do! More to read, more to learn, more everything—but I like it. I can have a sense of independence. People leave me notes—encouragement. Recently, people have brought my baby gifts—or see something that has hearts on it (they know I like hearts) and they give it to me—it amazes me. (Karen Bream)

Summary

We try to create a positive context for staff, using the same principles we use in work with families. We focus on eliminating barriers to our work with families, clarifying goals, expectations, and values, encouraging communication, maximizing involvement in decisions, and providing support and recognition. These factors minimize staff turnover and keep the organization running smoothly.

12
Recruiting and Screening Staff

Counselors and supervisors are the key components of any family preservation program. Without committed staff, programs cannot survive. These jobs are not for everyone. They entail long, unpredictable hours under pressure, dangerous conditions, and human pain. They also involve unsurpassed opportunity for personal growth and for contributing to the growth of others. Our challenge is to find individuals for whom the disadvantages are annoyances and the advantages are what make their lives worthwhile.

Recruiting Family Preservation Counselors

Next to recruiting and developing supervisors, which we will discuss later in this chapter, recruiting counselors for family preservation programs is probably our most difficult task. Young people are choosing careers in business over social services. Those who wish to do counseling are often more interested in private practice or medical settings where salaries may be higher. Child welfare is not a popular specialization in many universities. Those who do choose it are frequently women in their thirties, often with children. The unpredictable hours are difficult for them to coordinate with child care needs. Potential applicants for family preservation programs seem to find it much easier to envision the job's negative aspects—such as being on call all the time and going into dangerous neighborhoods than to envision the positive—such as having only two families at a time on their caseload and being able to watch those families make important changes in their lives. The family preservation approach is still unfamiliar to many potential applicants. It sounds risky. Some wonder if the approach is respectable and if programs will survive.

Our first choice for an applicant is someone with a masters degree in social services, with a cognitive–behavioral theoretical background, and several years' experience working with families. We rarely find our first choice. Increasingly, we must compete with other agencies for the few child welfare workers who enter the field. We develop relationships within Schools of Social Work, Psychology, and Counseling, and speak to their classes about family preservation. The University of Washington has been our best source of highly qualified applicants. The School of Social Work there is now beginning a joint project with us to develop a specialization in family preservation. We meet biannually with a group of 10 School of Social Work faculty members from schools throughout the country to increase their awareness of family preservation. We are working with them on curricula for inclusion in various classes they teach. We cooperate with the media and encourage anyone who is considering writing articles or doing television shows about family preservation. We make large charts to show at job fairs and collect flattering quotes to display. We advertise extensively in newspapers, professional papers, and employment services. We are developing a recruitment brochure that could easily be adapted for use by other family preservation programs.

As the number of these programs increases, so does the need for qualified staff. We are going to have to make recruitment for these programs a high priority to avoid having programs that are unable to begin because of their inability to hire, or having programs that are ineffective because they had no choice but to hire unqualified or unsuitable workers. We need to attract as wide a pool of applicants as possible, and we are usually disappointed by the low numbers that apply.

Selecting Counselors

Selecting good counselors is almost as difficult as recruiting good counselors. We would find it easier to select them if the characteristics that make a good family preservation counselor were easy to spot. In some ways, it seems that the reverse is true. Characteristics such as sex, age, race, marital status, parenthood, educational field, or degree have not been correlated with effectiveness on the job. Flexibility, sense of humor, intelligence, courage, and self-confidence are important, but are not easy to spot in an interview. We have developed a multilayered screening process to get the most information we can about these elusive characteristics.

Initial Screening

In the initial screening of resumes, we look for experience with troubled families, crisis intervention, cognitive–behavioral techniques, communications skills, and other learning approaches to problem solving. We assess the quality of the application itself regarding spelling, grammar, thoroughness, and neatness; we are looking for people who take pride in their work and who have high standards for themselves. We are also interested in people who have worked in innovative or unusual programs and settings. We like to hire people with similar theoretical approaches because those preferences often involve values, attitudes, and styles that indicate fundamental approaches to life and other people. If staff have large differences in how they view clients, it is likely they will differ about other agency policies, procedures, and ways they wish to relate to each other and to the community. Selecting staff for compatibility can minimize disagreements. We are concerned that our counselors be able to work together with individual families as needed, and to provide back-up for each other in times of sickness or during holidays and vacations. Congruence of theory and technique is important to avoid further confusing families who are already frequently confused. We are also concerned that our counselors learn to implement an approach really well. If the program as a whole includes too many theoretical approaches, we may end up with staff that understands a thousand interventions superficially, but is unable to successfully implement any one.

Phone Interviews

On the basis of their application, we talk to some applicants on the phone before scheduling them for a face-to-face interview. We do this to share more information about the job and to protect ourselves and the applicant from wasting time in an interview when they might not be interested in the job. We make sure applicants understand that they would be working with families in their homes. We ask if they would be willing to live in or very near the county where they would work, so they can be easily accessible to families. We check to see if they have a driver's license, car, and insurance and are willing to work some evenings and weekends. We make clear that they would give their home phone numbers to clients and be on call 24 hours a day, 7 days a week. We let them know the salary range and ask if this corresponds with their needs and expectations. If they are still interested in the job, and are willing to meet our requirements, we schedule a face-to-face interview.

Office Interviews

Applicants having the most relevant experience come for an hour-long discussion with a supervisor. We use part of this time to provide a realistic account of the job. We discuss flex time, being on call, living in the catchment area, and coping with clients who are sometimes dangerous or, at least, unpredictable. We want people to be very aware of the demands the program can make on their private lives, so that they may make the most informed choice possible. We also want applicants to know that we expect them to follow an already developed model, rather than inventing one as they go. Positive aspects of the job such as the high rate of success with clients, low caseload, clear-cut goals, training, and support are also discussed.

Two of our favorite initial areas of discussion involve applicants' descriptions of the most difficult client they ever had or the most difficult supervisor they ever had. We hope to find people who can be compassionate and specific in describing individuals who were problematic for them. We also want to know if they hold personal and professional values compatible to those of the program and program staff. We like people who want to be creative and who value autonomy and independence, and are at the same time able to function as part of a team. We want people who are flexible and can handle ambiguity. We want people who enjoy adventure. We look for those with good social skills who are comfortable relating to a wide variety of people, and who have an appreciation of and tolerance for the similarities and differences in families. At this point, if applicants look favorable, we ask them to bring a sample of their professional writing and to participate in a role play with our staff portraying a family in crisis.

Role Plays

Top applicants from the individual interviews are asked to return for sessions where members of the hiring team portray a family in crisis in a series of role plays. Other team members and agency administrators may sit at the back of the room. We want all team members to have input on potential new members. Watching others struggle and playing the role of client are excellent ways to learn what works and what doesn't work with families.

In role plays, family members are generally cooperative and under control. We recognize applicants are already under much pressure and we do not want the situation to be impossible for them. In the first role play, the applicant is to demonstrate his ability to defuse the crisis situation, gain the confidence and cooperation of family members, and clarify the issues. During the role plays, applicants are rated by staff on their performance in several areas. They get credit if they wait to be invited in, give clients clear messages regarding the purpose of the visit, and listen to family members without blocking or advising. We are looking for people who can remain calm, be supportive of all family members, and respect clients' decisions regarding their own participation in the session.

Applicants are marked down for ordering or commanding clients, ridiculing them, insisting on having all family members together, asking a lot of questions, and making too many inferences about "what's really going on" with family members.

After the first role play, applicants and Homebuilders who played family members debrief. We ask the applicants how well they think they did, and why. We give them feedback regarding their performance and watch how they take it.

In the second and third role plays, we ask applicants to pretend they are teaching skills to a teenager regarding cutting down absences at school, or teaching skills to a mother regarding controlling her depression. Often we ask them to try a particular interaction again after hearing our feedback. We want people who won't argue and who can utilize information rapidly to improve their skills. We also continue to evaluate applicants' social behavior. Do they make appropriate light conversation? Smile? Have good eye contact? A sense of humor? Do we like them? Would we like to become friends with them?

We look at the professional writing sample to see if the applicant will be able to write records without intensive training. Are their spelling and grammar reasonable? Do they know about sentences and paragraphs? We are also looking for signs of GLOP and poor attitudes regarding clients or supervisors.

Meals with Potential Counselors

If there are any doubts about an applicant, he will be called back one more time, usually for a meal with the supervisor and possibly an agency administrator. We like to talk in a less formal setting. We want to express every doubt we have about some applicants' suitability for the job, both to give them a chance to convince us our doubts are inappropriate, and to get further information about how they will behave in a challenging, stressful situation. We are concerned about putting too much pressure on applicants, but we are more concerned that the people we hire will ultimately be facing circumstances where lives may be at stake. We need to know that they can remain calm and think clearly in difficult situations.

Once applicants have completed this grueling screening, we express our appreciation for their endurance. Those we do not hire receive feedback only if they request it. Those we wish to hire are encouraged to express their feelings about the process and the potential job. If they are still positive about the position, they receive detailed feedback about their performance during the screening as part of their initial training.

Selecting Supervisors

Hiring supervisors is even more difficult than hiring counselors. We want them to have all the attributes of good counselors, and supervision experience besides. We prefer to hire supervisors from our counselor ranks. Although they may have problems learning to supervise their former peers, they know how to do the job and are in the best position to help others learn it. If we are forced to hire from outside because none of our current staff is willing to move to a certain location, or because existing counselors lack the skills or interest needed to become supervisors, we request that the new supervisor go on line and see cases for at least 3 months before beginning his or her supervisory role. In cases where it is impossible for new supervisors to have a caseload for 3 months because no one is available to provide backup supervision, we will still try to have the new supervisor see one case at a time to get some actual experience in the field. Willingness to see cases is a good screening device. We are looking for supervisors who are interested in clients and like being with them. If going back on the line is "beneath" the applicant, or too much trouble, the applicant probably will not be the hands-on kind of supervisor we would like. We are also looking for people who love to learn. If applicants already think they know everything, they are not for us.

Interviews

In interviews with supervisor applicants, we want to hear their theoretical approaches to change and their ideas about management. We are looking for someone who views supervision as teaching as well as management. We present supervisor candidates with dilemmas such as "What's more important, meeting your numbers for a grant, or preventing staff burnout?" or "What's more important, meeting the numbers for a grant, or quality of care?"

We also present them with samples of supervisory problems they might encounter, and ask what they would do. For example, "one of your staff comes to you and says, 'Don't tell anyone that I told you, but Tony isn't filling out his time sheets honestly." 'or "I think this rapid treatment is just a band-aid. What these families really need is psychoanalysis. I want some of my cases to go for at least a year so I can make some significant change." When we hire supervisors, we are concerned about their attitudes regarding being "on top." We are looking for people who value open communication, teamwork, flat organizations, and consensus decision making. We want to know how they view their worst previous supervisee for the same reason we ask potential counselors about their worst clients. Are they compassionate? Do they accept part of the responsibility for problems? Have they thought of ways they could have handled situations differently?

Role Plays

We also ask our supervisor candidates to role play. Team members they would be supervising also attend. We want to observe at least one role play where a counselor comes to the supervisor with a problem, such as how to feel less overwhelmed, and another where the supervisor has a problem with a supervisee's behavior, such as ridiculing a client, or avoiding paperwork. We give applicant's feedback, and ask for replays incorporating the feedback to see how fast they can learn and how open they are to changing their behavior.

Summary

We devote many hours to screening job applicants and selecting new staff. Candidates for both counselor and supervisor positions go through a multilevel screening process involving lengthy interviews by teams and role plays involving teams and agency administrators.

13
Training and Supervising Staff

As we grow, training becomes a bigger and bigger priority for us. The more differentiated our roles become, and the more geographically and culturally different our locations, the more work we have to do to articulate goals, values, and methods. Appendix "B" lists the training and consultation we provide for our own administrators, managers, supervisors, and counselors, as well as those from other programs. Appendix "C" shows more details regarding line staff modules. This chapter will summarize the training and supervision we provide for counselors. We recommend that anyone beginning family preservation programs provide training for their staff.

It's just too hard to start from scratch. People don't know what to expect, what works and doesn't work, how to cope with the demands of the job, or how to intervene in a situation. Starting a new program is difficult. Even with the training, new staff are often overwhelmed. Some people feel intimidated by the demands of the job. Some are skeptical about the model working with their client population in their agency in the state. Mostly, they are excited, enthusiastic, and appreciative of the training, but tired and a little scared.

The training doesn't make everything easy. Trainees still have to put the ideas into practice. They can't learn from hearing about it, or role playing, or watching videos. They still have to practice and experience the families firsthand, hopefully with supervision before they will really "get it." (Don Miner)

Family preservation is still new enough that we don't find staff who are totally ready for the job. New employees do best if they are given considerable training and support during the whole first year of their employment. Like our hiring process, the training occurs in several phases. These phases do not always happen in exactly the following order, because we try to do formal workshop training with a number of new staff from our own and other agencies. Hiring dates are not always the same, and we often have to wait until everyone is on board. The line staff training almost always happens within the first month or two of employment. New staff never begin seeing families without a supervisor or senior counselor along with them.

Initial Training

First Line Staff Training Session

The first line staff training session usually lasts 4 days. We talk about beliefs and strategies of family-based services. We want staff to understand how the model developed the way it did. We want them to understand the advantages and disadvantages of keeping children in their homes and of placing them. We teach workers how to engage and defuse families in crises, and how to prevent violence before, during, and between sessions. We address assessment and goal setting, and begin to work on how to teach families cognitive–behavioral and communications skills. We also discuss termination and follow-up issues. The training involves some lectures, but role play, videotapes, and other experiential modes are emphasized.

During the initial training, counselors' own stress management is a high priority. The job can have some definite low points that would severely tax anyone's morale.

I had a family with 5 children, four of them boys who were constantly fighting and rough-housing. The home was unpleasantly filthy. One day I took three of the four boys to the park to have fun!! One boy refused to come home while the 4 year old proceeded to poop in his pants while in my car!! The parents were not home when we got back. I went to help the 4 year old in the bathroom, but I was met with such stench I could not manage. Meanwhile the eldest brother was threatening the younger ones with a stick and looking totally out of control. Then the smell of something burning filled the house, and just as I was trying to figure out how to get them all out the father arrived home. Thank God!! The house did not burn down and I am not sure whether that was a blessing or not!! (Joanne Swanson)

Counselors need to know how to keep themselves together under pressure before they will be able to help others. We spend a number of hours teaching and helping them practice using Rational Emotive Therapy and other cognitive and environmental approaches. We want to decrease self-talk that is anxiety-provoking, such as,"If I can't do it perfectly, I shouldn't do it at all," or "I have to do this exactly right, all the time, or it will prove I'm not good enough." We encourage self-talk along the lines of "I will never do it perfectly. My work can still be worthwhile even if it's not perfect," or "Making mistakes is one way I learn. Everyone else here has made many mistakes and is continuing to make some. That's how it is, and I can grow from it without being humiliated."

We also work on new counselors' feeling of inadequacy about the job, which often arise from comparing themselves to those who are more experienced. We want new staff to go from "I will never be good enough" to "I may not ever be as good at certain aspects of counseling as some others, but that doesn't mean that my work isn't worthwhile, or that I'm a worthless person. I can try to improve my performance as I gain experience and knowledge."

New counselors also frequently need help with ambiguity and lack of cooperation from families. We try to help them shift from "Others' expectations should always be clear for me" and "This family should be more motivated," to "The world is not always clear. I can function without perfect clarity," and "If these families were effective and easy to help, they wouldn't need me. They have good reasons for appearing reluctant. I will make the situation worse if I pressure them. I may be able to give them hope even though they do not appear motivated right now."

Another way counselors learn to decrease their stress is through mental rehearsal. What goes on in our minds isn't just talk; we can also visualize ourselves. Workers can learn to develop mental movies for themselves where they watch themselves coping calmly or making positive statements in difficult situations. They can also "replay" events in the past they didn't handle as well as they would have liked. In the reenactment, they can visualize themselves dealing with the situation the way they wished they had.

We encourage new workers to develop good support networks for themselves both inside and outside work, and to get exercise, eat well, and to take time for themselves. We stress the need for them to let others know when they need help, so that help can be provided.

Initial Meeting with the Administrators

Administrators generally meet with new staff either in a group or individually within the first 3 months of employment. During these sessions, we talk about program and agency history and development, and how participatory management is interpreted. We also encourage "stupid questions," regarding any issues people have been wondering about, or that they felt uneasy asking. We want workers to have the information about the agency, but more important, we want them to feel some personal tie with agency administrators. We want to demystify roles and encourage getting to know each other as individuals. We want to begin some communications so if there are problems in the future, employees will have at least a little experience dealing directly with top managers.

Initial Plan

Shortly after the initial training, new staff meet with their supervisors to develop an initial plan for individualized on-the-job-training. Staff are given many materials: personnel policies, a resource guide with interventions for common client problems, an overview of the program, a book written jointly by Homebuilders administrators and various School of Social Work faculty members throughout the country, and a reading list.

The supervisor goes over a checklist with the new employee, regarding skills he is expected to learn within the first year of employment. A copy of this initial plan is attached as "Appendix D."

First Cases

Supervisors or senior counselors always accompany new staff on visits to their first families. Sometimes supervisors go along for the first several families, gradually phasing out as new counselors gain experience and skill. With the first family, the supervisor carries the bulk of the responsibility. She will discuss the family with her supervisee before the visit, then model skills and gradually begin coaching the trainee. She will give the trainee feedback after each session, and provide individual tutorials as needed, or, if her schedule precludes that, arrange for the trainee to meet with training staff to increase skills.

During the first case, trainees observe their supervisor, try new behaviors, ask questions, and listen to feedback. We stress that there are no stupid questions and that we expect them to let us know if they are having trouble with any aspect of the job.

Second Line Staff Training Session

Usually in the third or fourth month, trainees go through another 3-day session of formal group training. During these days, we focus more intensively on how to teach families to communicate and to change their own behavior. We present assertiveness training, and anger management, problem solving, and negotiating working with depressed and suicidal clients. We discuss what to do if progress isn't occurring, and how to use Multiple Impact Therapy. We continue to work on trainees' own listening and stress management skills. As in the first group training sessions, role playing is emphasized, and trainees receive a good deal of individual coaching as they develop skills.

Ongoing Training

We are always trying to learn more. Several times a year we will have outside experts come in and provide training for us, or send staff to workshops. We also set aside money for staff to attend outside workshops.

Staff Supervision

Staff training is an ongoing function. Counselors need intensive training for the entire first year, and all of us continue to learn as long as we are on the job. After the initial formal training has occurred, additional training is coordinated by the supervisor who meets individually with each supervisee at least monthly to discuss additional training needs and personal and professional growth plans. Other training occurs routinely through individual and group case consultation, other group training events, and individual training stipends for staff. This training is important for continued staff learning, but it is also necessary to bring new perspectives to the agency and to provide a break from the demanding work with families.

Case Staffings

Group Case Consultation. Team members meet at least one morning a week, sometimes two, with their supervisor to discuss each family they are seeing. We have a supervisor for approximately every six counselors. Group sessions foster professional growth by increasing options available for clients, identifying professional strengths and weaknesses in each team member, improving skills in weak areas, and developing supervision skills for present or future job positions. We also want to foster team building and to keep team members up to date on one another's families so they can be helpful if they are called to accompany or provide backup for another worker.

In case consultation, counselors first give a concise account of the case, including the source of the referral, the presenting problems, the social history, goals, and goal attainment scaling. General updates keep others informed of timelines, new ideas that did or didn't work, and progress on goals. Feedback is solicited from other team members as well as from the supervisor. Team members who are not presenting listen for feelings as well as content, reinforce the presenting counselor's attempts to deal with his or her situation, and offer ideas when they are requested.

Individual Consultation.   Staff routinely seek consultation from supervisors and teammates outside regular group meetings. There are certain situations when counselors are required to seek consultation: if they don't know if a case is appropriate to accept, if they are having difficulty defusing family members, or if they are having difficulty formulating goals after 1 week. We also encourage staff to contact supervisors if they don't like the family, if little progress is being made on goals, or if they think placement may be the best option for family members. And we want counselors to consult with their supervisors if they are putting in lots of overtime— say, more than 10 hours in a week—or if they find themselves staying awake nights or obsessing about a family. Any time a counselor feels pressured to make a decision and thinks a better decision could be made with help, he should call a supervisor or manager. Supervisors and other teammates are also available to accompany counselors on home visits when they feel anxious about safety, or just unsatisfied with the amount of progress being made.

Emergency Consultation.   Supervisors and administrators are on call 24 hours a day, 7 days a week just like counselors. In some offices, they carry beepers. Other offices rely on supervisors from other teams if one in unavailable. Staff *must* immediately contact supervisors if at any time they become concerned for the safety of any family member or themselves. If their supervisor is unavailable, they must contact other agency administrative staff. Any families with members who present serious threats to themselves or others must be discussed daily with supervisors.

Prevention of Burnout

Our approach, organization, training, and supervision are all designed to make it feasible for counselors to do their work over a long period of time. A fair number of our staff stay indefinitely, getting promoted or moving to other divisions, or gaining more expertise in their current jobs. Some take parental or other leaves of absence and return after one or more years.

The best way to cope with burnout is to prevent it, but counselors do sometimes become discouraged and overwhelmed. As in so many phases of our work with clients, the key to changes in behaviors and attitudes is a foundation of trust and respect between the helper and the helpee. At these times, we do the same thing we do with clients who are overwhelmed; listen, clarify concerns and issues, and help break problems down into small enough chunks that we can address them. We work toward individualized solutions rather than general ones. Encouraging some employees to take time off can be helpful. With others, time out can increase a sense of isolation and inadequacy. It is risky to encourage all employees to develop hobbies, because if they don't like hobbies they may feel guilty for not complying and not wanting to comply.

When counselors are discouraged, we encourage them to talk at length with their supervisors. If staff look upset, but do not initiate contact, supervisors will seek them out. When a supervisor takes several hours, and uses good active listening skills, "burnout" usually becomes reinterpreted. Some counselors take on too many responsibilities with too little time. Some are confused about job requirements. Some have irrationally high expectations regarding their job and their performance. Others are in disputes with peers or loved ones at home. Some get bogged down when everything seems to be going well; they are ready for new challenges. Sometimes, usually after working with particularly demanding families, counselors are physically exhausted. Obviously, each of these problems requires a different solution. Interventions could range from redefinition of job duties to time management training, time off work, or individual time with a Rational Emotive Therapist or other specialist.

Some issues are troublesome enough to appear fairly frequently. If getting calls at home is beginning to overwhelm someone, we might help them learn more structuring techniques to help families cope better on their own. We might encourage staff to tell families that on certain nights they will be unavailable and remind families of supervisors' numbers. They may also benefit from learning how to better structure phone calls to find out what is needed and respond, rather than feeling like they have to listen endlessly whether the call is urgent or not.

We continue to remind staff why we accept calls at home; it means a lot to family members that counselors respond to them when they are hurting. The calls are a wonderful opportunity to find out what's happening and to intervene before the situation gets out of control. At the same time, counselors do not have endless reserves of energy, and we support them telling clients they are too tired to talk if routine calls come at difficult times and client issues are not urgent.

If some staff become bothered working evenings and weekends, others on the team may remind them that they can sleep in when they want, they can usually attend their own children's school functions during the day, the lines to do things during the week are shorter, and there is more control over their schedule than most jobs. Obviously, this type of reconceptualizing doesn't always help. Some staff exchange coverage with others for certain weekends. Some make sure to schedule time off during the day or after sessions to do something fun. Some counselors who are parents like to encourage weekend work because their children can be with their spouse rather than a sitter. Other counselors make certain never to do paperwork or other routine tasks during the weekend. Most learn not to overcommit themselves to too many long days in a row.

When some of us become frustrated by not accomplishing as much as we would like with all families, we might tell ourselves "It's not my objective to take them to their destination, but just to put them back on track," or "Any progress made is better than none at all," or "If this wasn't a 4-week service it wouldn't be affordable." We might also review what we did get done and what interventions did or did not work, reevaluate whether the goals were reasonable, and remind ourselves that people have the right to change however and whenever they want.

Many of us also feel vulnerable in light of others' high expectations of us. Sometimes community leaders' and funding agents' enthusiasm can lead to unrealistic expectations and extra pressure on everyone. We must constantly remind ourselves that nobody at the agency is perfect or will ever come close. We try to unhook ourselves from outsiders' expectations of our curing families overnight. We can focus on educating others about small steps and shaping. If we expect too much, families won't feel successful either, and the whole point of the service will be lost.

Summary

Because Family Preservation Services are so new, we are not able to hire people who are ready to do the job. Intensive training is necessary during the first year of employment and continued training is helpful as long as the employee is on the job. Because the work is demanding and the issues staff confront may, literally, be life and death, close supervision is essential. Supervisors must understand and embrace the work of counselors, and must be as available and responsive to the counselors as the counselors are to families.

14
Program Evaluation

From the beginning, Homebuilders has been heavily evaluated. We had to have feedback on its effectiveness in order to decide whether it was worth continuing to do. Once we began to get information that it appeared effective, we, and others, were interested in subjecting it to more stringent tests. We have been interested in both understanding the process of the Homebuilders service and the treatment outcomes. The feedback from both these areas provides the rudder for management decisions and agency policy.

In this chapter we present an overview of results of Homebuilders success rates in preventing placement and cost effectiveness, as well as the methodology of several major studies that have been conducted to measure various aspects of Homebuilders' effectiveness in preventing unnecessary out of home placement, and in helping families to resolve their problems. We will compare and summarize results from these studies. We will also discuss program evaluation as a management tool, critical for continuing evolution of the model and the agency.

Overview of Homebuilders Success in Avoiding Out-of-Home Placement

For families with at least one child at imminent risk of placement, Homebuilders success in avoiding placement at 12 months following the initiation of service has varied from 73 to 91% of families served, depending on the definition of placement, client population, geographic location, program maturity, and other factors.

Definition of Placement. We consider placement to be the official, long-term placement of a child into state-funded care. If a child goes to live with a relative, such as a grandparent, aunt, or older sibling, for example, we do not consider this living arrangement to be placement because it is not official, state-funded placement.

185

Table 4. Homebuilders' Success in Avoiding Placement (All BSI programs)

Presenting problem	Placement avoided 3 months after intake (percent)	Placement avoided 12 months after intake (percent)
Child abuse and neglect	95	80–91
Families in conflict	94–96	80–88
Mental health	86–94	80–82
Developmental Disabilities	94	80
Delinquency	91–92	73–80

Geographic Location.   The location of our programs presents a variety of challenges to the measurement of program effectiveness. Client families who live in inner-city environments often must cope with dilemmas that may differ from client families who live in suburban and rural environments. Activity that contributes to crime, the safety of clients within their communities, the safety of therapists, and the availability of public transportation to clients living in rural areas who need access to community resources are a few examples of geographic factors that can affect short- and long-term success.

Program Maturity.   Each time we expand the service to a new program site, that site must work through the inevitable challenges posed by such expansion before functioning with the same smoothness of a program that has been operating for years. Maturity of a program cannot be overlooked when evaluating program effectiveness.

Overview of Cost-Effectiveness

Washington State cost-effectiveness

From a fiscal perspective, the cost of Homebuilders during 1989 averaged $2,700 per child considered to need placement in Washington State. Helping families learn effective skills for coping with problems costs significantly less than out-of-home placement (see Table 5).

Based on the figures in the table, the difference between the cost of Homebuilders and placement in Washington state is seen in Table 6.

The cost to the State of Washington to fund the Homebuilders program is easily recouped. Using the Washington costs (Washington State Department of Social and Health Services, 1989), a three-therapist

Table 5. Washington State Cost per Placement

Type of placement	Average cost/month (in dollars)	Average length of stay (months)	Average cost (in dollars)
Foster care	403	19.4	7,813
Group care	1,721	13.0	22,373
Residential treatment	2,206	13.0	28,678
Acute psych. hosp.	11,250	4.0	45,000
Long-term psych.	7,350	14.0	102,900

Table 6. Average Costs of Placement

Foster care	$ 5,113
Group care	$ 19,673
Residential treatment	$ 25,978
Acute psych. hosp.	$ 42,300
Long-term psychiatric	$100,200

unit costing $145,800 per year could be funded through reallocation of funds "saved" by preventing only 19 foster-care placements, or 7 group-home placements, or 5 residential-treatment placements, or four acute-psychiatric hospitalizations, or two long-term psychiatric placements. Three Homebuilders therapists can generally avoid placement of at least 60 children per year. Thus:

> 60 × $2,700 = $162,000/year
> children Cost of
> Homebuilders
> per child

That may seem like a large sum of money. However, compare the $162,000 cost of Homebuilders to that of foster care, the least-expensive type of state-funded placement, for those same 60 children:

> 60 × $7,813 = $468,780/year
> children Cost of
> foster care
> per child

Bronx Cost-effectiveness

An initial analyses of the first six months of the Bronx Project has many limitations in terms of sample size, length of follow-up and lack of a control group, as well as serious difficulties in retrieving data from New York systems. It is also impossible at this time for us to know if clients referred to Homebuilders would have been in placement for average lengths of stay, or if clients who ultimately are placed following Homebuilders remain for average lengths of stay. Nevertheless, we can get a very rough idea of Homebuilders' potential for cost-effectiveness. Table 7 shows average costs of out of home placement in New York.

Projected placements and costs for Homebuilders clients are shown in Table 8.

Costs for Homebuilders services during this period were $211,892, or $2,306,048 less than average costs of placement would have been. Even if we figure in average costs of placement for the five Homebuilders clients who were placed during this period (1 foster infant—$34,649; 9 year old, foster care,—$35,763; and 3 group home placements— $294,909) costs for Homebuilders clients are $1,940,747 less than if they had all been placed.

A more conservative assessment of potential for cost effectiveness would not assume that all clients would be placed without Homebuilders involvement. In more and more communities, placements do not exist, and even families whose problems are so severe that they should be placed often struggle along for years, or find the children living on the street indefinitely. Even so, it is certain that some of the cases referred to Homebuilders would have been placed. Even a few placements would justify the program's costs. For example, Homebuilders'

Table 7. Average Costs per Placement per Child in New York

Placement type	Average cost/year ($)	Average length of stay (years)	Average cost per child ($)
Foster home 0–3 years	10,794	3.21	34,649
Foster home 4–5 years	10,302	3.21	33,069
Foster home 6–11 years	11,141	3.21	35,763
Foster home 12–15 years	12,091	3.21	38,812
Foster boarding home over 16	12,220	3.21	39,226
Group home	30,624	3.21	98,303
Psychiatric residential facility	60,225	1.5	90,338

Table 8. Projected Placements and Costs for Homebuilders Clients May 1, 1987–October 31, 1987

Projected placement	Number of Homebuilders cases	Cost Per case ($)	Total projected costs ($)
FH 0-3	5	34,649	173,245
FH 4-5	2	33,069	66,138
FH 6-11	7	35,763	250,341
FH 12-15	1	38,812	38,812
FH 16-18	1	39,226	39,226
Group homes	18	98,303	1,769,454
Psychiatric institute	2	90,338	180,676
Total	36		2,517,892

first six months' costs in New York (including large amounts of startup costs) were $211,824. In terms of average costs of placements, it would be necessary to avert only 2.2 group home placements, 2.3 psychiatric placements, or 6.1 infant foster care placements.

Summaries of Major Studies

Over the years we have received a number of public and private grants that have allowed us, and others, to study our program in some detail. These efforts have often been humbling experiences. Research endeavors are never as simple, inexpensive, or definitive as they might first appear.

Each of the studies has limitations. Many have small samples. The studies are difficult to compare with one another because the definitions of avoidance of placement vary. In some, only official placements for any length of time documented by the State are counted. In others, any targeted children living for 2 weeks or more outside the home are counted as service failures or "placement cases." Follow-up times vary, from termination, to 1 year after intake. Probably our most serious problem has always been, and remains, the assumption that children we serve really would have been placed outside the home if Homebuilders had been unavailable. Quasiexperimental studies indicate between 76 and 100% of overflow cases do get placed, we have not yet been able to obtain the funding necessary to do a tight control study with random assignment of cases and a follow-up period long enough to assess placement rates the way we would like. We will discuss some of the specific difficulties we have had regarding control group attempts in an effort to give some perspective regarding the difficulty of implementing this type of study in the field, where referring workers' priorities rightly rest with individual clients' welfare rather than abstract concerns about cost-effectiveness.

Despite all these caveats, based on our collective work and the research of those associated with similar programs across North America (McDonald & Associates, Inc., 1987), there is reason to believe that programs like Homebuilders hold great promise as effective and efficient mechanisms that contribute to increased improvement, at least over the short run, in child and family functioning, as well as decrease or postpone the need for children to enter long-term out-of-home placements.

Homebuilders Juvenile Delinquent and Status Offenders Study.   In 1976 we received a grant from what was then the U.S. Department of Health, Education, and Welfare, Office of Child Development, to do a randomly assigned controlled research study to evaluate Homebuilders treatment effectiveness. We worked closely with the Washington State Department of Social and Health Services (DSHS) Office of Research. We were to get all our referrals from Pierce County (Tacoma) Juvenile Court. Whenever we got a referral, the design of the study called for us to contact our DSHS referral liaison who would then look at a table of random numbers and tell us whether to assign the case to the control or treatment condition.

The referring caseworkers from the juvenile court rapidly learned to hate the research referral system. Due to fears that the whole project might not have enough caseworker support to continue, we changed the procedure so that cases referred when we were open were treated by Homebuilders, and cases referred when we had no openings were assigned to the comparison group.

Caseworkers were very creative in developing ways to "beat the system." Some of the methods are described below:

1.   Some courtworkers would not refer a child and family unless the courtworkers were sure ahead of time that they could get clients that they felt needed the Homebuilders service into the treatment group. They learned how many therapists we had and developed pretty good hunches as to when we would have an opening and when our cases were being terminated based on discussions with their peers at the juvenile court. Due to a design flaw that assigned a case to the treatment or control condition *before* taking the client's name, it was possible for court workers to call in referrals to the program with a list of client names—some they wanted in the treatment group and some they

wanted in the control group. When they learned the condition of the case (treatment or control) they would shuffle through their list and then give the intake coordinator the name of a family that they wanted to receive the Homebuilders service if the condition was "treatment" or the name of a family that did not "need" the service if the condition was "control." Once we realized what was happening, the procedure was changed so that a client name had to be given *first*, then the condition was assigned.

2. Caseworkers would also tell families they thought were really appropriate to self-refer through another channel into our regular Homebuilders program, which was not part of the research study, thereby circumventing all the research hassle.

3. Caseworkers would stop referring all together if several cases were put in the control group.

4. Some caseworkers perceived placement of comparison cases as personal failure and reported using extraordinary means in an attempt to have their comparison group cases avoid placement.

In the second year of the study, due to a change in the jurisdiction for status-offending youth by the Washington State Legislature, the responsibility for these juveniles suddenly became the responsibility of the Washington State Department of Social and Health Services (DSHS). This change in jurisdiction also forced Homebuilders to move the subject pool for the research project over to DSHS. Fortunately, we were able to negotiate the research procedure with the staff at DSHS and continue the study.

An additional problem in this study was related to follow-up data. Especially in the comparison group it was difficult to locate the families to determine outcomes for the children targeted for placement.

The results of this study showed that 30 of the 41, or 73% treatment cases averted out-of-home placement for 12 months after intake. In the comparison group 5 of the 18, or 28% of the youths targeted for out-of-home care avoided placement. Average cost for treatment cases was $2,182 per case. Average cost per comparison was $4,991, for an average difference of $2,809 per case (Kinney, 1982).

Homebuilders Children's Mental Health Study. In 1979, Homebuilders began a demonstration project funded by the Washington State Legislature to evaluate the effectiveness of the Homebuilders model with mentally ill and severely emotionally disturbed children and youth. Thirty youths (25 treatment and 5 "overflow" comparison group cases) from Pierce County were referred to Homebuilders from the Office of Involuntary Commitment as an alternative to inpatient psychiatric hospitalization.

It was predicted that these children and their families would need a higher impact service and the basic Homebuilders model was supplemented in the following ways: The three most experienced Homebuilders were used most frequently for the Children's Mental Health cases and received twice as much supervision time. It was expected that the cases would extend beyond the normal 4 weeks so the three counselors were responsible for seeing only the 25 "mental health' cases during the year, as opposed to 54 regular Homebuilders cases. The counselors received additional training in psychotropic medication, suicide, and dealing with violent clients. In addition, psychiatric consultation was available, as needed.

Improvement in Functioning

Improvements in individual and family functioning were measured by Achenbach's (1974) Child Behavior Checklist (CBCL) and through Global Assessment Scales (GAS). Average scores are reported. Because the data are reported in aggregate form, it is not possible to provide additional statistical information. The original data are currently unavailable for access due to changes in Homebuilders' parent agency.

CBCL Scores.   Average "pre" score = 81.7; average "post" score = 43.9. The higher the CBCL score, the more problematic the child's behavior. A score of 38 indicates the high end of the "normal range" so these children, with an original score of 81.7, were demonstrating severe behavior problems. At the end of treatment they were approaching the "normal" range.

GAS Scores.   Average "pre" score was 29.1, "moderate" impairment in functioning, average "post" score was 57.6 closer to "slight" interference with functioning.

Parent Ratings of Improvements.   Parents were asked at termination to rate their children's presenting problems as "better," "worse," or "the same." Their ratings are presented in Table 9.

Placement Status

Children's living situations were tracked by research staff for twelve months after intake. They are as follows:

19 (76%) of the 25 youth remained at home
 2 (8%) were placed in psychiatric hospitals

3 (12%) were placed in group homes
1 (4%) was placed in juvenile detention

Cost-Effectiveness

Project cost effectiveness was evaluated by a comparison of Home-builders costs with costs of clients who were assessed as appropriate for hospitalization by the Office of Involuntary Commitment, referred to Homebuilders, but not accepted because the program was full. Home-builders costs were calculated by dividing the first year budget ($128,240) by the number of clients (25) to yield an average cost by client of $5,130.

All five comparison cases were immediately placed, four in psychiatric hospitals, and one in a correctional institution. Costs were projected using average costs and lengths of stay for those settings. This was $12,463 more than the costs for Homebuilders.

Homebuilders Critical Incident Study

Using a modified Critical Incident Technique (Flanagan, 1954), this study evaluated the process and outcome of the Homebuilders program (Fraser and Haapala, 1987-88; Haapala, 1983). Forty-one mothers, children and the therapists who served these families were interviewed following targeted therapy sessions. These interviews occurred once a week. Treatment was considered successful only if children had remained continually in the home from the initiation of treatment through the 3-month, posttermination follow-up period. Cases in which children were placed, ran, or lived with relatives or friends outside the home were defined as failures.

A one-page interview guide was developed to gather client and therapist descriptions of critical incidents occurring during treatment sessions. Interviews were conducted independently with mothers, children, and therapists. Participants were asked to describe as many behaviorally discrete incidents that positively or negatively influenced the helpfulness of the most recent treatment session (within 24 hours) as could be remembered. Audio tapes of each research interview were made for subsequent coding of reported critical incidents. This interview and taping method allowed interviewers to gather rich and detailed information.

Through the interview process, 1,200 critical incidents from therapy sessions were reported. Moments of conflict, joy, insight, and other events such as interruptions, behavioral charting, and practice of new skills were reported. Each incident was rated by respondents on a seven

Table 9.   Parent and Therapist Ratings of Client Improvement at Termination[a]

| | | Parent and therapist's ratings of condition at termination | | |
| | Number of cases with problem | Worse | Same | Better |
Problems	at intake	(%)	(%)	(%)
Disorientation	5			100
Delusions	3			100
Hallucinations	2			100
Inappropriate affect	8			100
Assault to others	13			92
Social isolation	9		44	56
Lack of cooperation	11		10	90
Lack of motivation	7			100
Dependency	12			100
Depression	16	6	6	88
Drug abuse	6	16.5	16.5	67
Alcohol abuse	6		75	25
Learning disability	4		75	25
Sexual assault to others	1			100
Thought disorder	1			100
Affective disorder	5			100
No school	10		30	70
Anxiety	17	6	18	76
Medical problems	2		100	
Problems with anger	17	6		94
Sleep disturbance	3		33	67
Hyperactivity	7		14	86
Impaired judgement	15		20	80
Obessional rituals	2			100
Speech impairment	2		100	
Delinquent acts	8	12	25	63
Poor impulse control	12		25	75
Psychosomatic illness	3		33	67
Phobias	7			100
Peer problems	11		36	64
Physical handicap	1		100	
Averages		1.5	17	81.5

[a] $N = 20$. Five cases were still open at the time of this report.

point Likert scale of helpfulness (extremely helpful to extremely unhelpful). The incidents themselves were categorized by independent judges using the constant comparative method (Glaser and Strauss, 1967). This method provided a coding and analytic procedure to classify the reported incidents into themes that characterize Homebuilders treatment. This qualitative method was selected for data reduction because it was most likely to preserve the rich character of the data and allowed categories to emerge from the data without a preconceived structure. The interrater reliability for all events scored was based on the agreement scores of two independent raters who sorted critical incidents into thematic categories. The interrater reliability for 1,200 events was 87.32%. In those cases on which judges did not agree on the placement of an event in a thematic category, the event was eliminated from further analysis. The final number of incidents used in the constant comparison was 1,120.

Individual events reported by each of the respondents were not qualitatively compared from each treatment session. Rather they were analyzed in the aggregate across respondents and all therapy sessions.

A comparison of the occurrences of each of the eight types of incidents that occurred during Homebuilders treatment resulted in two significant differences between the two outcome groups. In relation to mothers whose children were "placed" outside the home, a significantly higher proportion of mothers whose children remained in the home reported the provision of concrete services by therapists (Table 10).

Second, as shown in Table 11, a significantly higher proportion of mothers whose children remained in the home also reported treatment interruptions.

Clinically, the findings suggest the importance of expanding the definition of those activities that are considered to be therapeutic in a therapeutic relationship, and they distinguish the help given by professionals from that of neighbors, relatives, and friends. Although the provisions of concrete assistance may not in itself be sufficient as a treatment, it may play a larger role in setting the stage for successful

Table 10. Cross-Tabulation of Child Placement by Mother's Reports of Therapist-Provided Concrete Assistance ($N = 41$)[a,b]

Child placement	Concrete assistance	
	Yes	No
In-home	10	9
Out-of-home	3	19

[a] Taken from Fraser and Haapala (1987–88).
[b] Corrected $\chi^2 = 5,472$, $df = 1$, $p < 0.5$. Fisher exact test: p(2-tailed) $= .017$.

Table 11.   Cross-Tabulation of Child
Placement by Mother's Reports
of Interruptions during
Treatment Sessions ($N = 41$)[a,b]

| | Interruptions | |
Child placement	Yes	No
In-Home	12	7
Out-of-Home	2	20

[a] Taken from Fraser and Haapala (1987–88).
[b] Corrected $\chi^2 = 10,958$, $df = 1$, $p < .001$.
Fischer exact test: p(2-tailed) = .001.

intervention than previously believed. In this study and others, treatment that incorporated concrete assistance resulted in more successful outcomes (see, e.g., Hepworth and Larson, 1986; p. 541; Avison, Turner and Noh, 1986; Wahler, Leske, and Rogers, 1979; Wahler, 1980; and Whittaker and Garbarino, 1983). Family therapists who offered concrete services appear to have helped families solve important and stress–provoking problems. It appears that they were able to use this helping experience to establish a rapport with clients that created an entree to equally (and perhaps more) complex psychological and social problems. The strategic use of concrete problem-solving to build trust and to bring to bear clinical skills on sensitive, family interactional problems, distinguishes professional help from that provided by neighbors and friends.

Finally, one element of the home-based treatment approach was consistently rated as unhelpful, and yet it distinguished successful from unsuccessful outcomes. Interruptions during treatment sessions accounted for 10% of all incidents. As opposed to clinic-based models of treatment where the setting is controlled and interruption-free, the in-home model assumes that interruptions will occur in the course of contact. However, therapists are trained to take advantage of disruptions in order to demonstrate problem-solving. Such an approach is thought to enhance the generalizability of the intervention to home life.

Interestingly, mothers of children who remained in the home reported significantly more interruptions. This finding is consistent with the argument that family interventions are successful to the extent that therapists are able to deal with real-life family problems. For clients with successful outcomes, interruptions appear to have afforded therapists more opportunities to teach and demonstrate structured problem-solving. We hypothesize that mothers in the "success" group reported more interruptions as learning opportunities. In vivo interventions afford these opportunities by their very nature, but therapists must be carefully trained to make full use of them. Additional research on interruptions and the use of them by therapists is needed, for it is merely our suspicion that successful therapists took greater advantage of disruptions. No data were gathered on the way therapists responded to disruptions.

Homebuilders Developmental Disabilities Project

In 1981 we began a project to test whether Homebuilders could prevent a developmentally delayed client's move to a more restrictive environment, or to facilitate a client's move to a less restrictive placement. Thirteen out of fifteen, or 87% of the clients referred were able to prevent a move to a more restrictive setting. Two out of two, or 100% of those referred were successful in moving to a less restrictive placement with Homebuilders. Referring workers rated 88% of clients referred because of aggressive or destructive behavior as improved. Eighty-two percent of clients referred because of recurring episodes of problem behaviors such as stealing, tantrums, or self-injurious behavior had improved.

Homebuilders Special Needs Adoption Project

Homebuilders intensive, home-based Family Preservation Services were provided to 22 special needs children living in 20 adoptive family homes (Haapala, McDade, and Johnston, 1988). All adopted children were at imminent risk of out-of-home placement due to problems such as child's noncompliance, child's mental health problems, or poor parenting skills or lack of bonding. An average of 63 hours was spent by Homebuilders therapists in case-related activities for each of the 20 families. Cases were open for an average of 27 days. At the 3-month follow-up point, 77% of the children avoided formal out-of-home placements. These children were either living in their adoptive homes or with relatives. For 18 or the 20 families, Goal Attainment Scale scores were above 50, indicating that the goal was achieved at a level that was beyond the therapist's expectations. At termination, 12 families showed positive change, 6 families showed no change, and 1 family showed a worsened condition on the Family Risk Scales. According to referring caseworkers ($N = 17$), no progress was made on 9 of the caseworkers' family treatment goals, some progress was made on 9 of the caseworkers' treatment goals, and considerable progress was made on 14 of the caseworkers' treatment goals. Primary caretakers from 16 of the 20 families completed Goal Checklists at service intake, and 15 of them completed the Checklists at termination.

The status of these children looked much different at the 3- and 12-month follow- up points. Table 12 summarizes this information.

Of the 22 children, 10 (46%) had spent some time in at least one formal out-of-home placement. Another 4 (18%) had runaway or lived on the streets for some period of time. Only 8 (36%) of the 22 children completely avoided any time out of their adoptive family's or a relative's home.

Over the course of the 12-month follow-up period some of the children went through a series of placements and/or runaway episodes. It should be noted however, that at the point of 12-month follow-up only 32% of these youths were actually reported to be living in formal out-of-home care.

These findings support other research demonstrating less successful placement avoidance outcomes for children who have previously been formally placed in out-of-home care (Pecora, Fraser, and Haapala, 1988). Some of these children had experienced multiple placements and may, therefore, be at even greater risk for additional placement experiences.

Because little is known regarding the reasonable expectations for maintaining a disrupted special needs adoption placement once the child and/or family has seriously considered terminating the relationship, it is difficult to determine the potential placement avoidance impact of a service like Homebuilders. Based on other measures of treatment

Table 12.   Summary of Progressive Case Outcomes: Homebuilders Special Needs Adoption Project

| | Living situation of children at risk (N = 22)[a] | | |
	Termination	Three months after termination	12 months after termination
Adoptive home or relative's home	17 (77%)	14 (64%)	8 (36%)
On the street/ runaway or with friends	3 (14%)	5 (23%)	4 (18%)
Formal out-of-home placement	2 (9%)	3 (14%)	10 (46%)

[a] Once a child was a runaway or placed in formal out-of-home care, that outcome defined the child in all later assessments unless the child went into a less "socially desirable" living situation.

success gathered at Homebuilders termination (Goal Attainment, Family Risk Scale scores, etc.) there appears to be, at least initially, a success affect attributed to the Homebuilders service. This report did not collect extended longitudinal data on these measures so that it is not clear how long the discrete positive clinical affects lasted.

This approach may provide a valuable option to serving cases of special needs adoptions disruption, given the current state of effective services available to help adoptees and their families. Further study is needed to more clearly determine placement prevention as well as behavior change impact.

Family-Based Intensive Treatment (FIT) Research Project

The Family-Based Intensive Treatment (FIT) Research Project was designed to describe the outcomes of intensive home-based family treatment services based on the "Homebuilders" model. The research question that provided the focal point for the investigation was: "What factors are associated with family-based child welfare service failures?" Data on child, parent, family, service, and system characteristics were collected and used to describe the differences between successful and unsuccessful family-based treatment.

"Service failure" was defined in such a way as to include an unusually broad number of out-of-home conditions. Conventional out-of-home placements such as foster care, group care, and inpatient psychiatric hospitalization were included in the definition along with short-term placements such as shelter care, crisis or receiving care, and detention. In addition, if a child was on the run or moved out of the home to live with a neighbor, friend, or other non-relative, this was considered to be equivalent to an out-of-home placement. The "placement" of a child in any of these conditions outside the home for 2 weeks or more during the provision of family preservation services (FPS) or within 12 months following FPS intake was defined as "treatment failure." Based on follow-up interviews with parents and management information system reports, placement data were collected on all children in the families that participated in the study.

From these data, two kinds of placement outcomes were computed. First, a "family preservation" outcome was created by classifying families from which no child was placed as "successful." If even one child from the family was placed, the family's treatment was considered to have failed, i.e., Family Preservation Services were unsuccessful. Hence, this measure was called "family preservation." A second placement measure, based on individual children who were designated as being at risk of placement, was also used. It is a direct measure of the number of children at risk who were placed, regardless of whether they were in the same family. In this report, family preservation is used as the major outcome measure, and data analyses focus on identifying those system and family characteristics that distinguish successful from unsuccessful Family Preservation Services.

Research Design and Methods

A total of 453 families from the states of Utah and Washington participated in the study (Fraser, Pecora, and Haapala, 1989). The services in Washington were provided by Homebuilders in four counties; Pierce (Tacoma), King (Seattle), Spokane, and Snohomish. The services in Utah were modeled after the Homebuilders program and delivered through two public child welfare agency offices. The characteristics of services in each state were measured carefully using over 100 variables, and the key elements of service were identified and described.

A quasiexperimental longitudinal design was used, supplemented by a small case overflow control group ($N = 26$) in Utah. The control group was comprised of families that were referred for home-based services, met the criteria for admission, but could not be served because workers' caseloads were full. Data regarding child and family functioning for the total study sample were collected at four points in time: intake, service termination, 12 months after service intake, and whenever a service failure (child placement or runaway behavior) occurred. Of the 453 families, 263 started treatment sufficiently early in the study to permit 12-month follow-up. Outcome data for this group are reported separately.

Selected Findings

Intensive in-home services appear to improve child and family functioning. They also appear to affect placement rates.

Family Preservation and Child-based Placement Rates.   Even with a conservative definition of treatment success (failure defined as any non-relative placement or runaway episode for two weeks or more), the FPS workers were able to achieve success in preventing placement at the 12-month follow-up point with 71.4% of the children in the Washington sample, and 61.9% of the children in Utah at risk of placement in the total sample.

Parent and child changes in functioning. A variety of child and family outcome measures such as the Child Welfare League of America Family at Risk Scales (Magura, Moses, and Jones, 1987), as well as instruments that measured changes in family cohesion and adaptability (FACES III) and social support (Milardo, 1983) were used. As indicated earlier, the placement locations of children in the treatment and control group families were tracked using management information system reports and interviews with primary caretakers.

Based on FPS worker ratings of pre- and post-treatment functioning, families experiencing treatment success made significant positive changes on 21 measures. Results are shown in Table 13.

FIT study families who were service failures showed significant improvements on only nine measures during treatment, shown in Table 14.

Table 13. Successful Families

Families that were classified as successes made significant improvements during treatment on the 21 following measures:

1. Habitability of residence
2. Suitability of living conditions
3. Social support
4. Primary caretaker's mental health
5. Supervision of young children (primary caretaker)
6. Parenting of older children (primary and secondary caretakers)
7. Use of physical punishment (primary and secondary caretakers)
8. Verbal discipline (primary and secondary caretakers)
9. Motivation to solve family problems (primary and secondary caretakers)
10. Attitude toward placement (primary and secondary caretakers)
11. Knowledge of child care and development (primary and secondary caretakers)
12. Primary caretaker's abuse of substances (primary and secondary caretakers)
13. Child's mental health (first, second, and third oldest)
14. Child's physical health (second oldest)
15. Child's physical needs such as meals, clothing, bathing, and shots (first oldest)
16. Child's school adjustment (first, second, and third oldest)
17. Emotional care and stimulation of children (first and second oldest)
18. Child delinquency (first, second, and third oldest)
19. Child's home-related behavior (first, second, and third oldest)
20. Sexual harassment of child in the home (second oldest)
21. Adult relationships

Table 14.   Families That Experienced a Placement or Runaway Episode

---

Families that failed in the FIT Study made significant improvements on the nine following measures during treatment:

1. Parenting of older children (primary and secondary caretakers)
2. Use of physical punishment
3. Use of verbal discipline (primary and secondary caretakers)
4. Knowledge of child care and development
5. Meeting the physical need of the second oldest child
6. Child's school adjustment
7. Emotional care and stimulation of children
8. Child's delinquent behavior (first and third oldest children)
9. Child's home-related behavior (first and second oldest)

Family and Nonfamily Social Support.   Three stable and reliable dimensions of social support were found to characterize the social networks of primary and secondary caretakers. During the course of service, most caretakers' relationships with their spouses (when there was one) became less aversive. Primary caretakers reported that their contacts with extended family members and friends became more empathic and understanding. Successful and unsuccessful families were distinguished by a greater order of change in the aversive nature of their social interactions. Caretakers in families that avoided placement appear to have been relatively more effective in reducing negative contacts with spouses, extended family members, co-workers, and friends.

Consumer Ratings of Satisfaction with Services and the "Social Desirability" of Placement.   In terms of general satisfaction with FPS, primary caretakers rated home-based family treatment as very helpful. Even in families where a child had been placed, 78% of the primary caretakers felt that placement was the best alternative for their family. Conversely, when the child remained in the home, 89% of the primary caretakers thought that avoidance of placement was the best for their family. Primary caretakers rated both the home-based nature of service and its skills focus as important service elements.

Bronx Homebuilders Program

The Bronx Homebuilders program began serving families in May 1987, one year after the beginning of planning and preparation. Based on the same concept as the Behavioral Sciences Institute's Homebuilders

Programs in Washington State, the Bronx Homebuilders Program has been an experiment in many levels.

The information below serves to report some key preliminary information about the Homebuilders Program. It also compares some Washington State Homebuilders Program data with comparable data from the Bronx Homebuilders Program.

Data from the Washington State sample represents 376 families with 532 children an imminent risk of placement that were referred to Homebuilders Programs in King, Pierce, Spokane, and Snohomish counties from September 1987 through August 1988. Data from the Bronx represent 58 families with 101 children at imminent risk of placement referred to the Bronx Homebuilders Program from May 1987 through August 1988. Information is shown in Table 15.

Table 15. Demographic Information Regarding Washington State and Bronx Clients

Demographic characteristics	Washington	The Bronx
Age of children at risk		
0–5	130 (24%)	21 (21%)
6–10	127 (24%)	28 (28%)
11–14	166 (31%)	33 (33%)
15–17	106 (20%)	19 (19%)
Race of children at risk		
Hispanic	1%	56%
Black	8%	30%
Caucasian	80%	14%
Other (Asian, Native American)	11%	0
Family structure		
Percent of single-parent families	54%	72%
Income		
Percent with incomes less than $10,000/year	36%	50%
Case characteristics		
Average length of case in days	29.3	36.4
Average hours of direct contact with clients per case		
Face-to-face contact	38.3	42.7
Telephone contact	2.9	3.5
Placement status		
Percent of children in official placement 3 months after termination of Homebuilders	22 of 532 children = (4%)	13 of 101 children = (13%)

Whereas the age groupings of the Washington and Bronx client children appear quite similar, the race of the children, family structure, and family income are quite different.

The Bronx families are poorer, have more single parents, and the children are predominately Hispanic and Black.

The Bronx program serves its families for about a week longer than the Washington families are served. Staff in the Bronx program also spend more face-to-face and telephone contact time with their client families. The length of service and number of hours may represent a learning phase associated with the Bronx program being a new Homebuilders program.

Auditor's and Outside Evaluators

Over the years, Homebuilders has been more or less formally evaluated by many groups including American Criminal Justice Institute, a National Science Foundation Committee in conjunction with the Boys Town Centers for Youth Development, the National Institute for Mental Health, the Washington State Department of Social and Health Services, Division of Mental Health and Office of Research, the Washington State Legislature, and the Oregon Council on Crime and Delinquency. All reports have been highly positive.

Quality Enhancement Systems and Training (QUEST)

As our own programs have grown, and developed in different sites, some clear across the country from one another, it has become increasingly difficult to know what is going on in each site, and to convey the most important aspects of management to new managers with little exposure to the original site. Some of our trainees, such as those in New Jersey and Michigan, have begun many programs within a very short time frame.

In order to develop and maintain the quality we all would like, we have developed standards for programs, supervisors and therapists. This standards project, called Quality Enhancement Systems and Training (QUEST) includes definitions of desired qualities, rationales and methods for testing to see whether these qualities are occurring. We will also develop standards for administrators, intake workers, trainers and evaluators. Lists of standards for programs, supervisors and therapists are shown in Table 16.

Routine Program Evaluation Procedures

Homebuilders has wanted to know not only if we were achieving the outcomes we had hoped, but whether we were achieving them in a way that was satisfactory to all involved. We continuously gather feedback regarding our treatment methods and processes, using this feedback to revise and refine procedures.

Goal Attainment Scaling

Homebuilders has used Goal Attainment Scaling as the foundation of all their record keeping, to monitor client progress on individual presenting problems. Goal Attainment Scaling was first developed by Kiresuk and Sherman (1968) as an evaluation method for community mental health centers. It allows for the development and monitoring of individualized goals pertinent to each family as opposed to general criteria of improvement.

Goal Attainment Scales at Homebuilders are used to clarify goals, to retain an accurate index of events for record keeping purposes, and to assess whether change or progress is occurring in any one area of concern. The potential outcome levels are represented numerically by +2, +1, 0, −1, and −2. The qualitative differences of these ratings are as follows:

GOAL: Statement of specific goal

+2 = Best Anticipated Success
+1 = More Than Expected Success
 0 = Less Than Expected Success (in conjunction with treatment plan)
−1 = Less Than Expected Success
−2 = The Most Unfavorable Outcome Likely

The therapist works with the clients to insert potential outcome levels in the rating scale that are relevant to clients' specific goals. For example:

+2 = 80% school attendance this week
+1 = 60% school attendance this week
 0 = 40% school attendance this week
−1 = 20% school attendance this week
−2 = No school attendance this week

Table 16.   Program, Supervisor, and Therapist Standards

Program Standards
  1. Service provided in the natural environment
  2. Intensity of services
  3. Two-family caseload
  4. Short-term intervention
  5. Single counselor with team back-up
  6. Immediate intake
  7. Preventing unnecessary placement
  8. Emphasis on staff training and skill development
  9. Ecological approach
  10. Supervision for staff
  11. Goal-oriented, data-based decision making
  12. Unified agency philosophy
  13. Twenty-four hour availability

Supervisor Standards
  1. Clinical consultation
  2. Assessing and managing staff performance
  3. Administrative planning
  4. Decision making/judgment
  5. Hiring
  6. Community relations
  7. Teaching
  8. Support
  9. Leadership
  10. Time management
  11. Team membership

Therapist Standards
  1. Promoting safety
  2. Availability
  3. Engaging clients
  4. Interactive assessment
  5. Teaching
  6. Concrete services
  7. Interactive listening
  8. Facilitating change using behavioral strategies
  9. Facilitating change using cognitive strategies
  10. Constructive feedback
  11. Teamwork
  12. Community relations
  13. Advocacy
  14. Intervention quotas
  15. Documentation
  16. Termination

As the example specifies, a "0" or expected level of success is 40% school attendance, with the other scale points representing deviations from this expected level. It is desirable to calibrate the scale so there is equal distance between points. Outcome levels should ideally be expressed in clear, measurable terms.

Therapists must also be careful to avoid including numerous aspects or problems in one goal, and having too many goals per client. Four ongoing goals per family is probably the maximum number that is manageable. The potential outcome levels on a goal attainment scale are usually rated weekly in conjunction with a summary of the week's goal relevant activity to clarify and to substantiate the rating choice.

These ratings allow clients, therapists, supervisors and auditors to monitor progress on client presenting problems. The struggle for clarification of goals by therapists and clients can be an important treatment intervention. Written goals, monitored weekly, force therapists to be more focused in how they spend their time.

Client Feedback

We have solicited feedback from all client families since the beginning of the program. We always collect this information within 1 week of termination. Depending on personnel resources, we also collect feedback 3 and 12 months after intake. The method of data collection is also dependent on personnel resources. If we are tight, the therapists leave forms at the last visit for clients to mail in. Most commonly, secretaries and intake staff make phone call to families. When we have research grants we are able to send research staff to client homes for detailed interviews. We want to know if placement occurred, but also want to know how clients felt they were treated, whether our therapists did what we say they do, and, most important, whether the clients felt the intervention was helpful. Table 17 shows questions asked clients and a summary of responses for clients during the calendar year 1988.

Referring Worker Feedback

More recently, we have begun soliciting feedback from referring workers as well. Questions we are asking, and a summary of responses from 15 workers in Snohomish County in Washington are shown in Table 18.

Table 17.   Client Termination Survey

1. Respondents: Total: 367
   Mother/mother figure: 302 (82%)   PR   :   6 (2%)
   Father/father figure   :   59 (16%)   Other: 2 (1%)
2. Was it helpful that therapist came to your home for appointments?
   1   Yes   338—92%
   2   No   6—2%
   3   Sometimes   13—4%
   4   No opinion   6—2%
   5   No answer   4—1%
3. Did therapist schedule appointments for times that were convenient for you?
   1   Yes   349—95%
   2   No   7—2%
   3   Sometimes   9—2%
   4   No opinion   0—0%
   5   No answer   2—1%
4. Do you think therapist listened to and understood your situation?
   1   Yes   346—94%
   2   No   5—1%
   3   Sometimes   13—4%
   4   No opinion   1—0%
   5   No answer   2—1%
5. Did you ever feel hurried or pressured by the therapist?
   1   Yes   6—2%
   2   No   210—57%
   3   Sometimes   6—2%
   4   No opinion   1—0%
   5   No answer   144—39%
6. Did you have the feeling that you could depend or rely on therapist when you needed him/her?
   1   Yes   337—92%
   2   No   5—1%
   3   Sometimes   10—3%
   4   No opinion   2—0%
   5   No answer   13—4%
7. Did you feel that therapist knew what he/she was doing, that he/she was organized?
   1   Yes   297—81%
   2   No   1—0%
   3   Sometimes   9—2%
   4   No opinion   2—0%
   5   No answer   58—16%
8. Did therapist ever seem to take sides?
   1   Yes   18—5%
   2   No   321—87%

3 Sometimes   19—5%
4 No opinion   5—1%
5 No answer   4—1%

9. How is the situation for your family now, as compared with when you first began working with (therapist)?
   1 A lot worse now   2%
   2 A little worse now   2%
   3 About the same now   13%
   4 A little better now   32%
   5 A lot better now   51%

10. In general, how satisfied are you with the way you and (therapist) got along together?
   1 Very satisfied   86%
   2 Somewhat satisfied   6%
   3 Neither satisfied nor dissatisfied   2%
   4 Somewhat dissatisfied   2%
   5 Very dissatisfied   3%

11. Are target children living at home now? (indicate number)
   Yes   375   (89%)
   No   47   (11%)

12. How helpful was Homebuilders for your family?
   1 Not at all   4%
   2   3%
   3   11%
   4   23%
   5 Very helpful   60%

13. Did you have counseling before Homebuilders?
   Yes   64%
   No   36%

14. How helpful was the previous counseling?
   1 Not at all   36%
   2   19%
   3   26%
   4   8%
   5 Very helpful   11%

15. Would you recommend Homebuilders to a family in a similar situation?
   Yes   97%
   No   1%
   No opinion   1%

Table 18.   Referring Worker Feedback

1. How satisfied are you with the amount of contact (phone and in-person) you had with the Homebuilders therapist?
   1 (Not satisfied at all) = 0%
   2   = 0%
   3   = 0%
   4   = 33%
   5 (Very satisfied)   = 67%

2. How satisfied were you with the nature of the contact you had with the Homebuilders therapist? E.g. Was the therapist responsive, accessible, professional?
   1 (Not satisfied at all) = 0%
   2   = 0%
   3   = 0%
   4   = 25%
   5 (Very satisfied)   = 75%

3. How satisfied were you that the treatment goals set by the Homebuilders therapist were appropriate for this family? E.g. Consistent with those you identified in the referral.
   1 (Not satisfied at all) = 0%
   2   = 0%
   3   = 0%
   4   = 8%
   5 (Very satisfied)   = 92%

4. How satisfied are you with the amount of progress that was achieved with the family? Why?
   1 (Not satisfied at all) = 0%
   2   = 0%
   3   = 8%
   4   = 50%
   5 (Very satisfied)   = 50%
   No answer   = 8%

5. How satisfied were you with the termination letter? E.g. Too positive—balanced presentation: too long—enough detail; clearly written; useful/not useful assessment information?
   1 (Not satisfied at all) = 0%
   2   = 8%
   3   = 8%
   4   = 34%
   5 (Very satisfied)   = 50%

6a. Was there anything about the Homebuilder intervention that has made it more difficult for you to continue working with this family?
    Yes   = 14%
    No   = 72%
    No answer = 14%

6b. What do you think this family needs now to preserve the gains made during Homebuilder intervention?
Part I:
a. Does not need further services = 0%
b. Casework (respondent) can   = 0%
   keep the family at present
   level through routine
   contacts/services.
c. Needs additional professional = 100%
   help.
Part II: Do you think the family will get the follow-up help you think it needs?
Yes   = 60%
No   = 20%
Not sure = 20%
Part III: Was there anything about the Homebuilder intervention that has made your follow-up work with the family more difficult?
Yes =   0%
No = 100%

Staff Feedback

The Current Status Review.   The Current Status Review (Wetzel, 1989) has recently been employed by countywide therapist–supervisor units at BSI to review the activities of the team over the last year, and evaluate what seems to be working, what is not working, and what needs to be done next. In a half-day session, a facilitator draws out the opinions of staff and writes down the main ideas on butcher paper. The structuring of the meeting guides participants through a listing of important events over the last year. It also separates out and identifies what seems to be going well and what isn't related to any part of the program. For example, staff may point out that the janitor doesn't seem to be cleaning the office as well as he used to, they may identify a trend of low referrals, or frustration with the lack of success among clients who appear to share similar characteristics. From these findings brainstorming occurs to generate options to improve and maintain the program site. After the potential solutions are prioritized, an action plan is developed that establishes commitments among staff to try specific strategies to alter identified problems and assess their effectiveness.

"How's it Going? Questionnaire."   From time to time administrators send out short surveys to all staff that ask organization members to reveal their current status. Questions frequently revolve around compar-

ative satisfaction with job, perceived problems, possible solutions, feedback on specific newly implemented policies or procedures, etc. They are generally anonymous.

These surveys, once compiled, offer feedback to all staff, but particularly administrators and supervisors, that can be used to assess possible problem areas, degree of impact on staff, and potential solutions to be considered. This technique, over the years, has been a tremendously worthwhile tool in addressing morale problems, unpopular policies and procedures, as well as occasionally validating the sense that all is well. Table 19 shows a list of sample questions from "How's It Going?" Questionnaires.

Table 19.   Sample Questions from "How's It Going?" Questionnaire

---

1. Overall, on a 1–10 scale, where 10 is very satisfied and 1 is very dissatisfied, how would you rate your job satisfaction at BSI now?
2. Compared with other jobs you have had, are you more or less satisfied (1 = much less satisfied, 10 = much more satisfied)?
3. If you were to guess, how long would you predict you would stay at BSI?
4. What have been the three things you have liked the most about your job at BSI during 1988? Please rate them on a 1–10 point scale where 1 is mildly pleasant and 10 is wonderful, fantastic, one of the best things ever related to work.
5. What have been three worst things about your job at BSI during 1988? Please rate them on a 1–10 point scale where 1 is mildly unpleasant and 10 is horrible.
6. What are three things you would most like to see happen at BSI in the next year?
7. What are three things you would least like to happen at BSI in the next year?
8. How happy or sad are you about the quantity and quality of supervision you have been getting? 1 = Very poor, 10 = Very wonderful.
9. Are there things that you would like BSI administrators to do that they don't do? If so, what?
10. Do you feel you have had enough say in decisions that are made at BSI? If not, what decisions?
11. If you don't feel you have enough say in decisions that are made at BSI, how could we include you better?
12. Are there any other things you or others are trying to tell us that we're not hearing? If so, please tell us what they are.

Summary

Over the years, Homebuilders has been extensively evaluated in terms of outcomes of the intervention as well as the processes used to achieve the outcomes. Although all studies have limitations, and the lack of a rigorous control study over several years weakens any conclusions, there are many indications that Homebuilders does provide a less costly alternative to out-of-home placement of children, and does help families resolve their problems. Although these outcomes are highly desirable, it is also important that they be achieved in ways that are satisfactory to all involved. Methods of soliciting feedback from clients, referring workers, and staff are also discussed.

Appendix A
Development of the Homebuilders Program

1974   Project begins in Tacoma, Washington, with four counselors, under the auspices of Catholic Community Services. Serves children from any referral source as long as imminence of placement is documented. Success rate during the first year is 92% 3 months after termination.

1976   Project expands by three counselors with funds from U.S. Department of Health, Education and Welfare, Administration for Children, Youth, and Families. Referrals from the Pierce County Juvenile Court involve tracking of overflow cases to see if placement occurs. Success rate 12 months after intake is 73%. 73% of comparison cases are placed.

1977   Homebuilders Training Division begins providing training to other organizations as well as Homebuilders staff.

1978   Project expands to Seattle, Washington. Initial success rate 3 months after termination is 100%.

1979   Washington State Legislature funds mental health project to see if referrals from the Pierce County Office of Involuntary Commitment can be prevented from entering Western State Psychiatric Hospital. Success rate is 80%. 100% of cases that were not seen because the program was full were placed!

1980   Washington State Department of Social and Health Services funds pilot project to prevent placement of developmentally disabled children in more restrictive settings. Success rate 3 months after termination is 87%.

1982   Homebuilders create their own new parent organization, Behavioral Sciences Institute.

1983   Washington State DSHS expands program to Spokane County. First year success rate at 3 months after termination is 92%.

1984   Washington State DSHS expands program to Snohomish County. First year success rate at 12 months after termination is 86%.

1986   Administration for Children, Youths and Families funds joint
        project between Behavioral Sciences Institute and Medina
        Children's Services to test model with adoptive families with
        special needs children. Three month success rate is 86%.

1987   New York City Human Resources Administration and the Edna
        McConnell Clark Foundation fund program in the Bronx, New
        York. First year success rate is 87% three months after termina-
        tion.

1988   Washington State DSHS expands program to Kitsap and Whit-
        man Counties.

Appendix B
Homebuilders Consultation and Training Options

The following training and consultation options are designed to assist agencies develop funding, select and train staff, design administrative and referral procedures, provide high-quality service to families, and implement evaluation procedures.

Although this consultation and training is generic in that the components are applicable to a wide variety of family preservation service models, the training was developed within the context of the Homebuilders program of Washington State and reflects the values and beliefs of that program. Most training and consultation activities can be conducted either on site or at Behavioral Sciences Institute.

1. *Introduction to the Homebuilders Model* (1 Day)
   Overview of family-based services with emphasis on the components of in-home programs, client populations, and evaluations procedures. The Homebuilders program is presented as an example of a service model.

2. *Needs Assessment and System Planning* (1 Day)
   Consultation with agencies to maximize cost-effectiveness and quality of all services provided by developing appropriate client pathways and evaluation mechanisms. Development of a plan for implementation and integration of in-home services.

3. *Proposal Development and Program Preparation* (1–2 Days)
   Consultation with agencies interested in beginning to develop family-based in-home services. Selection of model best suited to their needs and interests. Development of a plan for program implementation and integration with existing agency programs and resources.

3. *Staff Screening and Selection* (1–5 Days)
   Consultation and assistance in the screening and hiring of key staff in an in-home program. The two primary positions of supervisor and counselor are addressed, including tasks of each

position and attributes of successful staff. Telephone consultation regarding advertising, evaluation of applicant resumes, and materials useful in selecting candidates from face-to-face interviews. The final round of staff selection is conducted on site, using a format that systematically evaluates job applicants using consistent criteria.

5. *Consultation/Visit at Behavioral Sciences Institute*
Intensive consultation with Homebuilder administrators, supervisors, therapists, and intake staff. Areas addressed include program development and implementation, administrative and supervisory issues, staff training, case consultation, referral and intake procedures, and program evaluation.

6. *Administrative and Supervisory Training* (2–3 Days)
Workshop or individual consultation regarding administrative and supervisory issues in operating in-home services. Areas addressed include staff selection and training, case consultation, record keeping, staff morale, time management, priorities and style, specific procedures for intake, follow-up, program evaluation, and marketing.

7. *Line Staff Training* (3–7 Days)
Workshop providing line staff/counselors with the basic knowledge and skills used in in-home services. Major areas covered include beliefs and strategies of family-based services, counselor stress management, engaging and defusing families in crisis, techniques for structuring the family situation to avoid violence, client-centered assessment and goal setting, teaching skills to families, cognitive and behavioral interventions, teaching communication skills, assertiveness training, working with depressed and suicidal clients, anger management, teaching problem-solving and negotiation, Multiple Impact Therapy, and termination issues.

8. *Monthly Review and Consultation*
Includes review of program records, intake materials, follow-up data, and reports from related community groups. Consultation regarding options for improvement in any areas where difficulties may be developing. Provided monthly during the first year of a new program. Provided on an as-needed basis during subsequent years.

9. *On-Site Follow-Up Consultation*
Review of materials and procedures. Case consultation and home visits with program counselors. Identification of staff problem areas, and strategies of intervening. Provided three to six times per year during the first year of a new program. Provided on an as-needed basis during subsequent years.

10. *Telephone Case Consultation*
Ongoing consultation regarding clinical, supervisory, and administrative issues. Provided two to four times per month during the first year of a new program. Provided on an as-needed basis during subsequent years.

Appendix C
Homebuilders Line Staff Training Modules

1. *Introduction*
   The history of the Homebuilders program, a description of Homebuilders' clients, and information on cost and treatment effectiveness. An introduction to crisis intervention and a discussion of the "headset" for training.
2. *Strategies of the Homebuilders Model*
   The strategies, characteristics, and guiding beliefs of the Homebuilders model.
3. *Stress Management for Counselors*
   Strategies counselors and others can use to maintain their physical and emotional well being. The use of cognitive restructuring in stress management. Trainees practice using "Rational Emotive Therapy" techniques.
4. *Defusing, Engaging, and Confronting Clients*
   The use of active listening and other skills to defuse and engage clients. Trainees participate in exercises and behavioral rehearsals to practice these skills.
5. *Assessment of the Potential for Violent Behavior*
   The major issues surrounding the prediction of violent and dangerous behavior and ideas for improving counselors' skills of assessing the potential for violence in families.
6. *Structuring before Visits*
   Strategies for structuring the family's situation to prevent violence from occurring prior to a visit. Participants practice specific structuring techniques in behavior rehearsal situations.
7. *Assessment and Goal Setting*
   The Homebuilders' method of assessing families and developing intervention goals. The use of active listening to obtain information and techniques for prioritizing problems and developing realistic goals.
8. *Structuring during Visits*
   The use of cognitive, environmental, and interpersonal strategies

221

for structuring the situation to prevent violence during a visit to a family's home.

9. *Structuring between Visits*
   Environmental and behavioral strategies for structuring the family's situation to prevent violence and other harmful actions from occurring between counselors' visits.

10. *Teaching Skills to Families*
    Three methods of teaching skills to families—direct instruction, modeling, and using consequences—and the use of additional aids to enhance the teaching process.

11. *Teaching Families Behavior Management Skills*
    The design and use of behavioral intervention strategies to encourage desirable behaviors and discourage problem behaviors. Specific behavior management skills to teach families including the use of contingent consequences, behavior charts, motivation systems, and contracts. Methods for tailoring the intervention to the family and helping families implement behavioral interventions.

12. *Teaching Communication Skills*
    Methods for teaching families the basic communication skills of active listening and using "I" messages.

13. *Teaching Families Cognitive Intervention Skills*
    Methods for helping clients recognize that their cognitions (their self-talk) can elicit feelings and behavior and how they can examine and change their cognitions.

14. *When Progress Isn't Occurring*
    Some issues to examine when the intervention is not progressing and when a counselor feels "stuck."

15. *Teaching Assertive Skills to Families*
    Use of a territorial model of assertiveness. How to teach clients to recognize levels of irritation, to respond with assertive behaviors, and to decide when to be assertive.

16. *Anger Management with Families*
    The use of cognitive and behavioral interventions in anger management and specific ideas for working with angry or assaultive clients.

17. *Depression and Suicide*
    Strategies for intervening with depressed clients.

18. *Multiple Impact Therapy*
    Multiple Impact Therapy (MacGregor, 1964), a structured multiple counselor intervention technique, used when a counselor is feeling stuck and when communication within the family is weak.

19. *Teaching Families Problem-Solving Skills*
    Basic problem-solving methods counselors can teach to parents and children. How counselors can help clients to use these problem-solving skills in their daily lives.
20. *Teaching Interactions*
    The use of the teaching interaction, a direct and positive approach for teaching skills and correcting behavior, and how to teach it to parents. The use of preventive teaching, corrective teaching, and dealing with ongoing behavior. Participants practice this skill in behavior rehearsal situations.
21. *Termination Issues*
    Guidelines for the termination of intensive, in-home services and for the extension of services. The process of termination and the use of networking and referrals to ongoing service.

Appendix D
Initial Plan for New Homebuilders

Information

OK	Needs Work	Don't Know	
——	——	——	The organization of BSI
——	——	——	The history of BSI
——	——	——	The history of Homebuilders
——	——	——	The Homebuilders Resource Guide
——	——	——	The Homebuilders Overview
——	——	——	The Homebuilders Policies and Procedures Guide
——	——	——	The Homebuilders grants

Skills

OK	Needs Work	Don't Know	
——	——	——	Active listening with individual
——	——	——	Active listening with family
——	——	——	Behavioral assessment
——	——	——	Ability to sell psychoeducational material
——	——	——	Ability to sell Homebuilders and desirability of keeping families together
——	——	——	Ability to be assertive
——	——	——	Ability to teach assertiveness
——	——	——	Ability to teach listening
——	——	——	Ability to control own emotions and think rationally
——	——	——	Ability to teach others to control emotions and think rationally

225

	Needs	Don't	
OK	Work	Know	
_____	_____	_____	Ability to organize own life to allow responsiveness to clients
_____	_____	_____	Ability to brainstorm options in difficult situations
_____	_____	_____	Ability to accept feedback
_____	_____	_____	Ability to present case clearly, concisely, and regularly
_____	_____	_____	Ability to keep paperwork up to date
_____	_____	_____	Ability to know when to contact supervisor for help
_____	_____	_____	Ability to handle ambiguity and complexity
_____	_____	_____	Ability to clearly self-disclose when appropriate
_____	_____	_____	Ability to recognize own strengths and weaknesses
_____	_____	_____	Ability to set up behavioral chart
_____	_____	_____	Ability to design anger management treatment plan
_____	_____	_____	Ability to structure daily routines
_____	_____	_____	Ability to implement no-lose problem resolution
_____	_____	_____	Ability to design and implement behavioral contracts
_____	_____	_____	Ability to creatively advocate to meet client basic need
_____	_____	_____	Ability to behave appropriately in meetings
_____	_____	_____	Appearance

Activities that will occur between ___DATE___ and ___DATE___ to enhance skill and information base.

References

Achenbach, T. M., (1979). *Child Behavior Checklist* (ADM 512). Bethesda, MD, National Instititute of Mental Health.

APA Task Force on Clinical Aspects of the Violent Individual (1974). *Clinical aspects of the violent inidividual: A report of the APA Task Force on clinical aspects of the violent individual.* Washington, D.C.: American Psychiatric Association.

Avison, W. R., Turner, R. J., and Noh, S. (1986). Screening for problem parenting: Preliminary evidence on a promising instrument. *Child Abuse and Neglect, 10* (2), 157–170.

Bach, G. R., and Wyden, P. (1969). *The intimate enemy.* New York: William Morrow.

Baker, W., and Holzworth, A. (1961). Social histories of successful and unsuccessful children. *Child Development, 32,* 135–149.

Bakker, C., and Bakker-Rabdau, M. K. (1973). *No trespassing! Exploration in human territoriality.* Novato, CA: Chandler and Sharp.

Becker, W. C. (1971). *Parents are teachers: A child management program.* Champaign, IL: Research Press Company.

Bootstani, M. and Tashakkori, A. (1982). Social maturity of children reared in an Iranian orphanage. *Child Study Journal, 12* (2), 127–133.

Caplan, G. (1964). *Principles of preventive psychiatry.* New York: Basic Book, Inc.

Castaneda, C. (1968). *The teaching of Don Juan: a Yaqui way of knowledge.* Berkeley: University of California Press.

Castaneda, C. (1971). *A separate reality: Further conversation with Don Juan.* New York: Simon and Schuster.

Castaneda, C. (1972). *Journey to Ixtlan: The lessons of Don Juan.* New York: Simon and Schuster.

Castaneda, C. (1974). *Tales of power.* New York: Simon and Schuster.

Churchill, N. C., and Lewis, V. L. (1983). The 5 stages of small business growth. *Harvard Business Review, 61* (3), 30–50.

Cole, E. (1988, April 14). *Basic values and the family preservation movement.* Presented at the Clark Foundation Grantees Conference, Clearwater, Florida.

Crary, E. (1979). *Without spanking or spoiling: A practical approach to toddler and preschool guidance.* Seattle: Parenting Press.

Crary, E. (1982). *I can't wait.* Seattle: Parenting Press.

Crary, E. (1982). *I want it.* Seattle: Parenting Press.

Crary, E. (1982). *I want to play.* Seattle: Parenting Press.

Crary, E. (1983). *My name is not dummy.* Seattle: Parenting Press.

Crary, E. (1985). *I'm lost.* Seattle: Parenting Press.

227

Dinkmeyer D. and McKay, G. (1976). *Systematic training for effective parenting: Parents handbook.* Circle Pines, MN: American Guidance Service, Inc.

Eisenberg, L. (1962). *The family in the mid-twentieth century.* Address to National Conference of Social Welfare. The social welfare forum: 1960, New York: Columbia University Press, 1960.

Ellis, A. (1973). *Rational emotive therapy.* New York: Springer Publishing Company.

Fahlberg, V. (1979). *Attachment and separation: Putting the pieces together.* Michigan: Vera Fahlberg.

Fanshel, D., and Maas (1962). Factorial dimensions of the characteristics of children in placement and their famililes. *Child Development, 33,* 123–144.

Fanshel, D., and Shinn, E. B. (1978). *Children in foster care, a longitudinal investigation.* New York: Columbia University Press.

Festinger, T., (1983). No One Ever Asked Us . . . A postscript to foster care. New York. Columbia University Press.

Flanagan, J. C. (1954). The critical incident technique in the study of individuals. In Traxler, A. E., *Modern educational problems,* 61–70.

Fraser, M. W., and Haapala, D. A. (1988). Home-based family treatment: A quantitative–qualitative assessment. *Journal of Applied Social Sciences, 12,* (1), 1–23.

Fraser, M. W., Pecora, P. J., and Haapala, D. A. (1988). *Families in crisis:* Findings from the family-based intensive treatment research project. Social Research Institute, Graduate School of Social Work, University of Utah, Salt Lake City, Utah and Behavioral Sciences Institute, Federal Way, Washington.

Gambril, E. D. (1977). *Behavioral modification: Handbook of assessment, intervention, and evaluation.* San Francisco: Jossey-Bass.

Gambril, E. D., and Wiltse, K. T. (1974). Foster care: Plans and actualities. *Public Welfare, 32,* 12–21.

Gelles, R. J. (1987a). *Family Violence (2nd ed.).* Newbury Park: Sage Publications.

Gelles, R. J. (1987b). A structural family systems approach to intervention in cases of family violence. *Family Relations, 36,* 270–275.

Glaser, B., and Strauss, A. (1967). *The discovery of grounded theory: Strategies for Qualitative research.* New York: Aldine.

Gold, J. A. (1981). *Parent adolescent communication training in groups: Evaluating a problem-solving model.* Doctoral Dissertation, University of Washington. Ann Arbor: University Microfilms.

Gordon, T. (1975). *P. E. T.: Parent Effectiveness Training.* New York: New American Library.

Greiner, L. E. (1972). Evolution and revolution as organizations grow. *Harvard Business Review, 50* (4), 37–46.

Haapala, D. A. (1983). *Perceived helpfulness, attributed critical incident responsibility, and a discrimination of home-based family therapy treatment outcome: Homebuilders Model.* Report prepared for the Department of Health & Human Services, Administration for Children, Youth, and Families, Behavioral Sciences Institute, Federal Way, Washington.

Haapala, D. A., McDade, K., and Johnston, B. (1988). *Preventing the dissolution of special needs adoptive families with children in imminent risk of out-of-home placement.*

Hauck, P. (1974). *Overcoming frustration and anger.* Philadelphia: Westminister Press.

Hepworth, D. H., and Larsen, J. A. (1986). *Direct social work practice: Theory and skills,* (2nd ed.). Chicago: Dorsey.

Hersen, M., and Bellack, A. S. (Eds.) (1976). *Behavioral assessment: A practical handbook.* New York: Pergamon Press.

Kazdin, A. E. (1980). *Behavioral modification in applied settings.* Homewood, IL: The Dorsey Press.

Kinney, J. M., and Haapala, D. A. (1984). *First year Homebuilder mental health report.*

Kiresuk, T. J., and Sherman, R. E. (1968). Goal attainment scaling: A general method for evaluation community mental health programs. *Community Mental Health Journal, 4,* 443–453.

Larsson, G., Bohlin, A. B., and Stenbacka, M. (1986). Prognosis of children admitted to institutional care during infancy. Sixth International Congress of the International Society for Prevention of Child Abuse and Neglect (1986, Sidney Australia). *Child Abuse and Neglect, 10* (3), 361–368.

Lehner, G. F. J. *Guidelines for giving and receiving feedback.* Unpublished paper. Los Angeles: Department of Psychology, University of California, n.d.

Lindemann, E. (1944). Symtomatology and management of acute grief. *American J. of Psychiatry, 101,* 141–148.

Lloyd, J. (1982). Prevention: At what cost? *Prevention Report,* National Resource Center on Family Based Service, The University of Iowa.

MacGregor, R. (1964). *Multiple impact therapy with families.* New York: Blakiston Division, McGraw-Hill.

Magura, S., Moses, B. S., and Jones, M. A. (1987). *Assessing risk and measuring change in families: The Bundy risk scales.* Washington D. C. Child Welfare League of America

Mash, E. J., Handy, L. C., and Hammerlynch, L. A. (1974). *Behavior modification approaches to parenting.* New York: Brenner/Mazel.

Mash, E. J., and Terdal, L. G. (Eds.) (1988). *Behavioral assessment of childhood disorders* (2nd ed.). New York: The Guilford Press.

Maslow, A. H. (1954). *Motivation and personality.* New York: Harper and Brothers.

McCord, J., McCord, W., and Thurber, E. (1960). The effects of foster home placement in the prevention of adult anti-social behavior. *Social Service Review, 32* (1), 5–17.

McDonald, W. R., and Associates (1987). *Evaluation of AB-1562 demonstration projects: Year one interim report.* Sacramento, California: Author.

Milardo, R. M. (1983). Social networks and pair relationships: A review of substantive and measurement issues. *Sociology and Social Research, 68* (1), 1–18.

Monahan, J. (1981a). The clinical prediction of violent behavior. *Crime and Delinquency Issues* (Monograph Series). Washington, D.C.: U.S. Government Printing Office.

Monahan, J. (1981b). *Predicting violent behavior: An assessment of clinical techniques.* Beverly Hills, CA: Sage Publications.

Olson, D. H., Portner, J., and Ravee, Y. (1985). *Focus 1*. St. Paul, Minnesota: Family Social Science, University of Minnesota.

Parker, G. (1979). Parental deprivation and depression in a nonclinical group. *Australian and New Zealand Journal of Psychiatry, 13*, 51–56.

Patterson, G. R. (1968). *Living with children: New methods for parents and teachers.* Champaign, IL: Research Press Company.

Pecora, P. J., Fraser, M. W., and Haapala, D. A. (1988). Intensive home-based family treatment: Client outcomes and issues for program design. In J. Hudson and B. Galaway (Eds.). *State Intervention of Behalf of Children and Youth.*

Peters, T. J. (1987). *Thriving on chaos: Handbook for a management revolution.* New York: Random House.

Pike, V., Downs, S., Emlen, A., Downs, G., and Case, D. (1977). *Permanent planning for children in foster care: A handbook for social workers.* Portland: U.S. Department of Health, Education, and Welfare.

Pringle, M. L. (1964). The emotional and social development of physically handicapped children. *Educational Research, 6* (3), 207–215.

Rogers, C. R. (1942). *Counseling and psychotherapy: Newer concepts in practice.* Boston: Houghton-Mifflin Company.

Rutter, M. (1979). Maternal deprivation: New findings, new concepts, new approaches. *Child Development, 50*, 283–304.

Solnit, A., and Cauce, A. (1982). "Foster families and the foster care system: Don't throw the baby out with the bath water." Unpublished manuscript.

Tharp, R. G., and Wetzel, R. J. (1969). *Behavior modification in the natural environment.* New York: Academic Press.

Turner, R. J., and McDonald, W. R. (November, 1985). Assessing risk factors for problem parenting: The significance of social support. *Journal of Marriage and the Family, 47* (4), 881–892.

Wahler, R. G. (1980). The insular mother: Her problem in parent treatment. *Journal of Applied Behavior Analysis, 13*, 207–219.

Wahler, R. G., Leske, G., and Rogers, E. S. (1979). The insular family: A deviance support system for oppositional children. In L. A. Hamerlynck (E.d.), *Behavioral systems for the developmentally disabled: School and family environments* (pp.102–127). New York: Burner Mazel.

Waters, V. (1980). *The anger trap and how to spring it.* New York: The Institute for Rational Living.

Weinstein, E. A. (1960). *The self-image of the foster child.* New York: Russell Sage Foundation.

Wetzel, R. J. (1989). Personal communication.

Whittaker, J. K., and Gabarino, J., and Associates (1983). *Social support networks: informal helping in the human services.* New York: Aldine.

Young, H. S. (1974). *A rational counseling primer.* New York: Institute for Rational Emotive Therapy.

Index